D0539985

The Dordogne & Périgord

The Dordogne & Périgord made to measure

The Dordogne & Périgord à la carte

Contents 14

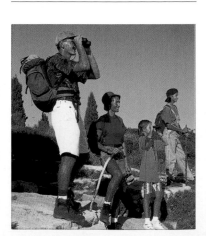

The Dordogne & Périgord in detail

A weekend
in Rocamadour

Y ou need a good two days to discover all the treasures of the number-two French tourist site. This clifftop holy city is surrounded by spectacular natural sights and a host of attractions for both adults and children.

For the most breathtaking part, start at the top – go up on foot or take the little train. Walk through the cliffside **shrines**, see the view from the **château** perched on the

Rocamadour's main shopping street

plateau or from the **Rocher des Aigles** (eagle's rock), accompanied by hundreds of birds of prey in spectacular flight. Halfway down the rock, stroll through the ancient shopping streets of the **medieval town**. This is also the place for a **great meal**. You can then amble gently down the pilgrims' way, to reach the hamlet of **L'Hospitalet**, opposite Rocamadour. Here you have not only an unforgettable view of the pilgrim city and the canyon, but also **animal parks**, spectacular **animations**, the **prehistoric caves** and **nature trails** to the waterfalls. Or take the easy way and go uptown in an open carriage (p. 170).

A weekend
in Conques

*Capital in the cloister
of the Abbaye de Conques*

Conques is a small village in Rouergue with narrow alleys and old timber-framed houses. It also boasts a masterpiece of medieval ornamental sculpture – the doorway of the **abbey-church of Sainte-Foy**, with its famous Last Judgment tympanon, whose 124 carved heads have watched over visitors for over 800 years.

N ot to be missed – the medieval treasures of Sainte-Foy, which include the abbey church and a reliquary statue covered with gold and precious stones.

Inside the abbey, note the **windows** by Pierre Soulages, made of a special glass that diffuses light. Go on to the cloisters to see one of the glories of medieval sculpture – the **reliquary statue of Sainte**

Foy in the Trésor, covered in gold and studded with precious stones. The town organises medieval festivals to celebrate its treasures. Choose your season – **classical music** in July, **films** in April. (p. 186)

Three days
in the Aveyron
gorges

T he road winds through the gorges for nearly 20 miles (32 km), giving plenty of time to enjoy nature's route through the limestone, overlooked by picturesque villages.

At the fine citadel of **Saint-Antonin-Noble-Val**, take a break to explore various nature trails or the **Bosc cave**. Then take the high road to follow the Aveyron gorges in the direction of the medieval château of **Bruniquel**. But don't miss out the picturesque villages on the way. And it's worth devoting a whole day to the joys of canoeing through this extraordinary landscape (p. 152).

Three days in Sarlat and the Périgord Dordogne

Three wonderful days from Sarlat to the Dordogne valley. If you're allergic to crowds, come out of season.

A medieval gem full of lovely houses, Sarlat is one of Périgord's most highly rated and therefore most visited tourist sites. See if you can you resist its charm. In summer, get up at dawn to whet your tastebuds at the **market**. After that, head to **Beynac** for a barge trip down the Dordogne. Don't miss the opportunity to visit the **Château de Marqueyssac** and its park, designed by a pupil of Le Nôtre, and the **Château de Castelnaud**. There is a superb view of one of the finest stretches of the valley (pp. 120 and 124).

Three days on the way to Cahors

Sample some great wines and the joys of the river – here, the two pleasures are side by side. The vineyards extend along the peaceful banks of the River Lot.

Relax on the river's serene slopes as you taste some of the *grands crus*. From the **Château de Mercuès**, which contains a notable restaurant, follow the course of the Lot from west to east. You can go **hang-gliding** at **Douelle**, visit the medieval town of **Luzech**, **go boating** at Caix, and discover the heritage and **arts and crafts** of **Puy-L'Évêque**, without forgetting the **ostrich farm** at **Duravel** (p. 158).

Cahors AOC vineyard, near Luzech

A week from Cahors to Figeac via the Lot and Célé valleys

Prepare for a stimulating week. Have your senses on alert on your journey from Cahors to Figeac via the Célé valley, returning via the Lot gorges.

Copy of the Rosetta Stone, Place des Écritures, Figeac

Luckily the historic heritage of **old Cahors** is well preserved. Stroll around the medieval city, and cast an appreciative eye over the **Romanesque Cathédrale St-Étienne** and the famous **Valentré bridge**. Pause for a little culture now and then – there's no shortage of things going on – and fill your basket with Quercy specialities at the market. You can get advice on **wine** at the Atrium (p. 154). Then it's off to the Célé valley. At **Cabrerets**, the **Pech Merle cave** contains inspiring rock paintings. From there, you are only 3 miles (5 km) from the Amis du Célé club, where you can go rock climbing, caving or

canoeing in total safety. After this brush with raw nature, get a scent of rural medieval life at the lively and informative **Quercy open-air museum**. Before leaving, sample some **bio produce** of the local farms and food firms, under the arches of an ancient priory. Paradise! (p. 162) Next stop is **Figeac**. Wander through back streets and arcades, making sure your route includes Rue Émile-Zola, where you can browse in the **craft shops**. Egyptologists should head for the **Musée Champollion**, the former birth-place of the whizzkid who deciphered hieroglyphics. If the younger generation is bursting for something more active, they will love **Surgié leisure park** with its pool and wave

machine, water chutes and trampolines. Unless of course they prefer to be seadogs at the **miniature port** in Capdenac-le-Haut (p. 164). Now you're on your way back to Cahors via the Lot valley. Keep your eyes peeled. From **Cajarc**, the gorges wind between impressive ochre and grey cliffs. After a break at the **Château de Cénevières**, you reach **Saint-Cirq Lapopie**. The sight of this village clinging to a rocky scarp is astonishing. Make your way down the narrow streets (crowded in summer) to reach the **towpath** by the Lot river. One of the best walks in the valley awaits you (p. 160). As you return to Cahors, leave a few hours to rediscover the magnificent gorges by **boat** or **barge**.

Château de Cénevières

A week
in the Grands Causses

This week can be spent visiting Templar townships, where you can enjoy story-telling, medieval fairs [banquets] and fireworks all summer, and guided walks on the Larzac and Combalou plateaux above Roquefort-sur-Soulzon.

Why not begin with **La Couvertoirade**? This is a medieval mini-city full of architectural treasures left by the **Templars** and **Hospitallers**. Explore its maze of alleys, covered passages and picturesque squares, pausing to buy **an authentic shepherd's bag** on the way. In summer, during the

Château de Montaigut

Estivales events at **Larzac**, night visits are organised. From here, take the road for the Larzac plateau, making your first stop **Homs-du-Larzac**,

where you can stock up on aromatic and medicinal plants grown locally. Try the local **pastis** – but don't overdo it! You then come to **La Calverie**, another Templar city, where a **medieval festival** awaits you, plus a theatrical **firework show** with narrative. You are now on the Larzac plateau. Spend half a day discovering the **wildlife**, **flora** and **geology** of this wild landscape in the company of an ONF guide (you'll need to make arrangements in advance). You'll then be ready for the next Templar fort at **Sainte-Eulalie-de-Cernon**, with its **concerts** and **light shows**.

Wild mouflon sheep

You might of course prefer an evening of **story-telling** and **medieval banqueting** at **Viala-du-Pas-de-Jaux** (p. 204). Head now for **Roquefort-sur-Soulzon**, where you can spend a day visiting the **cellars** where the celebrated marbled cheeses are matured in long galleries. The second day will provide time for a **nature stop** on the **Combalou plateau**, where lovely walks take you from sheepfolds to rocky peaks, passing some magnificent views on the way. At the end of this, **Saint-Jean-d'Alcas** awaits you. Smaller than La Couvertoirade, this Templar town is no less delightful. Not much further on is the **Pays de Bambi animal park** at **Saint-Félix-de-Sorgues** – a treat for the children. Push on to **Sylvanès** for a look at the remarkable **Cistercian abbey** and maybe go to a concert during the **international festival of church music**. You can finish an engrossing tour with a **great meal** at **Carayon**. This restaurant in the village of **Saint-Sernin-sur-Rance** is a real institution (p. 206).

A week
in the fortified towns of Rouergue

The region west of the Aveyron is noted for its fortified royal townships called bastides, which bring alive the drama of medieval history. Enjoy the architectural harmony of these 13thC. 'new towns' on foot, visit some of the buildings and browse in the craft shops, then go on to explore the varied countryside around, with plateaux alternating with valleys and gorges.

Cloisters of Saint-Sauveur monastery, Villefranche-de-Rouergue

Villeneuve is the most northerly of the four bastides. This town on the causse (limestone plateau) was founded by the counts of Toulouse. It has a very fine arcaded square, from where you can find the old houses and Romanesque church. Extend your stay here so as not to miss the **prehistoric park at Foissac**, just 4 miles (6.5 km) away, which will enthral the children. Then go south to **Villefranche-de-Rouergue**. Stunningly restored, this is the largest of the bastides and worth a whole day. It contains some architectural gems (notably the **Pénitents Noirs chapel**), lots of **shops** and an unmissable **Thursday market**. Not far from the town, the **Carthusian monastery** of **Saint-Sauveur** is a Gothic gem, and the little Renaissance **château** at **Graves** is also worth a detour.

From here, entrust yourself to the River Aveyron, taking the minor road running beside it. The landscape becomes craggier and craggier as the river digs deeper and narrows into a torrent. Halfway between Villefranche-de-Rouergue and Najac, you can take a break for a meal or an overnight stay at the **Relais** and **Château de Longcol**, a feast for both eyes and palate. Relaxed from the break, carry on to **Najac**. Its château is perched high on a hilltop

overlooking the flower-decked streets and quaint houses of the pretty village. A pleasant day can be spent here doing **outdoor sports** at the freshwater leisure centre (base de loisirs, p. 208). Your next road takes you eastwards to the last bastide, **Sauveterre-de-Rouergue**, which dominates the agricultural lands of the Ségala or 'rye country'. This is one

Tripoux Charles Savy – a tripe-based speciality from Naucelle

of the loveliest villages in France. Don't miss the arcaded square, and its **craft shops and restaurants** are attraction enough for a day or two (p. 212).

Place Centrale, Sauveterre-de-Rouergue

A week
in the Val de Garonne

I t's sheer heaven to wander among the market gardens of this gentle valley abounding in mellow fruit. The light is soft, the villages are serene, cradled by the River Garonne and the still waters of the Canal du Midi. A week to saunter through lower Quercy with never a dull moment, from Valence-d'Agen to Moissac.

Take to the waters of the Tarn and Garonne to reach the lake and Île aux Oiseaux (bird island) at **Saint-Nicolas-de-la-Grave** (p. 140). From there, you are just a step from **Moissac**. Don't just drive through: discover the town gradually over two or three days. Its magnificent **abbey** will tell you of a golden historical age, and its old streets will catch your eye. **Craft workshops**, **views** of the confluences of the rivers and canal, **walks** along the canal and **concerts** will fill your time. Not forgetting the more tangible pleasures of **chasselas**, the king of grapes, of which Moissac is the capital. If you need activity, head for the **outdoor leisure centre** at the 1,000-acre (166-ha) lake, which will satisfy both toddlers and sporty types (p. 144). From Moissac, you can also explore the countryside to the north, studded with conservation villages, fortified towns and craft centres.

Start in the ancient fortified town of **Valence-d'Agen**, where you should take a look at the old **lavoirs** (washhouses). Tuesday morning is best, when the **poultry market** is also on – it's one of the best in the region. To go with meat of this quality, nip out to **Donzac** to try the **'vins noirs'** ('black wines'). It comes as a cultural shock to pass the **nuclear**

power station at **Golfech** on the way, but budding physicists will want to go in and have it all explained to them.
After stirring the grey cells, relax as you explore **Auvillar**, one of the finest villages in the area. You will love its fine **covered market**, **museums**, **earthenware**, **wharves** and **footpaths** between riverbanks and vineyards . You then need only cross the Garonne to get an instant impression of being in the Loire valley, with the exuberant style of the **Château de Saint-Roch** deserving a closer look. At **Malause**, a change of transport.

To learn more about prehistoric man and his environment (see pp.22-25), visit Les Eyzies and the Vézère valley which offers almost 100 sites of interest including the Font-de-Gaume and Combarelles caves and museum of prehistory at the Château de Tayac (see pp.114-117). Don't miss the Grottes de Lacave (see p.181) which house an amazing collection of stalagtites and stalagmites as well as an underground lake.

A week
in Quercy Blanc

S outh of the Lot, on the huge limestone plateaux that smell sweetly of the Midi, the air is fragrant with lavender. Explore a countryside criss-crossed by waterways and studded with little villages full of charm and tasty delicacies.

Go straight to the heart of Quercy Blanc by basing yourself at **Lauzerte**, the finest medieval village in the region. This fortified town, which has always enjoyed a strategic position, has everything to stimulate your senses: half-timbering, arcades, wonderful food and splendid views (p. 148). Within a circumference of 12 miles (19 km), everyone will find an activity to suit

them. The boldest will go for **parachute-jumping** at **Bouloc** (p. 149), while families will prefer to hire **donkeys** for signposted **rambles** from **Cazes-Mondenard**. This is also the starting point of the **chasselas tour**, taking in vines and orchards (p. 149).
To the south, a special mention for three neighbouring villages, which can be seen in a day: first, a feast for the palate at **Saint-Nazaire-de-Valentane**, with its foie gras, magrets (duck breasts) and other farm specialities (p. 147). There's

also a sightseeing feast – the imposing 12th-C. **château** at **Brassac** (p. 147) and the fortified town of **Castelsagrat**, whose church contains a magnificent **retable** (p. 143). For children, west of Lauzerte is an **experimental farm** and **treasure hunt** at **Belvèze** (p. 148). Not far from there is the **lake at Montaigu-de-Quercy**, with its water sports and white-sand beach, suitable for young children (p. 147). From there you can go on to the **lavender distillery** at Servat (p. 147).

A wide range of pleasures awaits to the north and east. On Sunday morning, stock up at the **market** in the tranquil village of Montcuq (p. 146), go on to the **Roland cave** to see its underground lake (p. 146), or take the toddlers to **Castelnau-Montratier** (p. 146), where several amazing tours will keep them interested. Go on to Monpezat-de-Quercy, whose **Flanders tapestries** are worth a detour (p. 148). For a tasty finish, head for **Mirabel**, where you can sample various recipes made with **home-made plum products** (p. 150).

Lavender field

A fortnight
in Périgord

Y ou need a whole fortnight to explore
Sarlat, the Dordogne valley, the
Romanesque churches and medieval châteaux
and to sample the pleasures of Périgord . You can recharge your batteries
(trails on foot or by mountain bike) or fill your winter larder (wines, foie gras,
truffles, etc.). And immerse yourself in prehistory.

Give tribute to Caesar – your first visit must be to **Montaigne country**, where Périgord's most famous son grew up (p. 90). Then go and sample the **sweet wines** of **Monbazillac** (p. 92) before heading for **Bergerac**, the pretty tobacco capital of France (p. 94). You then enter the age-old **forests** of **La Double** (p. 98), re-emerging at Ribérac. Visit one of the local **farms** (p. 106) and the **domed Romanesque churches**. Or even hire a **bicycle** to do a tour of the local **châteaux**. In any event, don't miss the two at **Brantôme** (p. 108), which are worth a stopover. At **Nontron**, you can buy **knives**, take a dip in the pool at **Saint-Estèphe** (p. 110), then turn treasure-hunter and set off to find black gold at the **truffle museum** at **Sorges** (p. 113). Drop in on the **geese and duck farms** and stock up for the winter.

Jacquou le Croquant

Reserve at least half a day to wander around the fascinating streets of **Périgueux** (p. 100), especially if it's **market day**. See the attractive domes of the **Cathédrale Saint-Front**. If you like French gardens, head for **Hautefort** (p. 104). Not far from there, the **Auvézère gorges** are best appreciated on foot or by bike. Spend a few silent moments by the tomb of a **king of Patagonia** in **Tourtoirac** (p. 105) before plunging into the heart of Périgord Noir for some prehistorical therapy. Follow the **prehistory trail** from **Les Eyzes** to **Lascaux**. Some effort is required to see the 30,000-year-old **paintings** of **Cro-Magnon**

man. Breathtaking stuff. A visit to the **Préhisto-Parc** and **Espace Cro-Magnon** will complete your course in the origins of man (p. 114). Then it's on to magnificent medieval **Sarlat** (p. 120). You need a full day to explore the town, beginning early morning with the **market**. To round off your tour of Périgord, visit the **fortifications** of **Domme** and have a meal there (p. 129). The spectacular view of the Dordogne, lined here with numerous **châteaux and fortresses** (including **Beynac**, **Marqueyssac** and **Castelnaud**) will leave an indelible impression of this delightful valley (p. 129).

A fortnight
in northern Quercy

Y ou need at least a fortnight to visit northern Quercy. The region is full
of sights, from the Dordogne valley to Saint-Céré and its wonders.
The towns of Souillac, Martel and Rocamadour and the little gems of
Autoire and Loubressac are unmissable, not to mention the châteaux, museums
and leisure facilities or the celebrated and enormous pothole of Padirac.
Avoid July and August, if possible.

Château de la Treyne

If you have decided to come
in summer and reached
Souillac (superb **Benedictine
abbey church** with three
domes), get the what's-on list
from the tourist office. There
is something for everyone,
ranging from **jazz** to **classical
music** via a **festival of mime**.
It should be added that the
town houses a collection of
clockwork toys and robots that
is unique in Europe (p. 180).
Go on to **Martel**, the museum
city of **seven towers**. After a
visit to this exceptional piece
of architectural heritage, you'll
need a day to brush up on
reptiles and take a **steam** or
diesel train ride high up in

the Dordogne valley. If
possible, save a day to get lost
in a huge **labyrinth** in a maize
field (p. 168). Then, why not
head for **Carennac**, to test
your olfactory skills at the
stills museum (musée des
Alambics, p. 176). The next
stage takes you to the **feudal
château** at Castelnau, one of
the finest in France (p. 176).
Set up camp for several days
around Saint-Céré – possibly
in one of the magnificent little
villages of **Loubressac**, which
offers an uninterrupted view
of the region, and
Autoire, which has
a fabulous
cirque to
practise **rock-
climbing**
(p. 177). At
Saint-Céré, leave an evening
or two free for the singing
festival and a visit to the
Atelier des Maquis, where
you will undoubtedly unearth
a unique work of art. Find
time also for the **Jean Lurçat
tapestries** and the **Château de
Montal** (p. 174). Then the
moment comes when you
have to plunge 338 ft (103 m)
underground to the bottom of
the huge, stupefying **great
hole** of Padirac (p. 177).
Before setting off for
Rocamadour, drop in on
Arsène at **Gramat** to buy
some **pewterware** (p. 177).
Go on to the pilgrim town
of Rocamadour, where you
should pencil in two or three

days to uncover all its treasures
– it has, for example, no
fewer than seven
**Romanesque
churches** and
chapels. Leave
time for a stroll
round its medieval
streets and the **Merveilles
cave**, or to explore the paths
to the springs and waterfalls
and clamber up to see the birds
of prey at the **Rocher des
Aigles** and the monkeys at
the **Forêt des Singes** (p. 170).
To finish off your fortnight,
dine in style at the **Château
de la Treyne**, where, in the
shade of centuries-old cedars,
you can enjoy a well-earned
rest (p. 180).

Rocamadour

*Forêt des Singes,
Rocamadour*

A fortnight
in the Aveyron uplands

In the northwest of Aveyron département, the wild beauty of nature and distinctive landscapes are guaranteed to offer a change of scenery. It's a paradise of open-air activities, expert crafts and an array of gastronomic traditions – a full programme, in fact.

Enter the area from the east. The watery pleasures of **Olt** country (p. 188) and the **Truyère gorges** (p 194) mean you can canoe through some lovely villages, including the delightful small town of **Sainte-Eulalie-d'Olt, Saint-Côme-d'Olt, Espalion** – all in pink sandstone – and even the medieval village of **Estaing**. For the sake of your palate, don't forget the **strawberries** of **Saint-Geniez-d'Olt** and the local **wines** from the vineyards (p. 189). Further north, the scenery changes dramatically as you enter the huge volcanic Aubrac plateau. Here, keep your eyes skinned for an incomparable range of **wildlife** and **flora**, and be prepared for the

Aubrac wild pansies

traditional **cheeses**, the celebrated **knife factory** at **Laguiole**, vast numbers of country **trails** and even **skiing** in the winter season (p. 190). After some days of fresh air, descend via the **Causse Comtal**, where there are numerous spots for

a break before you get to **Rodez**. This old town and its surroundings will take a day or two because the architectural heritage here is plentiful, from the **Cathédrale Notre-Dame** to elegant old houses (p. 196). But there's more – Southeast of Rodez, the **Lévezou** area features some very large **lakes** and **dams** that are not to be missed, plus an amazing **insect city** at **Saint-Léons** (p. 198).

Save the last few days for the **glove factories** and **museums** of **Millau**, its remarkable ancient site at the **Graufesenque potteries**, or for practising your open-air sports techniques, from **rock-climbing** to **rafting** (p. 200). At the gates of Millau, you arrive at the most amazing limestone plateau of the département, the **Causse Noir**. You can reckon on a day or two to properly explore the fascinating **rock formations** of **Montpellier-le-Vieux** (p. 202) and the green **gorges** of **La Dourbie**, to sample the local honey or take a **camel** trip (p. 203).

Fields near Laguiole

The Dordogne &
Périgord à la carte

Gardens, lakes and wildlife parks

The region is rich in gardens and wildlife parks, most of which are best explored on foot. See also the interesting water parks.

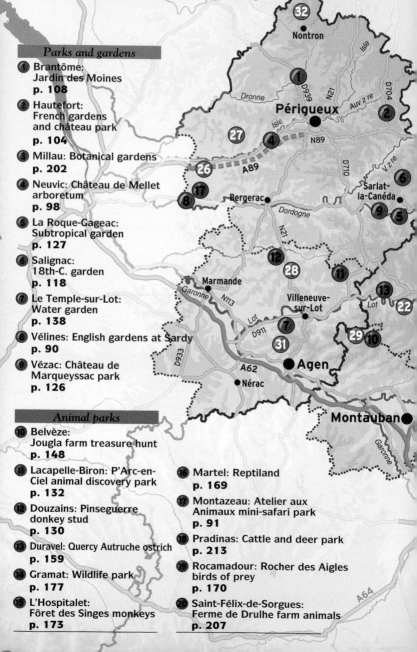

Parks and gardens

1 **Brantôme:** Jardin des Moines **p. 108**

2 **Hautefort:** French gardens and château park **p. 104**

3 **Millau:** Botanical gardens **p. 202**

4 **Neuvic:** Château de Mellet arboretum **p. 98**

5 **La Roque-Gageac:** Subtropical garden **p. 127**

6 **Salignac:** 18th-C. garden **p. 118**

7 **Le Temple-sur-Lot:** Water garden **p. 138**

8 **Vélines:** English gardens at Sardy **p. 90**

9 **Vézac:** Château de Marqueyssac park **p. 126**

Animal parks

10 **Belvèze:** Jougla farm treasure hunt **p. 148**

11 **Lacapelle-Biron:** P'Arc-en-Ciel animal discovery park **p. 132**

12 **Douzains:** Pinseguerre donkey stud **p. 130**

13 **Duravel:** Quercy Autruche ostrich **p. 159**

14 **Gramat:** Wildlife park **p. 177**

15 **L'Hospitalet:** Fôret des Singes monkeys **p. 173**

16 **Martel:** Reptiland **p. 169**

17 **Montazeau:** Atelier aux Animaux mini-safari park **p. 91**

18 **Pradinas:** Cattle and deer park **p. 213**

19 **Rocamadour:** Rocher des Aigles birds of prey **p. 170**

20 **Saint-Félix-de-Sorgues:** Ferme de Drulhe farm animals **p. 207**

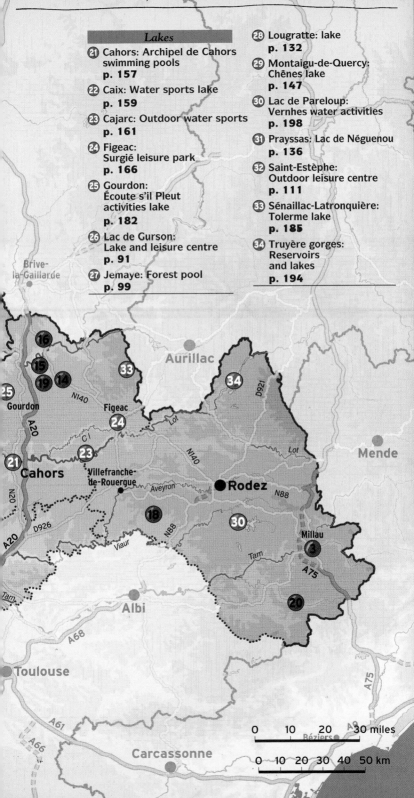

Flora of the Causses

Setting off to discover orchids in the grasslands of the Causses is just the thing to excite budding orchidophiles. Among the hundreds of species of orchids recorded in France, more than 40 are found in Lot alone. They are at their most splendid in spring. Don't let your excitement at seeing them blind you to the cadi sandwort, feather grass and carline thistles also closely associated with the Causses. Not forgetting downy oaks, the best sort for truffles.

An orchid in bloom

The lip's the thing

Orchids that reproduce by self-fertilisation need insects to bring the pollen and ovaries in contact. In exchange for this vital service, the flowers offer nectar, which they keep in a spur at the bottom of the lip (a much-altered petal). Thus evolution has equipped certain ophrys flowers with a very efficient method for attracting pollenising insects. The lip imitates the shape and pattern of the body of a wasp or bee, sometimes with amazing accuracy. Better still, some of them give off the smell of the female insect.

Cadi sandwort

This small plant grows on dry, limestone land at low altitudes on rugged terrains and scree. It has greatly suffered from a reduction and disruption of its biotopes (due to building work, dumping, quarrying etc.). Fortunately the Causses du Quercy provide a protected area for this plant to develop. The white flowers blossom in loose bunches, between May and July.

Causse du Larzac near Pierrefiche

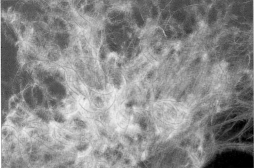

often short, crooked trunks, the full, rounded crown and their deeply cracked, blackish bark. Their shape and dimensions limit their use. The wood is dense and hard, making it difficult to work, but makes excellent fuel. And the trees are the best oak for truffles.

Feather grass

The scientific name for this beautiful grass is *stipa pennata*, but the people of the Causse call it 'angel's hair' or 'old lady's hair'. A landmark plant of the dry moor of the Causse in its windiest and stoniest areas, this hardy plant ripples in the wind like very fine tresses, and in the springtime its yellow-green spikelets take on a reflected silvery sheen in the low sun.

Acanthus-leaved carline thistle

Nothing is easier to recognise than *carlina acanthifolia*. It is almost emblematic of the dry, rocky grasslands of the Grands Causses. The broad, spiny, downy leaves of this stemless plant rest on the ground in a rosette. In the middle is a flowerhead 4-6 inches (10-15 cm) in diameter, made up of yellow flowers. Long picked for decoration (e.g. of the gates of sheepfolds), the plant is now a protected species and must not be picked. Be happy just to look at them, not least

because they are real natural barometers. When rain is on the way, the flowerhead closes up.

Downy (or white) oaks

Downy oaks, which are 30–80 ft (10–25 m) tall and have a lifespan of 500 years, can be recognised by their

HOW TO RECOGNISE ORCHIDS

Orchids have three petals and three sepals that rarely join together. The whole charm of these flowers lies in the central petal, the lip or labellum, which varies depending on the species. From spring, the flowers acquire a down and colours ranging from soft to brilliant. They also change to take on the appearance of miniature animals such as flies, spiders or even monkeys and frogs. Though some remain discreet, some take on extremely peculiar appearances, like the one called the Hanged man. Take time to explore them.

Protected wildlife of the Causses

In the heart of the Causses, wildlife has a refuge safe from the ravages of man, urbanisation and industrialisation. Here, birds, mammals, reptiles, amphibians and insects form a rich natural heritage, between cliffs, cloups, potholes, moors and forests where they can live and reproduce in peace. A number of species, some of them unique to France, like the black vulture or the ocellated lizard, have become emblematic of the landscape.

The return of the black vulture

Like its cousin, the griffon vulture, the black vulture had vanished from the area. In 1992 a score of these birds were re-introduced to the skies of the Causses, and once again the canyons of the Tarn and the high roads of the Causse Noir (especially the Jonte gorge in Aveyron) are witness to the noiseless, gliding flight of these exceptional birds. In winter, the amorous frolics of mating vultures are a quite extraordinary sight.

The great gravedigger

Specifically carrion-eaters, black vultures scan the plateaux and gorges looking for dead sheep, which they can spot several miles away thanks to their sharp eyes. Their role as natural butchers is vital. Without them, a number of viruses and bacteria would proliferate on the carcasses, polluting the rivers and spreading contagious diseases.

Peregrine falcons on the wing

Since 1950 the predatory activities of falconers and egg-collectors robbing nests, combined with the massive use of pesticides in agriculture, have reduced the number of peregrine falcons by 90%. The population of this threatened species in France has now stabilised at around 250 pairs. This small bird of prey nests in cliffs, especially in the Causses du Quercy. Here they have the

huge open space they need to hunt small birds (pigeons, cuckoos etc.), which they capture by nose-diving at speeds of over 170 mph (275 kph).

Short-toed eagles

Being fond of reptiles (especially snakes) but not immune to poison, these eagles prefer to hunt non-venomous species such as grass snakes. But at the rate of five snakes a day to feed a family, they are sometimes obliged to go for vipers, against which they protect themselves with scaly claws, thick plumage and their quick reactions. When hunting, they mostly circle around a likely spot at a height of 60-100 ft (20-30 m) and drop on their prey.
In France the estimated population of these migratory birds, which winter in the Sahara, is 1,000 pairs.

Stone curlews

With their sandy brown plumage strongly striated with black, these small wading birds live mainly on the ground in dry, bare, flat country. They have a squat body terminating in a long, slightly tapering tail. Their round heads display two large eyes ringed with black. Particularly shy during the day, stone curlews forage for insects, lizards or small rodents in the twilight or at night.

Ocellated lizards

The largest protected lizards in Europe, ocellated lizards are unique to southwest Europe.

Homelovers and great sun-worshippers, they are fond of dry, open terrain and live in holes, tree stumps or cracks in rocks. The destruction of their natural habitat has reduced their numbers and even scattered urbanisation sends this very wild species into retreat. The Causses du Quercy are one of the refuges of ocellated lizards, which have been completely protected in France by decree since 22 July 1993.

HOW TO RECOGNISE A VULTURE

Carrion-eating birds of prey, vultures can be identified by their small head attached a long neck adorned with a collar. The beak is thick and grey and hooked at the end, which is ideal for picking at carcasses. They nest in cliffs, but are quite often seen circling widely in the sky, using their wingspan of 6 ft (2 m) or more. Although they never attack people, they are always an impressive sight.

Caves and prehistoric sites

A visit to this region must include a trip to some of the fascinating sites to discover the prehistoric remains of Cro-Magnon man.

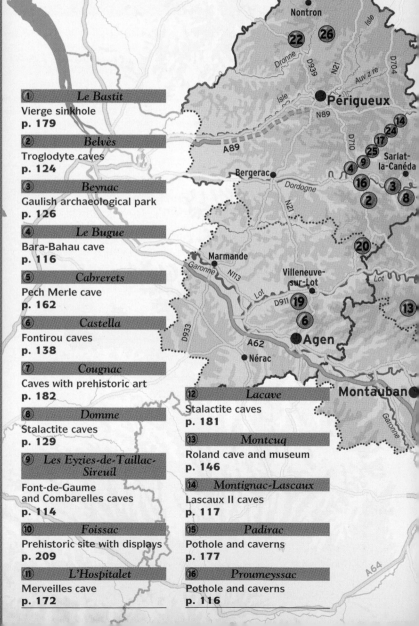

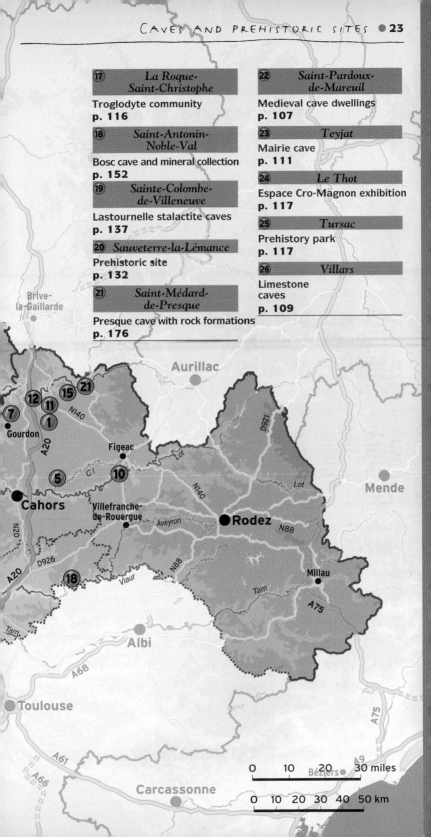

⑰ La Roque-Saint-Christophe

Troglodyte community
p. 116

⑱ Saint-Antonin-Noble-Val

Bosc cave and mineral collection
p. 152

⑲ Sainte-Colombe-de-Villeneuve

Lastournelle stalactite caves
p. 137

⑳ Sauveterre-la-Lémance

Prehistoric site
p. 132

㉑ Saint-Médard-de-Presque

Presque cave with rock formations
p. 176

㉒ Saint-Pardoux-de-Mareuil

Medieval cave dwellings
p. 107

㉓ Teyjat

Mairie cave
p. 111

㉔ Le Thot

Espace Cro-Magnon exhibition
p. 117

㉕ Tursac

Prehistory park
p. 117

㉖ Villars

Limestone caves
p. 109

Caves, potholes and dolmens

Villars cave

From Périgord to Rouergue, there are numerous underground sites beneath the limestone plateaux bearing witness to our prehistoric origins. Go back in time as you descend into the enchanting world of caves, follow underground streams or admire menhirs and dolmens.

Cradle of Cro-Magnon man

The Vézère valley all round Les Eyzies is the cradle of Cro-Magnon man, the *homo sapiens* who took up residence in these cliffs some 35,000 years ago. The great limestone plateaux and multiple geological folds in this landscape provided natural shelters to protect prehistoric man from bad weather and attacks from animals.

Magic of the underground world

This area's underground water features, whether rivers, sparkling pools or percolations, contrast vividly

Lacave cave

with the dryness of the surface. The result is a strange landscape whose famous formations were formed by dripping calcite deposits at a rate of 0.4 inches (1 cm) a century. The most famous are of course the stalactites (hanging from roof) and stalagmites (built up from the ground), but various other multi-coloured shapes fill the caves with columns, piers, transparent curtains or slender fans.

In the footsteps of man

Ever since the first underground expeditions led by Édouard Alfred Martel (1859–1938) in the early 20thC., modern experts have uncovered endless traces left by Palaeolithic man.

STALACTITES AND STALAGMITES

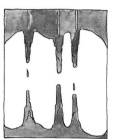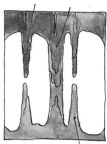

Rainwater filters into the caves after percolating through limestone beds, where it picks up calcium carbonate as it passes. As it drips from the roof of the cave, the water forms stalactites by depositing part of its limestone content. Stalagmites develop immediately below, formed by the accumulation of calcium carbonate in the remaining water. Over time, stalactites and stalagmites join up to form continuous columns.

Tools, skeletons, burials, pottery shards, carved objects, touching stencilled pictures of hands – not forgetting the ochre, red or brown frescoes, in which everyone can enjoy trying to identify bison, horses and mammoths.

Access made easy

It's no longer necessary to strap on ropes and lamps to go down. Without having greatly altered the natural surroundings, modern methods are used for guided visits, allowing you to descend 300 ft (100 m) underground without any trouble. Discreet lighting, lifts, guard-rails, electric trains or little boats are a feature of most tours.

The Mystery of megaliths

From the 4th and 3rd millennia BC, Neolithic civilisations in the Causses constructed hundreds of megaliths. With 500 dolmens, Aveyron tops the list. A distinction is made between menhirs, blocks of stone driven into the ground which are at the root of modern place names such as

Pierrefitte, and dolmens, consisting of upright supporting stones and a horizontal slab. One theory about the latter, some of which were buried under earth or stone mounds (tumuli), is they served as tombs. It remains a mystery how their builders acquired the techniques to manoeuvre blocks of stone weighing several tons (thousands of kg).

Dolmen at Tiergues (Saint-Affrique plateau)

ENIGMAS OF PREHISTORY

Over 3 million years, prehistory saw great changes in the evolution of the human species. The discovery of 'Lucy' in Ethiopia in 1974 triggered furious controversy about chronology. Previously, experts were agreed that we are descended from Homo habilis, who appeared in Africa 2.5 million years ago and is thus called because he used tools. Evolving progressively into Homo erectus, with the upright gait of a biped, he would then have colonised the ancient world and given birth to Neanderthal man and then Cro-Magnon man 300,000 to 400,000 years ago. But the discovery of Lucy and others upset these past certainties. An Australopithecus who lived 3 million years ago, she already walked upright. And she is either the missing link in the evolution of species (explaining the transition from monkey to man) or she is an entirely different but contemporary species of Homo habilis. In short, as things stand we are certain neither of the identity of our ancestors, nor of exact dates, nor even if modern man came from a single origin or from interbreeding. We await developments.

Nature trails and views

There is a wide range of possible country walks in the region, ranging from leisurely family strolls and serious day-long rambles to hikes lasting several days.

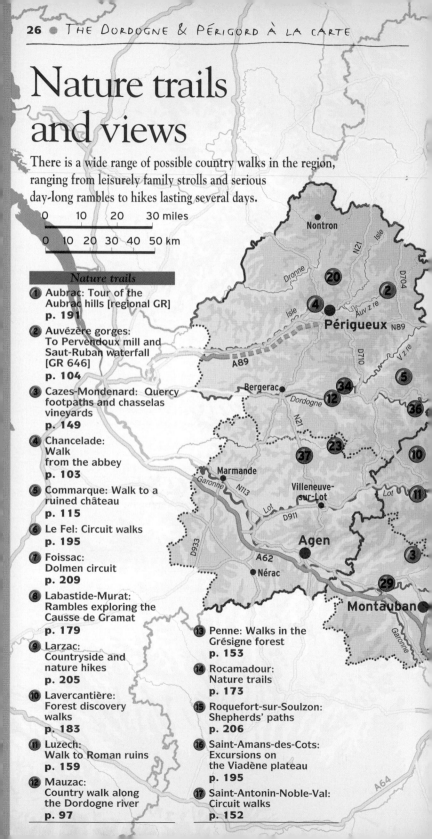

0   10   20   30 miles

0 10 20 30 40 50 km

Nature trails

1. **Aubrac:** Tour of the Aubrac hills [regional GR]
   p. 191

2. **Auvézère gorges:** To Pervendoux mill and Saut-Ruban waterfall [GR 646]
   p. 104

3. **Cazes-Mondenard:** Quercy footpaths and chasselas vineyards
   p. 149

4. **Chancelade:** Walk from the abbey
   p. 103

5. **Commarque:** Walk to a ruined château
   p. 115

6. **Le Fel:** Circuit walks
   p. 195

7. **Foissac:** Dolmen circuit
   p. 209

8. **Labastide-Murat:** Rambles exploring the Causse de Gramat
   p. 179

9. **Larzac:** Countryside and nature hikes
   p. 205

10. **Lavercantière:** Forest discovery walks
    p. 183

11. **Luzech:** Walk to Roman ruins
    p. 159

12. **Mauzac:** Country walk along the Dordogne river
    p. 97

13. **Penne:** Walks in the Grésigne forest
    p. 153

14. **Rocamadour:** Nature trails
    p. 173

15. **Roquefort-sur-Soulzon:** Shepherds' paths
    p. 206

16. **Saint-Amans-des-Cots:** Excursions on the Viadène plateau
    p. 195

17. **Saint-Antonin-Noble-Val:** Circuit walks
    p. 152

Nontron

Dronne

Isle

N21

Isle

D704

20

2

4

Auv z re

Périgueux N89

D710

V z re

Bergerac

Dordogne

34

12

5

36

A89

N21

10

23

37

11

Marmande

Garonne

N113

Lot

Villeneuve-sur-Lot

Lot

D911

Agen

D933

A62

3

Nérac

29

Montauban

Garonne

A64

Views

24 Autoire: Natural amphitheatre **p. 177**

25 Cajarc: **p. 161**

26 Combalou plateau: View of Roquefort country **p. 206**

27 Labastide-du-Haut-Mont: View of Auvergne hills and Pyrenees **p. 185**

28 Loubressac: Panorama of Quercy uplands **p. 177**

29 Moissac: Views of River Tarn and canal **p. 144**

30 Rocamadour: View of the château **p. 170**

31 Saint-Antonin-Noble-Val: **p. 152**

32 Saint-Cirq-Lapopie: view from La Popie rock **p. 160**

33 Saut de la Mounine: **p. 161**

34 Trémolat: Overlook of river bends **p. 96**

35 Le Vallon: Panorama of Truyère gorges **p. 195**

36 Domme: Jubilé clifftop path and view of châteaux and valley **p. 129**

37 Castillonnés: La Mouthe footpath and valley view **p. 131**

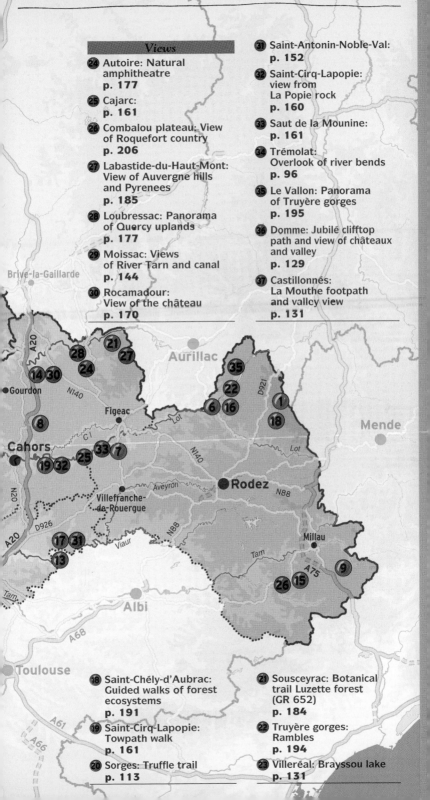

18 Saint-Chély-d'Aubrac: Guided walks of forest ecosystems **p. 191**

19 Saint-Cirq-Lapopie: Towpath walk **p. 161**

20 Sorges: Truffle trail **p. 113**

21 Sousceyrac: Botanical trail Luzette forest (GR 652) **p. 184**

22 Truyère gorges: Rambles **p. 194**

23 Villeréal: Brayssou lake **p. 131**

Water and the Causses
– a natural paradox

The Causses are areas of great contrasts, huge limestone plateaux punctuated by precipitous gorges. Paradoxically, beneath the dryness of the plateaux, there are rushing underground rivers. The plateaux are the open-air kingdom of walkers, potholers and climbers, but they are also the unchallenged realm of sheep – and, of course, the hallowed truffle oaks.

Sheep on the Causse du Larzac

Location...

The Causses are vast limestone plateaux, unique in Europe, extending south of the Massif Central. Bordered by the Cévennes range in the east and the Lot valley in the north, the Grands Causses extend south onto the plains of Hérault and lower Languedoc and west onto the Lévezou and Ségala plateaux and (at a lower altitude) the Causses du Quercy.

... and aspect

The limestone rock gives the landscape a character full of abrupt contrasts. The plateaux are harsh and dry, an endless succession of rock and close-cropped grass, scarred by deep valleys, huge canyons and natural sinkholes that are known as 'avens'.

Major and minor

The Causses are divided into two groups. First, there are the four 'major' Causses, the Grands Causses of Aveyron, which occupy a former marine gulf and vary in altitude from 1,600 to 3,300 ft (500 to 1,000 m). They are called the Causse du Larzac (the biggest), the Causse Noir ('black' because of its ancient pine forests), the Causse de Sauveterre and the Causse Méjean. Rainwater runoff and erosion have also created a series of attached mini-causses, isolated from the major plateaux by rivers, as for example Campestre, separated from Larzac by the River Virenque. The second, 'minor' group is formed by the extension of the Grands Causses to the west, in

View of the Causse du Larzac

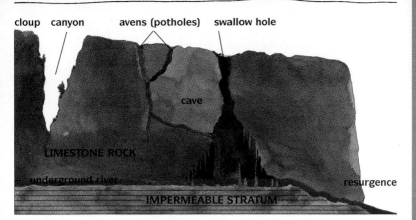

cloup   canyon   avens (potholes)   swallow hole

cave

LIMESTONE ROCK

underground river   resurgence

IMPERMEABLE STRATUM

Quercy. 'Minor' in the sense of being lower, their altitude rarely exceeding 1,000 ft (300 m), they include the causses of Martel, Gramat and Limogne.

Precipitous canyons

Canyons are narrow gorges cut into the limestone surface. They can reach depths of over 1,600 ft (500 m). The Jonte and Dourbie gorges in Aveyron are magnificent examples of canyons where suddenly, as you round a bend, immense horizons are interrupted by an alarming, vertical fissure.

A little geology

The limestone of the causses absorbs rainfall naturally like a sponge. The result is a sharp contrast between the dryness of the surface and the busy watery world beneath. The process is simple: water charged with carbonic acid dissolves the calcium carbonate in the limestone, creating small depressions known as 'cloups'. When these hollow out deep holes in the rock, they form pits or natural chasms called sinkholes, avens or 'igues'. These natural holes gradually become bigger, forming underground galleries that eventually interconnect and open up caves.

Underground rivers, resurgences and waterfalls

Sometimes a stream falls down an aven (pothole) or water filters through the limestone and collects deep down on an impermeable stratum. This is how substantial networks of underground rivers form. Depending on the gradient of the terrain, they may run for several miles, join up, hollow out galleries and continue in the form of waterfalls. Sometimes, when the impermeable layer returns to the surface, the streams emerge into the open and form springs. This is called a resurgence. Thus the underground river from the pothole at Padirac emerges

7 miles (11 km) away as the crow flies, its two resurgences running into the Dordogne.

Natural parks

Established more than three decades ago, the Parcs Naturels Régionaux (regional nature parks) are intended to maintain the ecological and economic equilibrium of the region. The creation of the Grands Causses park (1,150 sq miles/300,000 ha), around Roquefort country (Aveyron), in May 1995 took the number in the Midi-Pyrénées region to three. In the near future, a second natural park in the area, the Causses de Quercy, containing such treasures as Rocamadour, Padirac and Saint-Cirq-Lapopie, should also receive official blessing.

Mountain roads of the Causse Noir, Peyreleau

Rivers of the Dordogne

The Dronne, Isle and Dordogne rivers cross Périgord from east to west. They rise in the Massif Central before joining forces in Aquitaine. The Vézère is less tenacious and surrenders to the Dordogne at Limeuil. Further south, the temperamental and fickle Dropt waters a few Aquitaine bastides and the département of Lot-et-Garonne. In the north, the Bandiat idles around Nontron before setting off for the Charentes.

Did you say Dordogne?

Originally the Dordogne was called the Du-unna, a Celtic name meaning 'fast-flowing water'. During the Middle Ages, this was successively transformed into Duranna, Durunia, Dordoigne, and finally Dordogne. Occasionally it is referred to as the Espérance, after a well-known French TV series.

Mills

The waters of Périgord's rivers have long been put to work by man. In the 12thC., mention is made of a mill at Bigaroque on the Dordogne, while the squire of Bourdeilles left us a magnificent mill on the Dronne at Brantôme in the shape of a ship. The proliferation of these mills on the Dordogne, Dronne, Isle, Vézère and their tributaries bears witness to these rivers' history of commercial activity.

River transport

Rivers have been used as transport routes since the end of prehistoric times. Amphorae of Campanian wine have been found along the Dordogne, confirming the existence of a wine trade with ancient Rome before wine production developed in southwest Gaul. From the Middle Ages, river transport favoured commerce in valleys and the prosperity of merchants. Artisan trades developed, including marine carpenters, coopers, ropemakers, papermakers

and smiths. It was an era when wine and paper left Bergerac for Bordeaux, to be transported to England, Portugal or Holland. In the opposite direction, barges imported salt and dried fish, and from the 18thC. spices and silk were brought in from the colonies.

Development of gabare river barges

The gabares (river boats) had a flat-bottomed hull and very shallow draught so they could pass over shoals. The biggest could be 80 ft (25 m) long. Going upriver, they were towed by a team of oxen or horses. But in 1882, the railway reached Sarlat. Competition from the railway soon brought an end to gabare transport.

Not a pleasure trip

Sailing downriver was sometimes very dangerous because of hazardous channels and eddies. The opening of a 10-mile (16-km) lateral canal at Lalinde was greeted with relief by the bargees. The canal, interrupted by 10 locks with lockkeepers' houses, was only in service for 30 years from its opening in 1841, because of competition from the railway after 1870.

When a river meant fish...

The day has long passed when a decree prohibited the well-to-do from giving their servants salmon more than three times a week. But there was a time when the Dordogne heaved with fish. Weirs, installed more or less everywhere along its length since the 19thC., have prevented fish from migrating. Fish ladders had to be installed (notably at Bergerac) to allow shad and other species to

return upstream, but unfortunately such measures have been inadequate to restock the Dordogne. (At Tuilières, there is a lift to help fish past a 40-ft barrage.)

... and when a river meant fishing

There are still – or perhaps it's better to say – there are only 65 professional fishermen still setting their nets or placing their pots in the

Dordogne. Though the rivers of Périgord no longer feed the local population, they have by no means been deserted. Amateur anglers are the more active breed, with 30,000 a year fishing for pike, eels, lampreys and others.

Lamprey (above) and eel

Farm produce

Foie gras, duck breasts, prunes, Laguiole cheese,
not to mention Périgord caviar and ostrich steaks –
there's a wealth of local traditional foods for you to sample...

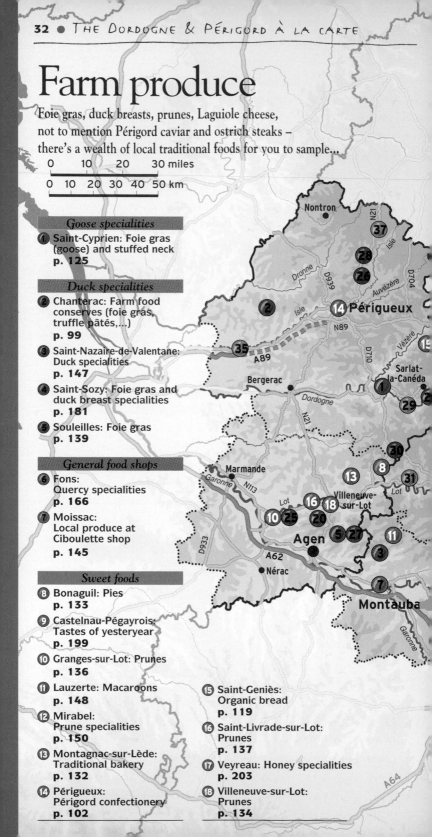

0   10   20   30 miles

0 10 20 30 40 50 km

Goose specialities

**① Saint-Cyprien: Foie gras
(goose) and stuffed neck
p. 125**

Duck specialities

**② Chanterac: Farm food
conserves (foie gras,
truffle pâtés,...)
p. 99**

**③ Saint-Nazaire-de-Valentane:
Duck specialities
p. 147**

**④ Saint-Sozy: Foie gras and
duck breast specialities
p. 181**

**⑤ Souleilles: Foie gras
p. 139**

General food shops

**⑥ Fons:
Quercy specialities
p. 166**

**⑦ Moissac:
Local produce at
Ciboulette shop
p. 145**

Sweet foods

**⑧ Bonaguil: Pies
p. 133**

**⑨ Castelnau-Pégayrols:
Tastes of yesteryear
p. 199**

**⑩ Granges-sur-Lot: Prunes
p. 136**

**⑪ Lauzerte: Macaroons
p. 148**

**⑫ Mirabel:
Prune specialities
p. 150**

**⑬ Montagnac-sur-Lède:
Traditional bakery
p. 132**

**⑭ Périgueux:
Périgord confectionery
p. 102**

**⑮ Saint-Geniès:
Organic bread
p. 119**

**⑯ Saint-Livrade-sur-Lot:
Prunes
p. 137**

**⑰ Veyreau: Honey specialities
p. 203**

**⑱ Villeneuve-sur-Lot:
Prunes
p. 134**

Vegetable oils

19 Martel: Walnut oil
p. 169

20 Pujols: Hazelnut oil
p. 135

21 Saint-Antonin-Noble-Val:
Walnut oil
p. 152

22 Sainte-Nathalène:
Walnut, hazelnut and
almond oils
p. 122

Cheeses

23 Laguiole: Fresh tomme
and Laguiole cheeses
p. 191-192

24 Roquefort-sur-Soulzon:
Roquefort cheese
Causses blue cheese...
p. 206

Museums

25 Granges-sur-Lot: Prune
delicacies museum
p. 136

26 Sorges:
Truffle museum
p. 113

27 Souleilles:
Foie gras museum
p. 139

28 Thiviers:
Foie gras museum
p. 112

29 Castelnaud: Périgord
walnut ecomuseum
p. 126

30 Villefranche-du-Périgord:
Chestnut
and mushroom
museum
p. 129

Others

31 Duravel: Eggs, pâtés
and ostrich meat
p. 159

32 Les Homs-du-Larzac:
Aromatic and medicinal
plants
p. 205

33 Le Mas de Monille:
Wild-boar specialities
p. 151

34 Le Montat:
Truffle-bed tour
p. 157

35 Montpon-Ménéstérol:
Périgord caviar
p. 99

36 Naucelle: Tripe
p. 213

37 Saint-Paul-la-Roche:
Apple juice, goat's
cheese...
p. 113

Free-range herds

The juicy pasture in the upper parts of the arid Causses sustains cows, sheep and goats, a common sight in the landscapes of Périgord, Quercy and Rouergue. Long essential for the survival of isolated communities, these local, rustic and individual breeds continue to be reared in the purest farming tradition. Some are kept for milk, others for 'red label' meat; either way they are still among the glories of the farming landscape.

herds of cows, decked out with cowbells, pennants and flowers, migrate up to the Aubrac plateaux for the summer. A friendly event, with much local colour.

Calves fed with milk

Looking at the grasslands of Lot or Aveyron départements, nothing appears to have changed in the lives of the herds. Brought up by their mothers and

Aubrac cattle

Known for centuries in northeast Aveyron, the breed was recognised in 1894. A typical sight on the Aubrac plateaux, the breed is easily distinguished because, though their coat may vary from brown to deep grey, they always sport elegant, lyre-shaped horns (used to make the handles of Laguiole knives) and eyes masked black. Aubrac cows provide high-quality milk and excellent meat that is sold by butchers in the region under the Fleur d'Aubrac label. Don't miss the **summer-pastures festival**, around 25 May every year, when

fed mainly on their milk for months, they are supposedly derived from well-known breeds such as the Blonde d'Aquitaine, Limousin or Gascon. To maintain the quality of the tender, pink and tasty meat, 850 breeders have joined forces under the auspices of the regional Aveyron breeders' association. Each year, the association certifies 7,000 calves with a unique 'geographical identity' (a kind of AOC for calves), a production zone limited to parts of Aveyron, Lot and Tarn départements.

Lacaune, star of Roquefort

At the outset, who would have risked a bet on this tall breed of cattle with hoofs, a short coat and hairless head and stomach? Kept in years gone by for its meat, it had no real dairy value. But from the 1970s its ability to adapt to a dry terrain drew the attention of researchers of the national institute of agronomic research (INRA). By selecting the best ewes and collaborating with producers, they turned the Lacaune into a world champion milker, and now their milk is used in the manufacture of Roquefort cheese. Today, there is great competition for the superstar breed and there are more than 1.2 million Lacaune cows in the region.

Caussenard ewe wearing 'glasses'

Sheep with spectacles

You can't miss these Caussenard sheep of Lot département, reared both for their milk and their meat. The black circles round their eyes contrast sharply with their white coat, and look a little like a pair of spectacles. Some say they wear them as sunglasses to protect them from the sun!

Tender lambs

Where you have sheep, of course ou have lambs. More specifically, farm lambs with a wild moorland flavour passed on through their mothers' milk. Bred from Lacaune or Caussenard ewes, they are kept for at least 5 months in the fold on a straw litter and fed solely by their mother for at least 70 days. They are sold under the regional 'Agneau del País' label.

Three cheers for tripe!

Typical of the Aveyron region around Naucelle, 'tripoux' is an uplands dish made from lamb or calf tripe that is constantly winning new fans.

A mixture of ham, calf tripe, strawberries and parsley is stuffed in a case made from a calf's stomach. This combination is slowly cooked for several hours in a beef stock with celery, carrots, onions and white wine. Once the fat is skimmed off, the mixture finishes up as little 4-oz (100-g) patties preserved in tins or glass jars which can be simply reheated in a bain-marie. This forms part of a traditional Sunday meal, served with potatoes or fried croutons – accompanied by, of course, a bottle of good red or dry white wine, preferably with an Aveyron label such as Marcillac or Entraygues.

All about foie gras

Did you know that the French word 'foie' (liver) comes from Latin 'fica' (fig). This is really quite logical, since Roman geese were virtually stuffed with the fruit. From Périgord to Quercy, you'll have plenty to choose from, including duck or goose foie, and other delicacies such as magret (duck breast), conserves and stuffed neck.

Force-feeding a goose

Force-feeding geese

The art of force-feeding has been preserved over the centuries and is claimed to be a reinforcement of the natural tendency of 'gras' (fat) geese and ducks to overeat before setting off on their long migrations. Force-feeding geese and ducks is considered perfectly reasonable and acceptable by the local people. You may feel revulsion at this practice, and we are certainly not advocating it, but it is a tolerated and inescapable part of the culture of the region.

Raw or cooked?

The liver of a fat adult goose weighs around 2 lbs (1 kg), while that of a duck only reaches 1-1.5 lbs (400-700g). They can be sold **cru** (uncooked) and vacuum-wrapped, or **frais** (fresh), i.e. lightly cooked. They only keep fresh for 5-6 days, but you can keep them several months in the freezer if they are **mi-cuit** (half-cooked) or **cuit** (cooked), having been sterilised.

Whole, mixed or reconstituted?

A **foie gras entier** (whole) consists of one or two whole pieces of salted and peppered liver. This is the ultimate in foie gras. The alternative is simply called **foie gras**. This refers to a preparation made

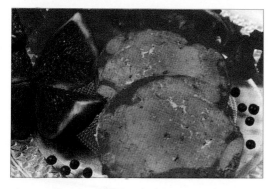

of pieces of liver from different birds mixed together. Finally, you can get a **bloc** (block) of foie gras made from reconstituted foie gras. Other foie gras products include 'parfaits', which must contain at least 75% foie gras, while

pâtés, mousses and 'galantines' of foie gras must contain at least 50% foie gras.

Make it yourself

Nothing could be easier. All you need to do is buy a whole foie gras from a farm (Oct. onwards) or from a market (labelled 'au gras') during the winter. Choose one that is firm but not stiff, evenly blond in colour and unveined. Soak the liver in slightly salted water for several hours. Separate the lobes, discard the membrane, the central vein and the blood vessels. Drain the liver, season it with salt, white pepper and a tumbler (30 cl) of wine or other alcohol (such as Armagnac). Set aside to chill for 24 hours. Put it into a terrine dish,

replace the lid and cook for an hour in a bain-marie in the oven at 200°C (400°F, gas mark 7).

Simplicity itself

A good foie gras is a joy on its own. Truffles are not essential, although they do add an undeniable extra flavour. First, chill the foie gras a few hours before eating, removing it from the chiller 30 minutes before serving. To cut it easily, it is best to use a sharp knife whose blade has been dipped in hot water. All you need to do then is taste it as it is,

along with a slice of good wholesome bread, toasted or fresh. A wide range of wines go well with it, but purists swear by Sauternes.

Other goose and duck products

It is not only the liver that can tickle your palate. Ducks and geese provide many other choice morsels. Offer your gourmets 'magrets' – plump, succulent fillets of duck breast served rare and cut into slices, served with sautéed potatoes and pieces of cooked apple. Processed when raw and vacuum-wrapped, you can also get your duck breasts smoked or dried. You can also get delicious duck thighs sold by the jar – very easy to reheat. And if there is any fat left at the bottom of the jar, don't throw it away. It will add flavour to fried food without harming your health: thanks to its natural richness in fatty polyunsaturated acids, it will not have any ill effects on your cholesterol levels.

The cheese platter

The creamy, scented milk from cows, goats or sheep bred on the Causses or upland slopes has been used to make cheeses since time immemorial. Often distinguished by an 'appellation' or a label, the output is diverse and of high quality, ranging from tiny delicate cheeses and solid cows' milk tommes to unusual marbled cheeses.

Cliff of Combalou plateau, Roquefort-sur-Soulzon

Roquefort, the product of air, milk and mould!

It all began 170 million years ago at Roquefort-sur-Soulzon, when the Combalou plateau rudely collapsed, bringing about the formation of 'fleurines', natural fissures that ventilate the underground caves with a humid breeze at a constant temperature, providing a natural air conditioning that favours fermentation. But the other secret of the most famous marbled cheese, protected by an AOC since 1925, is contained in two words – *penicillium roqueforti* – a natural mould that gives the cheese its greenish marbling, its subtle flavours, aromas and smoothness. Once the ewe's milk has been treated with the spores, the mass of white curds is cut into cubes and the surplus whey removed before the curds are sent for moulding and draining. The 'loaves' are sent to the salting room, then deposited on their oak stands to ferment. Three months later, the Roquefort is ready to be eaten (*see also* p. 206).

laurel and sweet-smelling plants. Made from raw milk, it can be eaten hot or cold, blending easily with other traditional foods of the region, such as truffles or Cahors wine. Its qualities were recognised in 1996 with the award of an AOC.

Its cousin, Causses blue cheese

This is a sort of cousin of Roquefort. Treated and made in the same way, it has two notable differences: the cheese is made with cows' milk, not ewe's milk. In addition, it is matured for three to six months in natural limestone caves, including of course the fleurines, but located outside the village of Roquefort. This has not prevented it from establishing its own separate right to an AOC.

Rocamadour, the cream of cheeses

Documented since the Middle Ages, Rocamadour is a soft little goats' milk cheese, creamy white with a smooth crust. Coming from the heart of the dry Causses du Quercy, it draws its aromas from the flowers grazed on by the sheep, mingling hawthorn,

Cabécou and pérail, tasty little morsels

From the Lot to the Aveyron, sheep's and goats' milk are both used to produced other little cheeses as tasty as Rocamadour. One such is the tiny, sheep's milk 'pérail': a small cake of cheese less than 1 inch (2 cm) thick, which acquires a pale, yellowish crust enclosing a milky fondant interior after maturing for 10-15 days. A delicacy to ferret out at farms or at the markets. Smaller still, only 2-3 inches (5-7 cm) in diameter is the 'cabécou', a word meaning 'goat', each cheese constituting only a single mouthful. Known in the 19thC. even in Paris, these cheeses with a fine and homogeneous consistency were on the decline. But one day a grocer

from Lot set to work, sending small fragile wooden boxes filled with the best cabécous to leading cheesemongers throughout France. Since then, these little goats' cheeses have made a comeback.

Laguiole, the grandad of cheeses

On the fringe of the Massif Central and spilling into Cantal, milk from Aubrac cows gave birth to Laguiole, a traditional cheese dating back to ancient times. The recipe was improved by the monks of the Middle Ages and kept alive by 'buronniers', people named after the 'buron' (shepherd's hut). Reviving the best of traditions, the Jeune Montagne co-operative relaunched the celebrated tommes made of raw whole milk. Matured for 4-12 months and weighing over 100 lbs (50 kg), they sport a fine,

amber-coloured rind, stamped with the symbol of a bull. Laguiole is the basic ingredient of aligot, a traditional Aubrac dish combining garlic, cheese and potatoes, served in a long, thick strip (p. 192).

Shepherds
– a pastoral symphony

Shepherds are still found on the high plateaux of the Causses. Despite the difficult way of life and depopulation, young people are trying their hand at it, supported by the dairy sector, the mainstay of the Caussenard economy. The presence of shepherds is vital for maintaining the vast upland terrain, as well as making it more attractive to tourists.

One animal, many uses

Sheep have always been present in these rocky landscapes, but not always for the same reason. Once reared for their wool, which supplied the cloth towns such as Saint-Affrique, or for their skins, used by the glove makers of Millau, they could also provide lambs for the butcher and manure for the vineyards of Languedoc. In the mid-19thC., however, competition from foreign wool forced shepherds of the Causses to put down their shears and get out their milking stools.

The rhythm of the seasons

Circumstances have changed, but shepherds still respect inherited traditions that are thousands of years old. For example, the management of the flocks follows an unchanging ritual. As soon as the fine weather arrives and warms up the high plateaux, the shepherd sets off every morning with his dog and his flock to cross the upland expanses to reach the steppes. The mountain pasturing is only brought to an end by the first frosts of winter, in November. From then on, the sheep are confined to the fold, where they eat fodder and cereals, waiting for the following spring.

Natural depressions and artificial ponds

Streams are a rare sight in the Causses, so its inhabitants soon altered the landscape to collect what little rain was available for his livestock. Taking inspiration from the natural

Lavogne on the Causse du Larzac

'dolines', small clay depressions where the grass is thicker, the shepherds created numerous circular, artificial ponds lined with stones, called 'lavognes', where they took their flocks twice a day.

Mechanised milking of ewes

The milking season

For six months, the ewes are milked twice a day in the fold. Previously done by hand, mechanisation now allows the milking of anything from 26 ewes per hour to more than 400 for advanced systems. Likewise, advances in health and nutritional practices have done much to increase production. Whereas in the 19th C. milk output was only a dozen or so gallons per sheep over the whole season, each animal now produces 42-50 gallons (200-230 litres).

Milk by tanker

It is now rare for shepherds to make their own cheeses as they once did. The milk which is obtained from the sheep is sent daily to the cheese manufacturers or co-operatives in tankers, where it arrives in a raw, pure and whole state. It is then immediately checked to determine its origin. The largest cheese makers can handle as much as 18,000 gallons (80,000 litres) of milk a day.

Red sheep

In the Camarès area, it is not uncommon to see flocks of sheep with strangely coloured ochre or red wool. You may think this a new species, or the work of a mad artist, but it is actually the result of a natural phenomenon. The land around this area is known as 'rougier' (redlands), because of the fiery colours of the soil.

Redlands seen from the Château de Montaigut

Gusts of wind pick up the pigmented dust, which floats in the air and eventually comes to settle on the white fleeces of the unsuspecting sheep.

Breeding and lambing

If you hear talk about the 'lutte' (struggle), don't imagine a punch-up between breeders. This is simply the name for the mating of the sheep, which begins in June. Five to six months later, the shepherds are busy helping the mothers and the new-born lambs through the main lambing season. Though some of the animals are destined to be sold for their meat, others remain to restock the flock. But the destiny of the young sheep, lambing also heralds the forthcoming milking season.

Milk delivery to the Jeune Montagne co-operative, Laguiole

Where to eat and drink

There follows a selection of places to sample regional cuisine or dine in exceptional surroundings, plus a selection of places to taste Cahors wine, Homs pastis and chestnut liqueur.

Outstanding restaurants

1. **Almont-les-Junies:** Restaurant Ferrières **p. 211**
2. **Belcastel:** Restaurant du Vieux Pont **p. 197**
3. **Bergerac:** La Flambée **p. 95**
4. **Cahors:** Le Bistrot du Cahors **p. 155**
5. **Chancelade:** Restaurant de l'Oison **p. 103**
6. **Domme:** L'Esplanade **p. 129**
7. **Espagnac-Sainte-Eulalie:** Les Jardins du Célé **p. 163**
8. **Les Eyzies:** Le Centenaire **p. 115**
9. **Le Fel:** Auberge du Fel **p. 195**
10. **Figeac:** La Cuisine du Marché **p. 166**
11. **La Fouillade:** Hôtel-restaurant Longcol **p. 209**
12. **Lacave:** Château de la Treyne **p. 180**
13. **Mercuès:** Hôtel-restaurant Château de Mercuèss **p. 158**
14. **Millau:** La Vieille Fontaine **p. 202**
15. **Lac de Pareloup:** Emmanuel III boat **p. 198**
16. **Le Puech-du-Suquet:** Michel Bras' restaurant **p. 192**
17. **Rocamadour:** Restaurant Beau Site **p. 171**
18. **Saint-Sernin-sur-Rance:** Carayon **p. 207**
19. **Sauveterre-de-Rouergue:** Le Sénnéchal **p. 212**
20. **Tursac:** Layotte farm inn **p. 117**

Wines and spirits

21 Cahors: Atrium wine centre
p. 156

22 21 Carsac-de-Gurson: Grappe de Gurson wine co-operative
p. 91

23 Donzac: Côtes-de-Brulhois 'black wines'
p. 141

24 Entraygues-sur-Truyère: Méjanassère estate (Entraygues and Le Fel AOC wines)
p. 195

25 Estaing: Vignerons d'Olt wine co-operative
p. 189

26 Les Homs-du-Larzac: Homs pastis
p. 205

27 Mercuès: Château de Mercuès (Cahors AOC)
p. 158

28 Monbazillac: Wine trail
p. 92

29 Monflanquin: Sept-Monts cellar (Agen wines)
p. 132

30 Montpezat-de-Quercy: Quercy wine centre; Gabachou estate; Vignerons du Quercy wine co-operative; Lafages estate
p. 150

31 Rocamadour: Périgord distillery (walnut wine, chestnut liqueur, morello cherries)
p. 171

32 Valady: Vignerons du Vallon de Marcillac cellar
p. 187

33 Villamblard: Reymond distillery (eaux-de-vie)
p. 98

Museums

34 Bergerac: Museum of wine, barrel-making and river transport
p. 94

35 Monbazillac: Wine museum
p. 92

36 Saint-Aulaye: Cognac and wine museum
p. 107

Cep mushrooms and truffles

fleshy umbrellas and black diamonds

One is visually striking, the other has to be sniffed out. Cep mushrooms and truffles (aka black diamonds) are the supreme forest products, their famous scents picked up by those who know where to dig. But it's easier to get them in the market place. And though nothing can beat them fresh from the ground, buying them deep-frozen or as conserves means they can be enjoyed throughout the year.

The king of ceps

There are 15 or so varieties of cep mushrooms, but the pick of the bunch are the Bordeaux cep and the black-headed cep, which are easy to recognise because they don't turn blue when touched. The Bordeaux cep, with a reddish-brown top and yellow pores and striated at the bottom, is firm, fleshy and fragrant. The black-headed cep has a brown top, contrasting with white flesh.

The dawn army

Ceps grow in mild, humid weather in autumn. The soil has to have been warmed up in July, watered in August, and all with a prevailing southerly wind. Picking them means getting up very early to beat the competition. Before the sun is even up, cars can be seen prowling the edge of the chestnut or oak forests, taking the 'dawn army' to 'their' cep patches, despite the warning signs of proprietors and farmers.

Market stalls

Many tons of ceps pass through the market at Villefranche-du-Périgord. When the price goes up or down here, the selling price throughout the region follows suit. You can, of course, look for good ceps on the stalls of many other villages in the region. The price is certainly high, but if you're feeling the pinch, you can always try the ceps in an omelette or salad.

Choosing and cooking ceps

Ceps should smell pleasant and have a firm, healthy texture. But some fans of ceps prefer them large and slightly soft to add to a sauce. Rather than wash the ceps, clean them carefully with a cloth or paper. If you want to keep

them, the best thing is to freeze them or place them in a jar of olive oil. Otherwise, nothing beats a pan of braised fresh ceps with a dribble of oil, a little garlic and some parsley to bring out all their flavour, together with a glass of red wine such as a Cahors or Marcillac.

Périgord truffles

These black diamonds shine with fire. Mysterious and rare, truffles captivated even the Pharaoh Cheops. The truffle is a gem that is born underground in early March beneath certain oaks, and grows and matures by December. An oddity of nature is that where truffles grow, the grass disappears as if burnt.

Harvesting truffles

Truffles are generally harvested between November and March. There are several methods, the most picturesque being 'à la mouche', using a very specific kind of 'mouche' (fly), which settles on the ground when attracted by the scent of the truffle. The better-known method is with a truffle sow, whose fondness for truffles and very precise

sense of smell leads her straight to the prize. The sow roots in the soil with her snout, but you must be on guard and get hold of the truffles before the animal swallows them. Finally, a well-trained truffle hound can also perform wonders with its acute sense of smell.

What to do next

The truffles, which weigh 0.5-7 oz (10–200 g), are brushed, washed and graded before being sold in the markets, the biggest being those at Saint-Alvère (Dordogne) and Lalbenque (Lot). You can buy them fresh – they can be kept for a week by immersion in a glass of oil to protect them from the surrounding air – or as conserves, which may be placed in an airtight, plastic container along with some

eggs. In this way you can make an omelette with a slightly truffled scent. It is also possible to acquire some excellent truffle oils, juice and sauces to add to omelettes and red meat.

Watch out for imitations

There are several varieties of truffle, but only one can be sold as a black Périgord truffle, or *Tuber melanosporum*, to give it its Latin name. This is found mainly in southwest France and the Dordogne and Lot areas. Unfortunately, it is very difficult for a non-specialist to identify. The high prices of truffles reflects the steady shrinkage of the areas in which they grow.

Fruit paradise

From spring to autumn, the whole region provides a festival of fruit. Full of sun, springing from fertile soils, carefully cultivated by people who respect tradition, the sweet, natural pleasures of the region include plums, grapes, peaches, apricots, red and black berries and melons.

The fruit of the vine

Golden and delicately scented, the chasselas grape of Moissac is cultivated solely by hand on sun-drenched slopes. The long, willowy bunches are easy to recognise from the red strip on the packaging.

The first fresh fruit to merit an AOC, these prestigious table grapes are grown in northern Tarn-et-Garonne département and a small area in Lot. But beware – chasselas 'doré' (golden) has a short season, available only in September and October. And as you should absolutely avoid putting them in the fridge, it is better to buy them in small quantities.

Walnuts from the east

Originally from the Near East, walnuts were introduced to the southwest of France by the Romans and the favoured areas remained the Dordogne and Lot. Several varieties are harvested, including the Corne, oblong in shape with a hard nut and delicate taste. There are also varieties that are easy to

crack open, such as the Franquette, Marbot or Grandjean, plus the splendid Nave walnuts from Lot. A pleasure to munch in autumn as you saunter through local markets. You can prolong the pleasure with tasty, healthy walnut oil, extracted from the pressed pulp and heated to 50°C (122°F). The recipe for the oil is often a family secret.

A basketful of red fruits

Strawberries from Saint-Geniez-d'Olt in northern Aveyron, also known as 'sanniés', are famous for their deep red colour, firm sweet flesh, wild scent and consistent quality. Note that they are harvested late – June – and there is a local prize, the strawberry 'Oscar', awarded to the best products.

Some weeks later, cherries come into season in two specially privileged areas – Moissac, where small morellos with a tangy, fruity taste are produced, and Aguessac, a site famous in Aveyron for its wealth of varieties, of which the best are the Burlat, Reverchon and the late Vignola.

Cantaloupe Melons

A quarter of all French melons come from the Midi-Pyrénées region. The champion in all classes is Tarn-et-Garonne, the leading producing area in France. And quantity is not all, because Quercy's range is celebrated for its quality. Grown in open fields, picked when perfectly ripe and respecting the specifications of the Plaisirs du Cocagne label, Quercy melons have orange flesh, are juicy and very sweet. They are best savoured from July to Oct. and should not be conserved. To preserve their aroma and firmness, they must be kept at a constant temperature between 10 and 12°C (50 and 54°F).

Royal greengages

The queen of eating plums, unchanged for 500 years and

supreme in Quercy, is the greengage, which gets its French name, 'reine-claude' (Queen Claude), from the wife of King François I. It is golden yellow and has succulent, sweet flesh. However, it ripens only at the end of August. Note that the fine white skin that sometimes appears on the greengage is only the residue of chemicals, which are used as a protection against the heat of the summer.

Ancestral prunes

Other larger varieties, such as the Ente plum, are used to make Agen prunes in the Lot valley. In a practice dating back to at least the 16thC., the sun-dried plums were withered in the bread oven. These days the fresh fruit benefits from modern technology that preserves the softness and energy content of the prunes, including the precious potassium. Steeped in Armagnac or wine spirits, filled with chocolate, made into jam or just as they come – the choice is yours.

Cahors wine
favoured by kings and popes

It has been called powerful, thoroughbred, noble and full-bodied. Cahors wine has won fame on the high tables of Europe since ancient times. Noted for its ageing ability, this AOC does wonders for the local economy. It should be tasted on the spot, between the banks and slopes of the Lot valley.

From the Romans to the tsars

Introduced during the era of Roman colonisation, Cahors wine was soon appreciated widely for its grand style. A great rival of Bordeaux wines in the Middle Ages, it conquered the English court before being adopted by the papal court as well. The Renaissance could not ignore such a recommendation. Cahors was crowned the equal of all wines in the courts of all the sovereigns of Europe, from François I, who had some acres planted with its vines, to the Russian tsars.

The fruits of endeavour

The ravages of war, the phylloxera disaster, catastrophic frosts ... the

Vineyards in Cahors, château Les Buysses

late 19thC. seemed set to destroy the vine. However, thanks to the efforts of a number of growers, who planted new, hardier strains and strictly protected their lands, the famous Cahors wine was 'reborn'. This rebirth was symbolised in 1947 by the establishment of a wine co-operative in Parnac. Since then, the wine has gone on to reap the benefit of the drive for quality, recognised with the award of an AOC in 1971.

On the banks of the Lot

For nearly 40 miles (65 km), the vines hug the bends of the River Lot between the villages

of Soturac, west of Cahors, and Arcambal to the east. The plantations are spread over three types of soil: valley alluvium, the argilocalcite of the slopes and plateau limestone. There are 500 members of the local professional winegrowers association, who plant 10,374 acres (4,200 ha) with vines.

'Vin noir'

Cahors wine is known as 'vin noir' ('black wine') because of its deep garnet colour with mauve glints. But that is not its only special feature, because Cahors has also body, thanks to the Cot grape (also known as Auxerrois) that makes up 70% of its content. Two other varieties go into the mix: Tannat, which gives the wine its structure and its remarkable ageing ability, and Merlot, which adds roundness and finesse of bouquet. Limited yields, manual harvesting and grading, ageing in oak barrels...these contribute to guarantee the quality of Cahors wine.

See it and drink it

Many vineyards in the area encourage visits to their cellars. The proprietors of châteaux, ancient rectories, royal hunting lodges, bishops' palaces or more modest estates will all explain with the same passion the slow development of the vines as well as the distinctive features of the various cuvées (vintages), which often carry prestigious historic names – all, of course, with a glass in your hand.

Aged for up to 15 years

Remarkable for their long life, Cahors wines are distinguished according to the land on which the grapes are grown. On the alluvial plain, the wines will develop all their aromas after three years. Wines from grapes grown on the plateaux need five years to reveal their fullness and velvetiness. So, have a little patience. The best vintages may stay in the cellar for 15 years.

TASTE TEST

When light, young and fruity, Cahors wine should be served at 14-15 °C (57-60 °F). It goes brilliantly with creamed vegetables, potages, soups and consommés. If the tannins predominate, it goes with foie gras, meats in sauces, cold meats and Roquefort. The oldest Cahors crus will express all their subtlety at a temperature of 16-18 °C (60-65 °F), with truffles, red meats, game and ceps, not forgetting local cheeses such as Rocamadour and Cabécou. A little tip: decant the wine into a carafe 30 minutes before serving.

Church architecture

From Romanesque chapels to Gothic churches, the region has some fine ecclesiastical buildings.

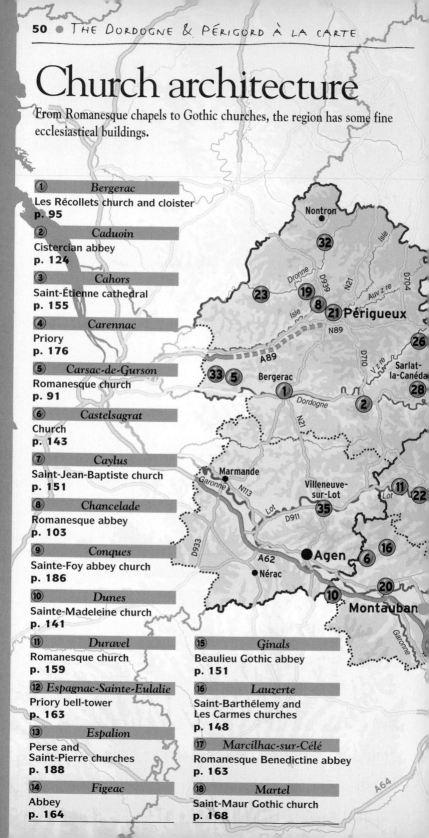

① *Bergerac*
Les Récollets church and cloister
p. 95

② *Caduoin*
Cistercian abbey
p. 124

③ *Cahors*
Saint-Étienne cathedral
p. 155

④ *Carennac*
Priory
p. 176

⑤ *Carsac-de-Gurson*
Romanesque church
p. 91

⑥ *Castelsagrat*
Church
p. 143

⑦ *Caylus*
Saint-Jean-Baptiste church
p. 151

⑧ *Chancelade*
Romanesque abbey
p. 103

⑨ *Conques*
Sainte-Foy abbey church
p. 186

⑩ *Dunes*
Sainte-Madeleine church
p. 141

⑪ *Duravel*
Romanesque church
p. 159

⑫ *Espagnac-Sainte-Eulalie*
Priory bell-tower
p. 163

⑬ *Espalion*
Perse and
Saint-Pierre churches
p. 188

⑭ *Figeac*
Abbey
p. 164

⑮ *Ginals*
Beaulieu Gothic abbey
p. 151

⑯ *Lauzerte*
Saint-Barthélemy and
Les Carmes churches
p. 148

⑰ *Marcilhac-sur-Célé*
Romanesque Benedictine abbey
p. 163

⑱ *Martel*
Saint-Maur Gothic church
p. 168

On the history trail

Château d'Estaing

History and travel have always gone together in Rouergue and Quercy. Explore history by following the dolmen trail or touring medieval châteaux, tracing the routes of pilgrims or the works of the Templars, or trailing in the wake of sailing barges or pack horses.

Dolmens

It's a little known fact, but with 500 dolmens from Foissac on the Saint-Affrique plateau by way of Salles-la-Source, Aveyron is top of the league in the number of its megaliths. However, the word 'dolmen' comes from the Breton 'dol' (table) and 'men' (stone), and the exact significance of these ancient burial stones continues to remain a mystery to us.

In the footsteps of Saint Jacques

According to legend, the apostle Saint Jacques le Majeur (St James the Great) evangelised Spain – in practice, Galicia. On returning to Jerusalem he was beheaded and

Statue de Saint Jacques, Espalion

his remains put on a ship by two of his disciples, which the winds and current miraculously returned to Galicia. The town of Santiago de Compostela grew up around his 'tomb' and became one of the three leading pilgrim destinations

Dolmen de Tiergues, Saint-Affrique plateau

of Christianity, along with Rome and Jerusalem. Four roads from France head that way. The one signposted as long-distance footpath GR6 starts from Puy-en-Velay and passes through Conques, Figeac, Cahors and Moissac before crossing the Pyrenees at Saint-Jean-Pied-de-Port. The route is dotted with numerous relics, churches, paintings and other survivals from the legendary pilgrims' way.

Saint-Eulalie-de-Cernon

Salt Road

In the Middle Ages, Rouergue had no salt of its own and had to negotiate with producer areas to obtain it. A salt tax was introduced and royal warehouses with a monopoly on its sale were set up, e.g. at Salmiech (which means 'salt centre'). In exchange for the 'white gold', villagers provided wood, poultry and livestock. In the last 15 years, history buffs have revived the Salt Road concept for tourists. You can follow the Salt Road linking Rouergue with the Mediterranean salt pans on foot, on horseback, in a carriage or by mountain bike. (Information from La Route du Sel, BP2, 12120 Salmiech ☎ 05 65 46 73 60).

Templars and Hospitallers trail

The orders of the Templars and Hospitallers were created in the early 12thC. to help pilgrims visiting the Christian sites in Jerusalem. Initially founded on the Causse du Larzac, the Templars established a base at Sainte-Eulalie-de-Cernon, followed by further fortified sites at La Couvertoirade, La Cavalerie and Viala-du-Pas-de-Jaux. For 150 years, the population of the plateau clustered around these sites and developed the farming and pastoral economy of the region. In 1312 the Templar order was brutally suppressed by Pope Clement V and its mantle passed to the Hospitallers, who in turn fortified these sites, which came in handy in the Hundred Years War. You can take either a car-based or a walking tour of them (GR71C) covering 75 miles (120 km). Guided visits of each site are organised every day of the year (info. from the Conservatoire Larzac Templier et Hospitalier, Place Bion-Marlavagne, 12100 Millau ☎ 05 65 59 12 22).

Baraque road

The D911 road follows the ridge from Villefranche-de-Rouergue to Millau. Its route was worked out in the 19thC. by Intendant Lescalopier, who wanted to replace the medieval roads with an official highway linking Montauban and Nîmes. To encourage traffic, 'baraques' (rudimentary inns and hostels for carters and carriages) were set up along the new road. Some of the better-placed baraques, sited at crossroads and trading places, flourished. Examples include Rieupeyroux, Baraqueville and La Primaube.

In the wake of the gabares

Dried cod is hard as wood and must soak in water for about eight days to be edible. It is said that boatmen working on the River Lot trailed them from their 'gabares' (barges) so they would be ready when they arrived. A nice story, but water transport undoubtedly helped to popularise the recipe for 'estofinado' (the Occitan word for dried cod), which has become the gastronomic symbol of Decazeville. From summer 2000 (around mid-Aug.), a rally of local gabares from Aveyron and Lot-et-Garonne will revive this tradition of river navigation. Tasting sessions of estofinado at each stage (information: R2 Organisation ☎ 06 09 71 91 32 or ODiCè Organisation ☎ 06 07 68 97 37).

Bastides and villages

The region has a wealth of fortified towns and villages surviving from medieval times. The sites are generally very picturesque and the villages have maintained their authenticity.

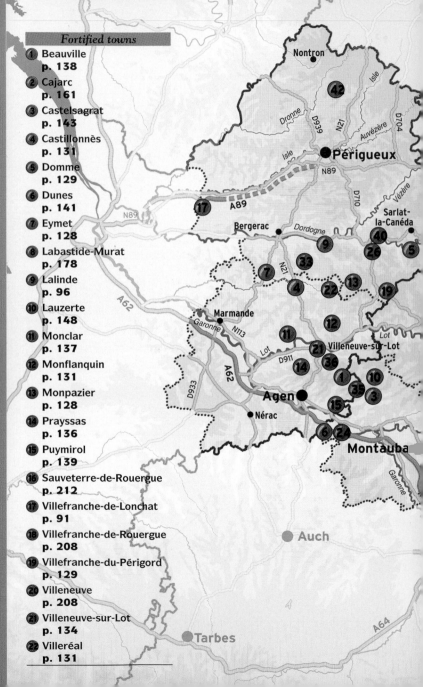

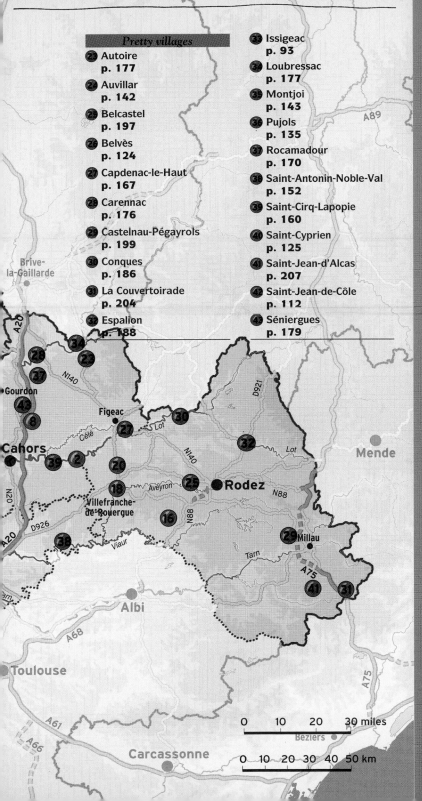

Bastides of Aquitaine

Place de Cornières, Lauzerte

In 1152 Eleanor of Aquitaine married Count of Anjou Henry Plantagenet, who became king of England a year later. The duchy of Aquitaine was part of her dowry, and the marriage created a political tangle. Aquitaine became an English-run seneschalsy under the sovereignty of the king of France. At each other's throats, the English and French sought to consolidate their positions. In order to concentrate their populations and establish their influence, they founded new towns called 'bastides' (fortified towns). Over 150 years, some 315 of these bastides were strung out across southwest France.

Why build bastides?

In addition to the political and military motives, the land had to be farmed and social life organised as well. In fact, various reasons prompted feudal lords, bishops and kings to develop a new policy for laying out their territory. In the 13thC., when the population was growing at an inordinate rate, the over-population of the countryside led to an influx of people into the large towns. The bastides arrived just in time to stem this exodus.

Profitable towns

The new towns, which typically had 1,000-2,000 inhabitants, made their founders rich. Fairs and markets flourished and so were taxed. In addition, travellers and merchandise passing through the bastides were charged tolls. Furthermore, justice was administered, with fines levied for all kinds for offences and crimes.

Places of safety...

In the troubled times of the Middle Ages, it was not wise

Villefranche-de-Rouergue

DISCOVERING THE BASTIDES

Starting from Monflanquin, you can visit the principal bastides of the Agen uplands in one day. A bastide exhibition is also on hand to present this astonishing urban planning phenomenon in a digestible way. Information from the tourist office at Monflanquin ☎ 05 53 36 40 19. Guided discovery visits are also available in Rouergue. Information from the Association des Bastides du Rouergues at the tourist office in Villefranche-de-Rouergue ☎ 05 65 45 13 18.

For the bastides of Périgord, see p.128.

... but to different plans

When the founders chose a site, they planted their flags and then started to scour the countryside for people to populate their town. Surveyors adapted the general design of the bastide to the particular terrain. Though normally rectangular, bastides could also be oval, circular or oblong. This was usually a matter of topography, but

Maison de l'Hébrardie, Cajarc

sometimes also reflected an existing settlement, as a bastide could be based on a developed community, like the rural 'sauvetés' (townships founded by monasteries to provide security and sanctuary, where offenders were liable to excommunication) or even 'castelnaus' (villages built under the protection of a specific castle).

to travel alone on deserted roads. Cutpurses, thieves and bandits even attacked people in villages. Within the strong walls of the bastides, however, the population could have some security.

... with revealing names

The names of the bastides can often give us a clue to their history or character: Villeneuve-sur-Lot, for example, indicates a new town on the Lot river, while the 'mont' of Monflanquin denotes the hill on which the bastide is built. Villefranche records the existence of 'franchises' (various privileges) and Beaumont was obviously built on a fine-looking hill, and so on.

Strictly planned...

The interior layout of a bastide left nothing to chance – you'll find no winding alleys here. The town plan provided a geometric, rectangular framework of streets and buildings. The central square was the soul of the bastide, the place for commerce and festivities; it was used as an exchange point for the produce of the whole agricultural region. Around this square were 'couverts' (arcades), protecting shopkeepers and craftsmen from rain and sun. Even after seven centuries of vicissitudes, and despite the ravages of weather and the imposition of different styles, the bastides of Aquitaine and Rouergue still retain a family air.

Place Centrale, Sauveterre-de-Rouergue

Châteaux

The medieval châteaux and Renaissance palaces dotted about the countryside of Périgord, Quercy and Rouergue are a fascinating testimony to the rich history of the area.

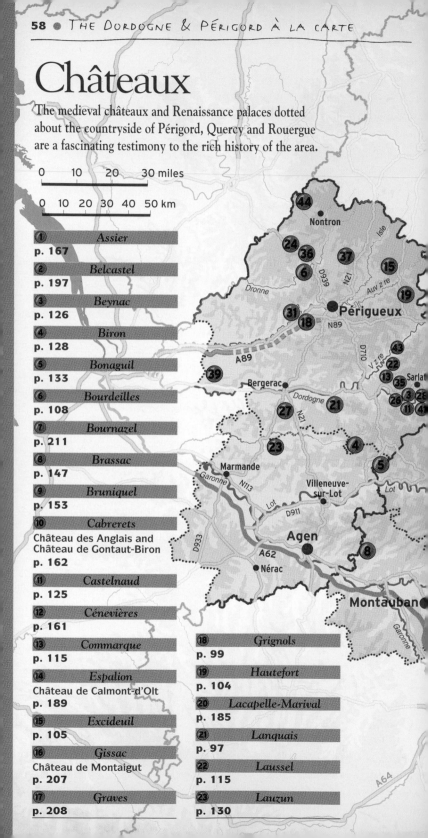

0   10   20   30 miles

0 10 20 30 40 50 km

Nontron
Périgueux
Dronne
Isle
Auvzre
Bergerac
Dordogne
Marmande
Garonne
N113
Villeneuve-sur-Lot
Lot
Agen
Nérac
A62
Montauban
Garonne
A89
N89
D999
N21
D710
Vzre
Sarlat
A64

Rural architecture

Farm and dovecote in Quercy

I n these traditionally agricultural regions of Quercy, Rouergue and Périgord, the rural architecture is among the finest in France. Often perfectly restored, rustic houses and their outbuildings compete in inventiveness and picturesque details. A harmony of colours, forms and materials in perfect accord with the landscapes. Ready for a spin in the country?

Le Cade farm, in the Causse Noir

Château-style houses...

In Périgord, half-timbered and cob-built farmhouses predominate, along with honey-coloured Sarlat stone beneath ample Mansart-style roofs. The most elaborate are more reminiscent of mini-châteaux or manor houses than classic farmhouses. A local speciality are the 'borderies', which often give their name to hamlets. These are humble sharecroppers' houses, which the squires of

fortified farms once rented to lowly tenants in exchange for their labour.

... or chalet-style

Around Sainte-Sabine in the Dordogne, there are 50 or so peculiar timber houses, very old but very substantial, with a distinct Nordic look. Resting on enormous blocks of flint, they are made of heavy beams stacked horizontally and secured at the corners by wooden joints. Their very narrow openings suggest that

they served some defensive purpose during the times of the bastides.

High-style living

Massive and solid, houses in Quercy and Rouergue opted for height, leaving the ground floor (called the 'en-bas' or downstairs) for the wine cellar and the sheep. The house proper was on the first floor, which was reached by wide flights of stone steps outside, which finished in a 'lou bolet', a platform protected by a

A roof made of lauze tiles

porch roof. This often extended into an open gallery, prettily described as a 'soleio', where linen and fruit were hung to dry. The building materials used include every colour found in the Causses, from white limestone and red Aveyron sandstone to brown tiles and dark grey lauze stone.

Stones upon stones

As you drive along the roads of the Causses, you might wonder why there are so many low drystone walls. In fact, rather than marking a boundary, they are often simply heaps of stones thrown up by ploughshares. That's why you can drive for miles between drystone walls that enclose even the smallest meadow or byre.

Bothies galore

The local word for these humble dwellings varies from region to region ('garrottes', 'cajolles', 'bories' or 'capitelles'), but they are all shepherd's bothies, small

dwellings whose idiosyncratic construction required a certain knack. These impressive circular structures are made of stone from top to bottom without using mortar, rising to a perfectly vaulted, tapering, conical roof. That they stay up at all is amazing. The structural secret is a large flat stone at the top, which stabilises the whole structure. The finest examples are now protected. Inside these stone 'igloos' is a single room which served as living quarters, as a store for foodstuffs and as a cheese loft.

Bread and water

When building a house, first the right site had to be found and was identified by the dowser with a hazel rod. Then came the masons, who taxed their imaginations in building the wells. The most inventive have conical or pyramidal roofs featuring wooden frames, tiling or strange domes. Generally not far away were the ancient bread ovens, which were just as essential. The masonry was so meticulous that they are often the last contructions to succumb to

the weather. The ovens were generally placed alongside the houses and their fine vaults sometimes still contain active bakeries.

Rich dovecotes

'Pigeonniers' (dovecotes) vary widely, being perched on columns or on top of a barn, round or square, and adorned by half-timbering or a turret. Many of those gracing the countryside of Périgord, Quercy and Rouergue have been well restored. Once

reserved for seignorial estates or more prosperous farms, these structures are as elegant as they are practical (the pigeons were kept for food and their droppings were highly sought after as a strong and very effective fertiliser). Understandably, the dovecotes became noted as a symbol of wealth.

Quercy's mills
revolving museums

Mills have been providing energy for two millennia. Today, their sails revolve in the wind once again and water flows over their wheels. The doors of Quercy's mills are open, ready to reveal the millers' secrets and their ancestral skills. Some are operational, others are undergoing restoration. All are worth a look when you're out and about.

Brousse mill, Castelnau-Montratier

In the current

The discovery of Quercy's mills is a pleasure to enliven any walk or hike. They occupy unusual or picturesque sites, clinging to cliffs or perched on riverbanks. Some of them are still operational, others have become fine homes.

Constructed on the side of a rock, the mill at Saut looms 33 feet (10 m) above the Alzou. The Vergnoulet mill at Mayrinhac-Lentour is still masterfully grinding rye, wheat, maize and buckwheat. The Brousse mill at Castelnau-Montratier is quite a sight. An 11.5-ft (3.5-m) fall works the hydraulic system for the flint grindstones. Finally, the mill at Martel (p. 169), housed in an ancient hunting inn, continues to press a fine golden oil with a delicate aroma.

The heyday of the mills

First documented in the 12thC., mills represent the first machines invented by man to help him make his daily bread. Once there were more than 1,000 of them, grinding wheat, rye, maize, buckwheat or walnuts, operated by water, wind or donkey power. This very

Interior mechanism of Seyrignac mill, Lunan

ancient industry barely survived beyond the early 20thC. Today, thanks to a number of enthusiasts, sails and wheels turn again in the Quercy sky or the waters of the Lot. The third Sunday in June is national mill day, when the doors of these superbly restored buildings are opened to the public to reveal the secrets of milling.

The language of the sails

To celebrate a miller's marriage, the sails of his mill were stopped in the sign of a St Andrew's cross and decorated with leaves and flowers. To honour him in death, the sails were stopped in the sign of a Latin cross.

Working the grindstones

As everywhere in Occitan territory, windmills with revolving calotte towers are always made of fine stones, standing on a broad base so as to resist the wind and the vibration of the mechanism and capped with an oak and chestnut roof. At first-floor level, the system of gauges enabled the fineness of

Boisse mill, Sainte-Alauzie

grinding to be regulated. On the second floor, the grindstones, the lantern, the wheel and shaft are driven by the mounted sails.

Giants with white sails

Thirteen windmills have retained their sails, but only six are still capable of grinding. Quercy's regional body for windmill enthusiasts (☎ 05 65 31 28 85) publishes

a very practical brochure that lists mills and restaurants in mills. Among the more notable are the Boisse mill at Sainte-Alauzie (5 miles/8 km NE of Castelnau-Montratier) – a listed historic monument and the archetypal Quercy windmill – and the mill at Carlucet, the only one possessing two pairs of grindstones, which is a type also known as an English mill (see p. 179).

WALNUT TREATS

Delicious in salads, walnut oil does wonders to pancake batter. And it's good for you! Rich in zinc and copper, it is recommended for cases of rickets, certain bone ailments, anaemia and rheumatism. To try a delicious traditional recipe with shelled walnuts, preheat your oven to 120°C (250°F, gas mark 4), then grind a large serving of walnuts and set them aside. Prepare a bain-marie (about 60°C/140°F) for the following mixture: 9 oz (250 g) of sugar, 4 egg whites and the juice of a lemon. Whisk in the bain-marie to get the meringue to rise. Take off the stove when it sticks to the whisk and gently drop the walnut pieces in. Put a teaspoonful of the mixture on greaseproof butter paper, keeping each little pile separate. Cook for 30 minutes and eat with walnut wine served chilled.

Sporting activities

The region offers a huge range of sporting activities accessible to everyone, from canoeing and paragliding to fishing or canyoning, and from family relaxation to high excitement.

0   10   20   30 miles

0   10 20 30 40 50 km

Water sports

1 Auvézère gorges: canoeing
p. 105

2 Brantôme: Canoeing
p. 109

3 Cahors: Water-skiing, canoeing...
p. 156

4 Caix: Water-skiing, canoeing
p. 159

5 Cajarc: Water-skiing, canoeing...
p. 161

6 Les Eyzies: Canoeing
p. 116

7 Le Liauzu: Canoeing
p. 163

8 Najac: Fishing, canoeing, rafting
p. 209

9 Saint-Antonin-Noble-Val: Caneoing
p. 153

10 Saint-Nicolas-de-la-Grave: Windsurfing, catamaran, sailing, canoeing...
p. 145

11 Tolerme lake: Water-skiing, canoeing...
p. 185

Aerial sports

12 Bouloc: Parachuting
p. 149

13 Bozouls: Microlights
p. 197

14 Douelle: Paragliding
p. 158

15 Loupiac: Ballooning
p. 167

16 Millau: Hang-gliding, paragliding
p. 202

Horse riding

17 Figeac
p. 166

18 Millau
p. 202

19 Salt Road
p. 53

Nontron

Périgueux

Bergerac

Sarlat-la-Canéda

Marmande

Villeneuve-sur-Lot

Agen

Nérac

Montauban

Auch

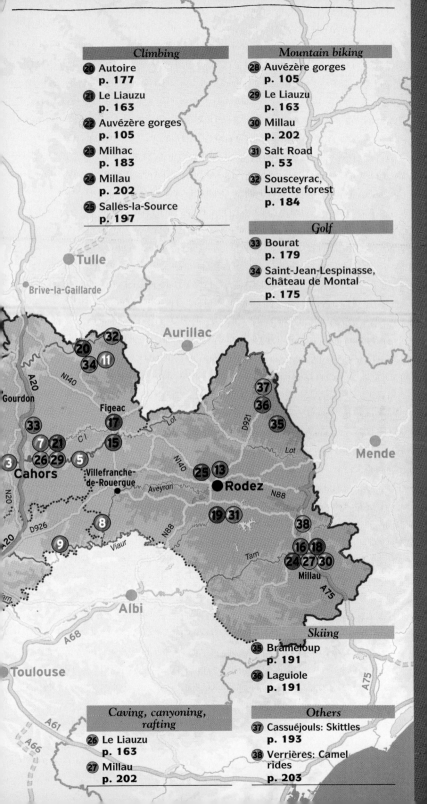

Climbing

20 Autoire
p. 177

21 Le Liauzu
p. 163

22 Auvézère gorges
p. 105

23 Milhac
p. 183

24 Millau
p. 202

25 Salles-la-Source
p. 197

Mountain biking

28 Auvézère gorges
p. 105

29 Le Liauzu
p. 163

30 Millau
p. 202

31 Salt Road
p. 53

32 Sousceyrac,
Luzette forest
p. 184

Golf

33 Bourat
p. 179

34 Saint-Jean-Lespinasse,
Château de Montal
p. 175

Skiing

35 Brameloup
p. 191

36 Laguiole
p. 191

Caving, canyoning, rafting

26 Le Liauzu
p. 163

27 Millau
p. 202

Others

37 Cassuéjouls: Skittles
p. 193

38 Verrières: Camel
rides
p. 203

Outdoor activities in the wild

Feeling jaded? Need some fun? Time for a breath of fresh air? The region's vast open spaces are just the place to explore the pleasures of outdoor activities that you've never tried before. You can make full use of the local resources, on the water, on the rockfaces or along the country trails.

Time for a paddle!

The host of rivers that criss-cross the surface of Périgord, Quercy and Rouergue are just the place to sample the pleasures of canoeing. For families, the calm waters of the Lot, Dordogne, Tarn, Célé and many other rivers still provide miles of channels that present no technical problems of any kind provided you respect the basic rules – being able to swim and wearing a lifejacket (provided by the clubs). If you have some experience, other sections will guarantee some splendid, fast thrills. But whatever your level, you will get the same pleasure from taking time for a dip in the reaches and discovering countryside inaccessible to landlubbers.

Rafting in the rapids

Unlike in canoeing, you're not alone when you take to the water on the inflatable boat, but in a group guided by a helmsman. Hold tight! Rafting is both fast moving and bumpy, but there's no danger. Most navigable rivers have rapids where you can discover a different side of the region hurtling down gorges or canyons.

Fishing

Trout, pike, zander, perch, carp, roach, black bass – the region's rivers harbour many different varieties of fish, allowing you to try out different angling techniques such as fly-fishing and others. This is the time for a relaxing break by a lake, or a more serious effort with both feet in the stream. You must get a permit, which can be obtained in most communes. Ask for a 'carte jeune' for under-16s and a 'carte vacances' (for which there is a charge) in shops selling fishing equipment. The latter authorises all forms

of fishing for any fortnight from 1 June to 30 September. Opening times are displayed in the town hall.

Up or down?

Maybe you dream of exploring the magic of the subterranean world, or

maybe your ambitions are to ascend a rock face. The multiple folds of the Causses provide entertainment for both cavemen and the upwardly mobile. There's something to suit all abilities, from the first steps for children to climbs or caves for experienced sportsmen, thanks to the supervisory set-up offered by the associations.

Taking to the air

Say farewell to mundane cares. Seen from above, everything seems lovelier. Paragliding, gliding, free flight in a hang-glider, microlights, parachuting and even ballooning – there's nothing like it for an outstanding panorama of contrasting landscapes. The sky is yours, just choose your mode of transport. Some offer a simple first-timer's option, but others require training and a minimum age before you can get away on your own. So it's best to find out in advance from qualified instructors and supervisors.

On foot, on horse-back or on two wheels

The whole region is open to exploration. Thousands of miles of footpaths and signposted trails, as well as numerous discovery circuits with guides and commentary,

enable you to enjoy the wilds of nature in full. Whether it's a few hours of family relaxation or a whole day's activity, boredom is out of the question given the variety of landscape, forests and mountain roads. Some will prefer a walking pace, others will choose freewheeling on a mountain bike, which can be hired more or less anywhere, and hardened riders can take to horseback. However, note that some clubs will not hand over the reins unless you have a riding hat and complete an initiation course, as a token of sincerity. Saddle up!

Festivals

Jazz festivals, film events, street theatre and poetry days are all examples of Périgord, Quercy and Rouergue in festive mood.

Music and song

① Bergerac: Jazz (Wednesday evenings in summer)
p. 95

② Cahors Blues Festival (summer)
p. 155

③ Conques: Classical and baroque (summer)
p. 187

④ Figeac: New music (May)
p. 70

⑤ Gourdon: Summer festival (classical, jazz...)
p. 183

⑥ Martel: Classical (July-Aug.)
p. 168

⑦ Millau: Jazz (July)
p. 200

⑧ Moissac: Festival of the human voice (July)
p. 145

⑨ Monflanquin: Classical music festival, Guyenne (second fortnight in July)
p. 132

⑩ Monpazier: Classical, jazz, variety (July-Aug.)
p. 128

⑪ Ribérac: Music and lyrics Ribérac-style (July-Aug.)
p. 106

⑫ Rodez: Occitan festival (July)
p. 196

⑬ Saint-Céré: Lyric festival (summer)
p. 175

⑭ Souillac: Jazz & classical (July-Aug.)
p. 180

⑮ Sylvanès (abbey): Church music (summer)
p. 207

⑯ Lot valley: Musical summer (mid-July to mid-Aug.)
p. 70

⑰ Villefranche-de-Rouergue: Europarade, brass bands (mid-July)
p. 208

⑱ Villeneuve-sur-Lot: Jazz (July)
p. 135

Sound and light shows

⑲ Flagnac (end July/early Aug.)
p. 211

⑳ Penne (July-Sept.)
p. 153

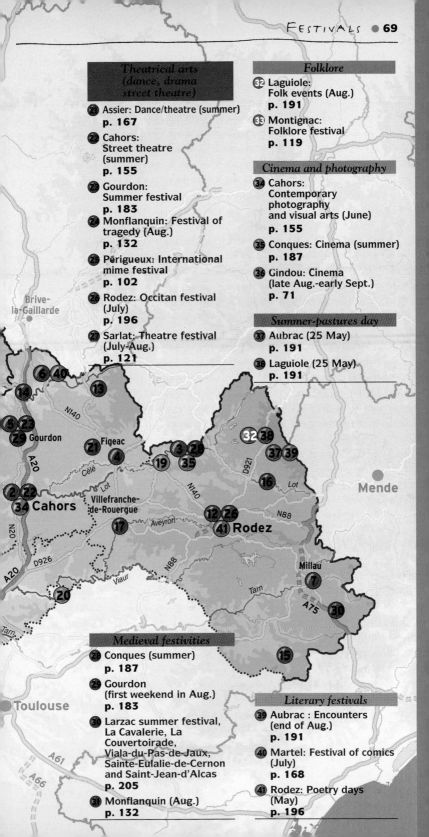

Theatrical arts (dance, drama, street theatre)

21 Assier: Dance/theatre (summer)
p. 167

22 Cahors: Street theatre (summer)
p. 155

23 Gourdon: Summer festival
p. 183

24 Monflanquin: Festival of tragedy (Aug.)
p. 132

25 Périgueux: International mime festival
p. 102

26 Rodez: Occitan festival (July)
p. 196

27 Sarlat: Theatre festival (July-Aug.)
p. 121

Folklore

32 Laguiole: Folk events (Aug.)
p. 191

33 Montignac: Folklore festival
p. 119

Cinema and photography

34 Cahors: Contemporary photography and visual arts (June)
p. 155

35 Conques: Cinema (summer)
p. 187

36 Gindou: Cinema (late Aug.-early Sept.)
p. 71

Summer-pastures day

37 Aubrac (25 May)
p. 191

38 Laguiole (25 May)
p. 191

Medieval festivities

28 Conques (summer)
p. 187

29 Gourdon (first weekend in Aug.)
p. 183

30 Larzac summer festival, La Cavalerie, La Couvertoirade, Viala-du-Pas-de-Jaux, Sainte-Eulalie-de-Cernon and Saint-Jean-d'Alcas
p. 205

31 Monflanquin (Aug.)
p. 132

Literary festivals

39 Aubrac : Encounters (end of Aug.)
p. 191

40 Martel: Festival of comics (July)
p. 168

41 Rodez: Poetry days (May)
p. 196

Festivals: art in all its guises

A ll summer, the valleys, churches and terraces of Lot and Aveyron resound with jazz, classical music and song, traditional parades and contemporary festivals of films, literature, dance and theatre, combining the magic of the arts with the natural magic of the region.

Cows decked out for the summer-pastures day festivities

Summer music in the valleys

A simple recipe: take the sublime scenery of Lot, Dordogne or Tarn; invite instrumentalists or top singers, plus some talented people destined for great things and have them play in medieval châteaux, cathedrals and abbeys. The result? Great concerts in the best of all possible settings. From mid-July to mid-August, music echoes through the valleys.

Lyric festival at Saint-Céré

A must for visitors to Lot, the lyric festival at Saint-Céré is dedicated to opera and vocal music. Bringing together young singers to create lyric productions aimed at a very wide public, it offers them the finest possible opportunity to launch their professional careers. At such venues as the Château de Castelnau-Bretenoux, the Romanesque cloister at Carennac, Gourdon church and Souillac abbey, the music of Mozart, Rossini and Schubert mixes with blues recitals and cabaret shows.

'Avis d'pas sage'

A festival of new music and new harmonies at Figeac, where artists present personal views of their time. Every May, Figeac honours these pioneers of new musical moods.

Jazz events

Whether in the orchards and gardens of the Château

The Marriage of Figaro, performed during the lyric festival at Saint-Céré

Europarade, Villefranche-sur-Rouergue

d'Assier (early August), at the foot of Souillac abbey (mid-July) or in the streets of Millau (mid-July), whether it's subtle and tuneful or swinging percussion, jazz is reborn every summer in all its styles. There's something for everyone.

Bandtime – 'Europarade' at Villefranche-de-Rouergue

With more than 1,000 musicians to liven up markets, stadia and terraces, Europarade is bandtime in Villefranche – with bands from all over Europe and across the Atlantic, ranging from the Bronx Tambours to the Foreign Legion band and the famous Trinidad carnival's top group to the Chinese Army band. Europarade is a pulsating affair, and adds terrific color to the street scene. Firework shows, music and flower-decked floats add to the festivities, so mid-July is the time to be in Villefranche-de-Rouergue.

Film fest

Gindou (14 miles/22 km SW of Gourdon) may be a long way from the sequins and chandeliers of Hollywood or Cannes premieres, but this is where the festival of young African and Mediterranean film talent ('Rencontres

Cinéma de Gindou') takes place. This festival has established a good reputation among cinema buffs. For a week at the end of August the event provides an

opportunity to discover high-quality, lesser-known films. There are drinks parties to meet the directors, debates, exhibitions and open-air screenings, all under the starry sky. Good fun.

Literary Aubrac

The Rencontres d'Aubrac is a literary event that takes place over the last weekend of August. The theme is the world of the plateau as seen through the eyes of its authors. The event brings together original writing, university studies and well-known personalities from film, theatre and music, to bring out the best of the region's culture.

Summer-pastures day festivities

Saint Urbain's day (25 May) is the day of the summer-pastures festivities (Fête de la Transhumance), when the russet-coloured cows with their black eyes leave the cowshed to spend four months in the fields. Starting at dawn, decorated with ribbons, flowers, leaves and pompoms, the herds troop out after Buttercup, the head cow, to start their 40-mile (65-km) amble to the alpine freshness of the Aubrac plateau. There the festivities get into full swing to the sound of bagpipes and accordion, with a gigantic, traditional aligot dish (*see* p. 39) made specially for the occasion. On that day, the six inhabitants of the village of Aubrac welcome 25,000 visitors who come to watch the traditional local event. You can win Laguiole knives, Aubrac cheeses, or a cow!

Making the huge aligot mixture

The Dordogne & Périgord for children

The region has a wide range of leisure activities to offer visitors small and large, ranging from leisure parks to prehistoric parks, rides in sailing barges and on heritage railways to unusual museums and courses in astronomy. (For animal parks and lakes, see p. 16.)

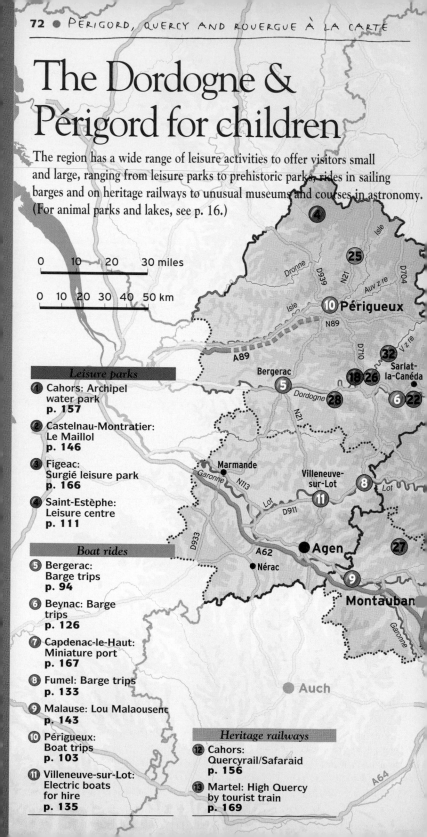

Leisure parks

① Cahors: Archipel water park **p. 157**

② Castelnau-Montratier: Le Maillol **p. 146**

③ Figeac: Surgié leisure park **p. 166**

④ Saint-Estèphe: Leisure centre **p. 111**

Boat rides

⑤ Bergerac: Barge trips **p. 94**

⑥ Beynac: Barge trips **p. 126**

⑦ Capdenac-le-Haut: Miniature port **p. 167**

⑧ Fumel: Barge trips **p. 133**

⑨ Malause: Lou Malaousenc **p. 143**

⑩ Périgueux: Boat trips **p. 103**

⑪ Villeneuve-sur-Lot: Electric boats for hire **p. 135**

Heritage railways

⑫ Cahors: Quercyrail/Safaraid **p. 156**

⑬ Martel: High Quercy by tourist train **p. 169**

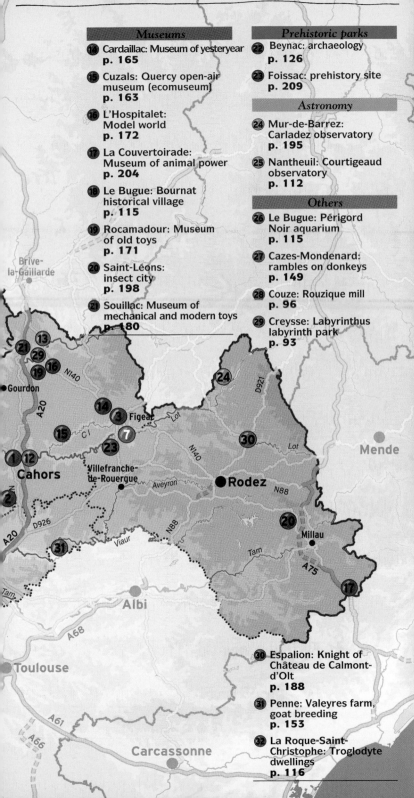

Museums

14 Cardaillac: Museum of yesteryear
p. 165

15 Cuzals: Quercy open-air museum (ecomuseum)
p. 163

16 L'Hospitalet: Model world
p. 172

17 La Couvertoirade: Museum of animal power
p. 204

18 Le Bugue: Bournat historical village
p. 115

19 Rocamadour: Museum of old toys
p. 171

20 Saint-Léons: insect city
p. 198

21 Souillac: Museum of mechanical and modern toys
p. 180

Prehistoric parks

22 Beynac: archaeology
p. 126

23 Foissac: prehistory site
p. 209

Astronomy

24 Mur-de-Barrez: Carladez observatory
p. 195

25 Nantheuil: Courtigeaud observatory
p. 112

Others

26 Le Bugue: Périgord Noir aquarium
p. 115

27 Cazes-Mondenard: rambles on donkeys
p. 149

28 Couze: Rouzique mill
p. 96

29 Creysse: Labyrinthus labyrinth park
p. 93

30 Espalion: Knight of Château de Calmont-d'Olt
p. 188

31 Penne: Valeyres farm, goat breeding
p. 153

32 La Roque-Saint-Christophe: Troglodyte dwellings
p. 116

Land of legends

Mounine's leap

Whether because of their grandeur or their peculiarity, the natural phenomena of this region have long inspired the human imagination. In Quercy and Rouergue, the wind, water and stones seem to murmur poetic tales of fairies, hermits, devils and lovers. Once upon a time...

exhaustion our man retraced his steps. Back at the cave meanwhile his bread had acquired a fine layer of mould, and the curd was streaked a delicate green. No matter, he was famished. He took a bite, swallowed and – lo and behold, loved it. Roquefort cheese was born.

The shepherd's tale

A very long time ago, a young shepherd from the Causses was sheltering with his flock in a cave. When a delightful maiden passed by, he abandoned his sheep, hunk of bread and curds to follow her. After walking for some days and not finding the girl, famished and shattered with

Mounine's leap

On the road to Saujac, at the foot of the cliff, is a place called Saut de la Mounine (Mounine's leap). The story goes like this... In the 15thC. a girl called Guislaine was greatly taken with a fine young man. But her father would rather his daughter were dead than married to the man she

loved. Not far away lived a hermit and his monkey, called Mounine. Hearing of Guislaine's plight, the monkey decided to sacrifice itself, and threw itself from the cliff wearing the young lady's clothes. The father believed his daughter was dead and regretted his behaviour. When he discovered that she was alive after all, he organised a splendid wedding for the happy couple.

Doves of Figeac

All that remains of the ancient abbey of Figeac, which in the Middle Ages was the equal of Conques, is the church of Saint-Sauveur once attached to it – and a story of strange miracles. Pepin the Short was passing through Quercy, looking for a place to build a monastery, when he is said to have heard voices whispering the name of Figeac. Two doves then drew the Sign of the Cross in the sky, before depositing an olive branch at the king's feet. Better still, it was God

Covered market in Thémines

Saint-Sauveur church, Figeac

himself, escorted by angels, who is supposed to have consecrated the nave.

Clovis' javelin

Certainly the foundation of monasteries never failed to stir spirits. Take Moissac, for example. The ancient belief was that Clovis himself was to decide the exact spot to build it by throwing a spear from the top of a hill. Unfortunately the weapon landed in a swamp, and as a result the building had to be built on piles. Whether this is true or false, no-one knows, but one thing is sure: the present abbey does suffer greatly with problems of rising damp from the soil.

The miraculous bell

If you visit the Chapelle Notre-Dame, in the pilgrim town of Rocamadour, pause for a moment by the small bell beneath the chapel's lantern tower. Cast in the 9thC., it was said to have the power of announcing miracles of shipwreck victims. Each time a sailor in difficulty called on the Virgin and promised to go on a pilgrimage, the was said to bell ring of its own accord.

The fairy of the Ouysse

Between Rocamadour and Figeac, the road runs through the village of Thémines, where the stream of the same name disappears down a swallow hole, only to reappear 15 miles (24 km) downstream, near the source of the Ouysse. A legend claims that the ground opened to release the waters, but that a fairy remains trapped in this underground prison.

Satanic abyss

The enormous 'great hole' of Padirac is quite terrifying as it is said to be diabolical in origin. The tale goes that Saint Martin was riding his donkey when Satan appeared before him with a bag stuffed with hellbound souls. He offered a deal: if the Saint could overcome the obstacle that Satan produced, the souls would be saved. As he spoke, he stamped with his heel to create a yawning hole. Saint Martin commended his soul to God, spurred his donkey – and sailed across the chasm, landing on a slab – and you can still see the marks of the donkey's hoofs.

Miraculous bell of the Chapelle Notre-Dame, Rocamadour

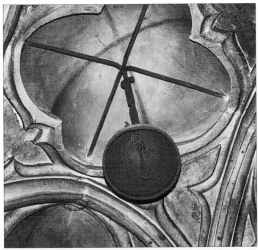

Crafts

Some fantastic ideas for gifts – there's no shortage of quality products on offer: ceramics, earthenware, umbrellas, boater hats, knives or even Aveyron skittles.

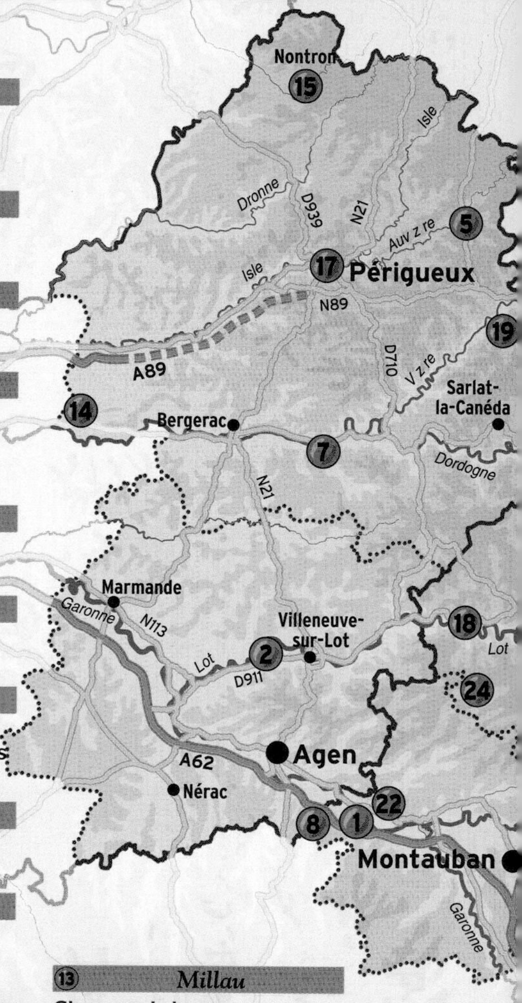

① *Auvillar*
Wool, gloves, mohair scarves
p. 142

② *Brugnac*
Mohair pullovers and socks
p. 137

③ *Caussade*
Hat makers
p. 150

④ *Cavagnac*
Sculptures, glass blowing, Hameau Pélissié knives
p. 169

⑤ *Cherveix-Cubas*
Lacoste umbrellas
p. 105

⑥ *La Couvertoirade*
Shepherd bags
p. 205

⑦ *Couze*
Handmade paper from Larroque and Rouzique mills
p. 96

⑧ *Dunes*
Pottery studio
p. 141

⑨ *Figeac*
Nadine Miniot earthenware studio and shop
p. 165

⑩ *Gramat*
Pewterware by Arsène Maigne
p. 177

⑪ *Laguiole*
Cutlery studios
p. 192

⑫ *Mechmont*
Earthenware miniatures and pottery by Mylène Cros
p. 157

⑬ *Millau*
Glove workshops
p. 201

⑭ *Montcaret*
Pewterware
p. 90

⑮ *Nontron*
Porcelain and knives at Hermès boutique; Nontron knives; workshop of Louis Martin, master glassmaker
pp. 110-111

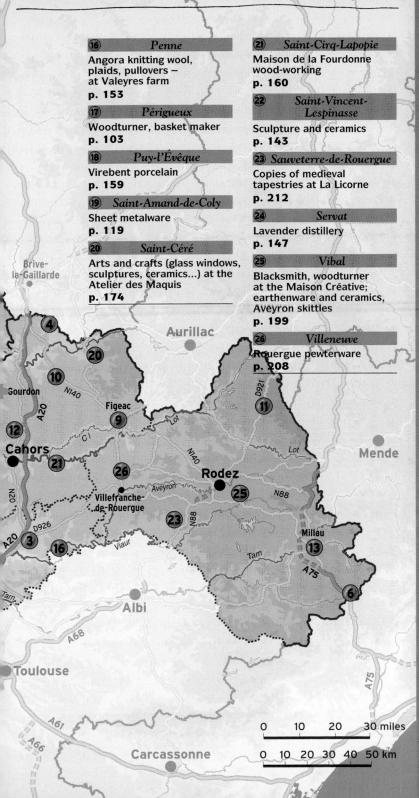

⑯ Penne

Angora knitting wool, plaids, pullovers – at Valeyres farm
p. 153

⑰ Périgueux

Woodturner, basket maker
p. 103

⑱ Puy-l'Évêque

Virebent porcelain
p. 159

⑲ Saint-Amand-de-Coly

Sheet metalware
p. 119

⑳ Saint-Céré

Arts and crafts (glass windows, sculptures, ceramics...) at the Atelier des Maquis
p. 174

㉑ Saint-Cirq-Lapopie

Maison de la Fourdonne wood-working
p. 160

㉒ Saint-Vincent-Lespinasse

Sculpture and ceramics
p. 143

㉓ Sauveterre-de-Rouergue

Copies of medieval tapestries at La Licorne
p. 212

㉔ Servat

Lavender distillery
p. 147

㉕ Vibal

Blacksmith, woodturner at the Maison Créative; earthenware and ceramics, Aveyron skittles
p. 199

㉖ Villeneuve

Rouergue pewterware
p. 208

Millau gloves
passion for leather

Has France been taken over by machine-made leather goods and skins of mediocre quality? Certainly not. At the foot of the majestic Larzac plateau, a small Aveyron town still holds out against international competition. At Millau, the capital of French gloves, a handful of hardy glovemakers perpetuate a unique expertise. The great couturiers who make up most of their clientele are not mistaken.

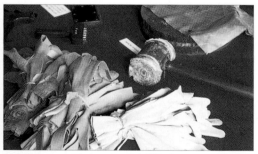

Mallet for ornamenting gloves (musée de Millau)

70 operations for a single glove

Cutting, slitting, refining, ornamenting, stitching, stretching, trimming, sleeking... From stripping the hide to making a pair of gloves involves 70 operations. These including soaking the skin, removing the fleece, pieces of flesh and fat, tanning it, stretching it to make it supple, dying it, slicing it, removing the wrinkles and finally dividing it into pieces large enough to make a glove each. This last operation, called 'dépeçage', is the prerogative of the cutter and requires an infallible eye in order to avoid any waste.

Glovemaking – from father to son

Working in skin and leather is a tradition dating back to the 12thC., but it was in the 17thC. that the business really got off the ground, encouraged by the compulsory need to wear gloves at all ceremonial occasions. In the 19thC., Millau had 80 taweries and 20 glove-makers, and in 1963 the industry still employed 60,000 people and produced a record 5 million pairs of leather gloves.

tanned the skin of kids and lambs, i.e. fine, supple hides, but the glove-makers of Millau also used exotic materials such as the skin of the Singapore python, peccary and ostrich.

From tanned hides to tawers

Tawers were craftsmen who dressed hide before it was processed further. They

The skins used are exceptionally supple

Cutting the gloves (glove workshop, Millau)

sport, work and orthopaedic) represent 50% of production, gloves 30% and other leather goods 20%.

Glove forms (Musée de Millau)

The piece of leather is then placed on a template and slit to separate the fingers. Then skilful hands assemble, stitch, sew on the buttons and adorn with embroidery.

the international competition and the evolution of fashion, which have hit the business hard, the 14 remaining taweries are attempting to diversify, while still maintaining the discipline and quality. Now leather garments (haute couture,

Sewing the gloves (glove workshop)

Trademark Millau leather

The skins tanned in Millau enjoy an international reputation for quality. The raw material is exceptional here, being derived from Larzac lambs. Aware of the value of this quality, the tawers have created a common trademark, the Peaux de Millau, which commits them to maintaining rigorous standards in selection and processing and allows the consumer to easily identify their work.

Leather pros

Today, Millau continues to influence the top end of the leather trade. However, given

LEATHER SHOWS ITS CLAWS

There has been a remarkable swing towards skin products. Though models may parade with bare hands, they are often dressed in leather and top couturiers swear by dipped lambskin. Jackets, dresses, coats, trousers – from head to toe, the original creations that prance down the catwalk for the top designers, from Dior to Saint-Laurent via Chanel, Kenzo, Lacroix and Hermès, rely on the traditional expertise of Millau's craftsmen. What is their strength? The originality of the designs, the quality of workmanship and the sophisticated overcast stitching. Top couturiers know that they can ask for ultra-sophisticated work here, even just a single item, and present the most challenging tasks – a piece of fur, silk or crocodile skin added here or there, unexpected shapes or gloves that hug the whole arm. Every workshop has its speciality and its stories about its prestigious clients. Pay them a visit and admire the quality of their designs.

Window display of gloves by top couturiers (musée de Millau)

Laguiole knives
Aubrac blades

La Forge: where the Laguiole knife is made

Born in 1829, the Laguiole knife is much more than a simple folding knife with a horn handle. It is both a mark of the people of the plateau and the Rouergue product that is most widely exported in the whole world. The top product of France's cutlers allies tradition and modernity, good taste and quality. Redesigned by the greatest designers, it carried off the EC's design trophy.

Entrance hall at La Forge

Descendant of the Catalan flick-knife

The idea of making this little knife with a curved handle came to Pierre-Jean Calmels in 1829. He decided it would be easier to carry than the ancient kitchen knife, which was carried in a sheath or sometimes strapped to the forearm. It was undoubtedly inspired by the Catalan 'navaja', a folding flick-knife, and the 'capuchadou', a fixed blade with a beech handle.

A matter of life and death

It was farmers and shepherds who assured the success of this fine knife, which was both practical and elegant. In 1840 a handy bodkin was added that breeders could use to take care of the rumina of cows that were swollen with accumulated gas. In 1880 came the corkscrew, indispensable to Aubrac natives who ventured up to Paris to become café owners. When the knife became fashionable among the bourgeoisie, the handle was often dressed in ivory and the plates that held it were adorned with chequered patterns. In the golden age of the Laguiole,

Pré-salé (agneau de) lamb raised on salt marshes
Primeur young vegetable
Profiterole puffs of *choux* pastry, filled with custard
Provençale (à la) Provençal style: tomatoes, garlic, olive oil, etc.
Prune plum
Pruneau prune
Quenelle light dumpling of fish or poultry
Queue tail
Queue de boeuf oxtail
Quiche lorraine open flan of cheese, ham or bacon
Raclette scrapings from specially-made and heated cheese
Radis radish
Ragoût stew, usually meat but can describe other ingredients
Raie (bouclée) skate (type of)
Raifort horseradish
Raisin grape
Ramier wood pigeon
Rapé(e) grated or shredded
Rascasse scorpion fish
Ratatouille aubergines, onions, courgettes, garlic, red peppers and tomatoes in olive oil
Réglisse liquorice
Reine-Claude greengage
Rémoulade sauce of mayonnaise, mustard, capers, herbs, anchovies
Rillettes (d'oie) potted pork (goose)
Ris d'agneau lamb sweetbreads
Ris de veau veal sweetbreads
Riz rice
Robe de chambre jacket potato
Rognon kidney
Romarin rosemary
Rôti roast
Rouget red mullet
Rouget barbet red mullet
Rouille orange-coloured sauce with peppers, garlic and saffron
Roulade (de) roll (of)
Roulé(e) rolled (usually crêpe)
Sabayon sauce of egg yolks, wine
Sablé shortbread
Safran saffron
Saignant(e) underdone, rare
St-Jaques (coquille) scallop
St-Pierre John Dory
Salade niçoise tomatoes, beans, potatoes, black olives, anchovies, lettuce, olive oil, perhaps tuna
Salade panachée mixed salad
Salade verte green salad
Salé salted
Salmis red wine sauce
Salsifis salsify (vegetable)
Sandre freshwater fish, like perch
Sang blood
Sanglier wild boar
Saucisse freshly-made sausage
Saucisson large, dry sausage
Saucisson cervelas saveloy
Sauge sage
Saumon salmon
Saumon fumé smoked salmon

Sauvage wild
Scipion cuttlefish
Sel salt
Soja (pousse de) soy bean (soy bean sprout)
Soja (sauce de) soy sauce
Soubise onion sauce
Sucre sugar
Tapenade olive spread
Tartare raw minced beef
Tartare (sauce) sauce with mayonnaise, onions, capers, herbs
Tarte open flan
Tarte Tatin upside down tart of caramelized apples and pastry
Terrine container in which mixed meats/fish are baked; served cold
Tête de veau vinaigrette calf's head vinaigrette
Thé tea
Thermidor grilled lobster with browned béchamel sauce
Thon tuna fish
Thym thyme
Tiède mild or lukewarm
Tilleul lime tree
Tomate tomato
Topinambour Jerusalem artichoke
Torte sweet-filled flan
Tortue turtle
Tournedos fillet steak (small end)
Touron a cake, pastry or loaf made from almond paste and filled with candied fruits and nuts
Tourte (Tourtière) covered savoury tart
Tourteau large crab
Tranche slice
Tranche de boeuf steak
Traver de porc spare rib of pork
Tripoux stuffed mutton tripe
Truffade a huge sautéed pancake or galette with bacon, garlic and Cantal cheese
Truffe truffle; black, exotic, tuber
Truite trout
Truite saumonée salmon trout
Turbot (Turbotin) turbot
Vacherin ice-cream, meringue, cream
Vapeur (à la) steamed
Veau veal
Veau pané (escalope de) thin slice of veal in flour, eggs and breadcrumbs
Venaison venison
Verveine verbena
Viande meat
Vichyssoise creamy potato and leek soup, served cold
Viennoise coated with egg and breadcrumbs, fried (usually veal)
Vierge litteraly virgin (best olive oil, the first pressing)
Vierge (sauce) olive oil sauce
Vinaigre (de) wine vinegar or vinegar of named fruit
Vinaigrette (à la) French dressing with wine vinegar, oil, etc.
Volaille poultry
Yaourt yogurt

© Richard Binns

Noyau sweet liqueur from crushed stones (usually cherries)
Oeufs à la coque soft-boiled eggs
Oeufs à la neige *see* Île flottante
Oeufs à la poêle fried eggs
Oeufs brouillés scrambled eggs
Oeufs cocotte eggs cooked in individual dishes in a bain-marie
Oeufs durs hard-boiled eggs
Oeufs moulés poached eggs
Oie goose
Oignon onion
Ombrine fish, like sea-bass
Onglet flank of beef
Oreille (de porc) ear (pig's)
Oreillette sweet fritter, flavoured with orange flower water
Origan oregano (herb)
Orléannaise Orléans style: chicory and potatoes
Ortie nettle
Os bone
Osso bucco à la niçoise veal braised with orange zest, tomatoes, onions and garlic
Pain bread
Pain complet/entier wholemeal
Pain de campagne round white loaf
Pain d'épice spiced honey cake
Pain de mie square white loaf
Pain de seigle rye bread
Pain grillé toast
Pain doré/Pain perdu bread soaked in milk and eggs and fried
Paleron shoulder
Palmier palm-shaped sweet puff pastry
Palmier (coeur de) palm (heart)
Palombe wood pigeon
Palomête fish, like sea-bass
Palourde clam
Pamplemousse grapefruit
Panaché mixed
Pané(e) breadcrumbed
Papillote (en) cooked in oiled paper or foil
Paquets (en) parcels
Parfait (de) mousse (of)
Paris-Brest cake of *choux* pastry, filled with butter cream, almonds
Parisienne (à la) leeks, potatoes
Parmentier potatoes
Pastèque watermelon
Pastis (sauce au) aniseed based
Pâte pastry, dough or batter
Pâte à choux cream puff pastry
Pâte brisée short crust pastry
Pâté en croûte baked in pastry crust
Pâtes fraîches fresh pasta
Pâtisserie pastry
Paupiettes thin slices of meat or fish, used to wrap fillings
Pavé (de) thick slice (of)
Pavot (graines de) poppy seeds
Paysan(ne) (à la) country style
Peau (de) skin (of)
Pêche peach
Pêcheur fisherman
Pèlerine scallop
Perche perch
Perdreau young partridge

Perdrix partridge
Périgourdine (à la) goose liver and sauce *Périgueux*
Périgueux sauce with truffles and Madeira
Persil parsley
Persillade mixture of chopped parsley and garlic
Petit gris small snail
Pétoncle small scallop
Picholine large green table olives
Pied de cheval large oyster
Pied de mouton blanc cream coloured mushroom
Pied de porc pig's trotter
Pigeonneau young pigeon
Pignon pine nut
Piment (doux) pepper (sweet)
Pintade (pintadeau) guinea fowl (young guinea fowl)
Piperade omelette or scrambled eggs with tomatoes, peppers, onions and sometimes ham
Piquante (sauce) sharp tasting sauce with shallots, capers and wine
Pissenlit dandelion leaf
Pistache green pistachio nut
Pistou vegetable soup bound with *pommade* (thick smooth paste)
Plateau (de) plate (of)
Pleurote mushroom
Poché(e), pochade poached
Poêlé fried
Poire pear
Poireau leek
Pois pea
Poisson fish
Poitrine breast
Poitrine fumée smoked bacon
Poitrine salée unsmoked bacon
Poivre noir black pepper
Poivron (doux) pepper (sweet)
Polonaise Polish style: with buttered breadcrumbs, parsley, hard-boiled eggs
Pomme apple
Pommes de terre potatoes
  château roast
  dauphine croquettes
  frites chips
  gratinées browned with cheese
  Lyonnaise sautéed with onions
  vapeur boiled
Porc (carré de) loin of pork
Porc (côte de) loin of pork
Porcelet suckling pig
Porto (au) port
Portugaise (à la) Portuguese style: fried onions and tomatoes
Portugaises oysters with long, deep shells (*see* Huîtres)
Potage thick soup
Pot-au-feu clear meat broth served with the meat
Potimarron pumpkin
Poularde large hen
Poulet chicken
Poulet à la broche spit-roasted chicken
Poulpe octopus
Poussin small baby chicken

mushrooms, pasta
Jalousie latticed fruit or jam tart
Jambon ham
Jambonneau knuckle of pork
Jambonnette boned and stuffed
(knuckle of ham or poultry)
Jarret de veau stew of shin of veal
Jarreton cooked pork knuckle
Jerez sherry
Joue (de) cheek (of)
Julienne thinly-cut vegetables: also ling
(cod family)
Jus juice
Lait milk
Laitue lettuce
Lamproie eel-like fish
Langouste spiny lobster or crawfish
Langoustine Dublin Bay prawn
Langue tongue
Lapereau young rabbit
Lapin rabbit
Lard bacon
Lardons strips of bacon
Laurier bay-laurel, sweet bay leaf
Léger (Légère) light
Légume vegetable
Lièvre hare
Limaçon snail
Limande lemon sole
Limon lime
Lit bed
Lotte de mer monkfish, anglerfish
Loup de mer sea-bass
Louvine (Loubine) grey mullet, like a
sea-bass (Basque name)
Lyonnaise (à la) Lyonnais style: sauce
with wine, onions, vinegar
Mâche lamb's lettuce; small dark green
leaf
Madeleine tiny sponge cake
Madère sauce *demi-glace* and Madeira
wine
Magret (de canard) breast (of duck);
now used for other poultry
Maïs maize flour
Maison (de) of the restaurant
Maître d'hôtel sauce with butter,
parsley and lemon
Manchons *see* Goujonnettes
Mangetout edible peas and pods
Mangue mango
Manière (de) style (of)
Maquereau mackerel
Maraîchère (à la) market-gardener style;
velouté sauce with vegetables
Marais marsh or market garden
Marbré marbled
Marc pure spirit
Marcassin young wild boar
Marché market
Marchand de vin sauce with red wine,
chopped shallots
Marengo tomatoes, mushrooms, olive
oil, white wine, garlic, herbs
Marennes (blanches) flat-shelled oysters
(*see* Huîtres)
Marennes (vertes) green shell oysters
Marinières *see* Moules
Marmite stewpot

Marrons chestnuts
Médaillon (de) round piece (of)
Mélange mixture or blend
Ménagère (à la) housewife style: onions,
potatoes, peas, turnips and carrots
Mendiant (fruits de) mixture of figs,
almonds and raisins
Menthe mint
Merguez spicy grilled sausage
Merlan whiting (in Provence the word is
used for hake)
Merlu hake
Merluche dried cod
Mesclum mixture of salad leaves
Meunière sauce with butter, parsley,
lemon (sometimes oil)
Meurette red wine sauce
Miel honey
Mignon (de) small round piece
Mignonette coarsely ground white pepper
Mijoté(e) cooked slowly in water
Milanaise (à la) Milan style: dipped in
breadcrumbs, egg, cheese
Mille-feuille puff pastry with numerous
thin layers
Mirabeau anchovies, olives
Mirabelle golden plums
Mitonée (de) soup (of)
Mode (à la) in the manner of
Moelle beef marrow
Moelleux au chocolat chocolate dessert
(cake)
Montmorency with cherries
Morilles edible, dark brown,
honeycombed fungi
Mornay cheese sauce
Morue cod
Moule mussels
Moules marinières mussels cooked in
white wine and shallots
Mousseline hollandaise sauce with
whipped cream
Moutarde mustard
Mouton mutton
Mûre mulberry
Mûre sauvage (de ronce) blackberry
Muscade nutmeg
Museau de porc (de boeuf) sliced muzzle
of pork (beef) with shallots and parsley
with vinaigrette
Myrtille bilberry (blueberry)
Mystère a meringue desert with ice-
cream and chocolate; also cone-shaped
ice cream
Nature plain
Navarin stew (usually lamb)
Navets turnips
Nid nest
Noilly sauce based on vermouth
Noisette hazelnut
Noisette sauce of lightly browned butter
Noisette (de) round piece (of)
Noix nuts
Noix de veau topside of leg (veal)
Normande (à la) Normandy style:
fish sauce with mussels, shrimps,
mushrooms, eggs and cream
Nouille noodle
Nouveau (Nouvelle) new or young

Estragon tarragon flavoured
Farci(e) stuffed
Farine flour
Faux-filet sirloin steak
Fenouil fennel
Fermière mixture of onions, carrots, turnips, celery, etc.
Feuille de vigne vine leaf
Feuilleté light flaky pastry
Fève broad bean
Ficelle (à la) tied in a string
Ficelles thin loaves of bread
Figue fig
Filet fillet
Financière (à la) Madeira sauce with truffles
Fines de claire oyster (see Huîtres)
Fines herbes mixture of parsley, chives, tarragon, etc.
Flageolet kidney bean
Flamande (à la) Flemish style: bacon, carrots, cabbage, potatoes and turnips
Flambée flamed
Flamiche puff pastry tart
Foie liver
Foie de veau calves liver
Foie gras goose liver
Fond d'artichaut artichoke heart
Fondu(e) (de fromage) melted cheese with wine
Forestière bacon and mushrooms
Four (au) baked in the oven
Fourré stuffed
Frais fresh or cool
Fraise strawberry
Fraise des bois wild strawberry
Framboise raspberry
Frappé frozen or ice cold
Friandise sweets (petits fours)
Fricassée braised in sauce or butter, egg yolks and cream
Frisé(e) curly
Frit fried
Frites chips/French fries
Friture small fried fish
Fromage cheese
Fromage de tête brawn
Fruit de la passion passion fruit
Fruits confits crystallised fruit
Fruits de mer seafood
Fumé smoked
Galette pastry, pancake or cake
Gamba large prawn
Ganache chocolate and crème fraîche mixture used to fill cakes
Garbure (Garbue) vegetable soup
Gâteau cake
Gauffre waffle
Gelée aspic gelly
Genièvre juniper
Gésier gizzard
Gibelotte see Fricassée
Gibier game
Gigot (de) leg of lamb; can describe other meat or fish
Gingembre ginger
Girofle clove
Glacé(e) iced, crystallized, glazed
Glace ice-cream
Gougère round-shaped, egg and cheese choux pastry
Goujon gudgeon
Goujonnettes (de) small fried pieces (of)
Gourmandises sweetmeats; can describe fruits de mer
Graisse fat
Gratin browned
Gratin Dauphinois potato dish with cheese, cream and garlic
Gratin Savoyard potato dish with cheese and butter
Gratiné(e) sauced dish browned with butter, cheese, breadcrumbs, etc.
Gravette oyster (see Huîtres)
Grenouille (cuisses de grenouilles) frog (frogs' legs)
Gribiche mayonnaise sauce with gherkins, capers, hardboiled egg yolks and herbs
Grillade grilled meat
Grillé(e) grilled
Griotte (Griottine) bitter red cherry
Gros sel coarse rock or sea salt
Groseille à maquereau gooseberry
Groseille noire blackcurrant
Groseille rouge redcurrant
Gruyère hard, mild cheese
Hachis minced or chopped-up
Hareng herring
    à l'huile cured in oil
    fumé kippered
    salé bloater
    saur smoked
Haricot bean
Haricot blanc dried white bean
Haricot vert green/French bean
Hollandaise sauce with butter, egg yolk and lemon juice
Homard lobster
Hongroise (à la) Hungarian style: sauce with tomato and paprika
Huile oil
Huîtres oysters
    Les claires: the oyster-fattening beds in Marennes terrain (part of the Charente Estuary, between Royan and Rochefort, in Poitou-Charentes).
    Flat-shelled oysters: *Belons* (from the river Belon in Brittany)
    Gravettes: from Arcachon in the South West); both the above are cultivated in their home oyster beds.
    Marennes are those transferred from Brittany and Arcachon to *les claires*, where they finish their growth.
    Dished oysters (sometimes called *portugaises*): these breed mainly in the Gironde and Charentes estuaries; they mature at Marennes.
    Fines de claires and *spéciales* are the largest; *huîtres de parc* are standard sized. All this lavish care covers a time span of two to four years.
Hure (de) head (of); brawn, jellied
Île flottante unmoulded soufflé of beaten egg with white sugar
Imam bayeldi aubergine with rice, onions, and sautéed tomatoes
Infusion herb tea
Italienne (à l') Italian style: artichokes,

Cabillaud cod
Cacahouète roasted peanut
Cacao cocoa
Café coffee
Caille quail
Cajou cashew nut
Calmar (Calamar) inkfish, squid
Campagne country style
Canard duck
Caneton (Canette) duckling
Cannelle cinnamon
Carbonnade braised beef in beer, onions and bacon
Carré chop
Casse-croûte snack
Cassis blackcurrant
Cassolette small pan
Cassoulet casserole of beans, sausage and/or pork, goose, duck
Cèpe fine,delicate mushroom
Cerise (noire) cherry (black)
Cerneau walnut
Cervelas pork garlic sausage
Cervelle brains
Champignons (des bois) mushrooms (from the woods)
Chanterelle apricot coloured mushroom
Chantilly whipped cream with sugar
Charcuterie cold meat cuts
Charcutière sauce with onions, white wine, gherkins
Chasseur sauce with white wine, mushrooms, shallots
Chateaubriand thick fillet steak
Chaussons pastry turnover
Chemise (en) pastry covering
Chicon chicory
Chicorée curly endive
Chipiron see calmar
Choix (au) a choice of
Chou (vert) cabbage
Choucroute souring of vegetables, usually with cabbage (sauerkraut), peppercorns, boiled ham, potatoes and Strasbourg sausages
Chou-fleur cauliflower
Chou rouge red cabbage
Choux (pâte à) pastry
Ciboule spring onions
Cidre cider
Ciboulette chive
Citron (vert) lemon (lime)
Citronelle lemon grass
Civet stew
Clafoutis cherries in pancake batter
Clou de girofle clove (spice)
Cochon pig
Cochonailles pork products
Cocotte (en) cooking pot
Coeur (de) heart (of)
Coing quince
Colin hake
Compote stewed fruit
Concassé(e) coarsely chopped
Concombre cucumber
Confit(e) preserved or candied
Confiture jam
Confiture d'orange marmalade
Consommé clear soup

Coq (au vin) chicken in red wine sauce
Coque (à la) soft-boiled or served in shell
Coquillage shellfish
Coquille St-Jacques scallop
Coriandre coriander
Cornichon gherkin
Côte d'agneau lamb chop
Côte de boeuf side of beef
Côte de veau veal chop
Côtelette chop
Coulis de thick sauce of
Courge pumpkin
Couscous crushed semolina
Crabe crab
Crécy with carrots and rice
Crème cream
Crème anglaise light custard sauce
Crème brûlée same, less sugar and cream, with praline (see Brûlée)
Crème pâtissière custard filling
Crêpe thin pancake
Crêpe Suzette sweet pancake with orange liqueur sauce
Cresson watercress
Crevette grise shrimp
Crevette rose prawn
Croque Monsieur toasted cheese or ham sandwich
Croustade small pastry mould with various fillings
Croûte (en) pastry crust (in)
Cru raw
Crudité raw vegetable
Crustacés shell fish
Cuisse (de) leg (of)
Cuissot (de) haunch (of)
Cuit cooked
Datte date
Daube stew (various types)
Daurade sea-bream
Décaféiné decaffeinated coffee
Dégustation tasting
Diane (á la) pepper cream sauce
Dieppoise (à la) Dieppe style: white wine, cream, mussels, shrimps
Dijonaise (à la) with mustard sauce
Dinde young hen turkey
Dindon turkey
Dorade sea-bream
Doux (douce) sweet
Échalotte shallot
Écrevisse freshwater crayfish
Émincé thinly sliced
Encre squid ink, used in sauces
Endive chicory
Entrecôte entrecôte, rib steak
Entremets sweets
Épaule shoulder
Épice spice
Épinard spinach
Escabèche fish (or poultry) marinated in court-bouillon; cold
Escalope thinly cut (meat or fish)
Escargot snail
Espadon swordfish
Estouffade stew with onions, herbs, mushrooms, red or white wine (perhaps garlic)

Menu decoder

À point medium rare
Abats offal
Abricot apricot
Acarne sea-bream
Affiné(e) improve, ripen, mature (common term with cheese)
Africaine (à l') african style: with aubergines, tomatoes, ceps
Agneau lamb
Agrumes citrus fruits
Aigre-doux sweet-sour
Aiguillette thin slice
Ail garlic
Aile (Aileron) wing (winglet)
Aïoli mayonnaise, garlic, olive oil
Algues seaweed
Aligot purée of potatoes, cream, garlic, butter and fresh Tomme de Cantal (or Laguiole) cheese
Allemande (à l') German style: with sauerkraut and sausages
Alsacienne (à l') Alsace style: with sauerkraut, sausages and sometimes foie gras
Amande almond
Amandine almond-flavoured
Amer bitter
Américaine (à l') Armoricaine (à l') sauce with dry white wine, cognac, tomatoes, shallots
Amuse-gueule appetizer
Ananas pineapple
Anchoiade anchovy crust
Anchois anchovy
Ancienne (à l') in the old style
Andouille smoked tripe sausage
Andouillette small chitterling (tripe) sausage
Aneth dill
Anglaise (à l') plain boiled
Anguille eels
Anis aniseed
Arachide peanut
Arc-en-ciel rainbow trout
Artichaud artichoke
Asperge asparagus
Assaisonné flavoured or seasoned with; to dress a salad
Assiette (de) plate (of)
Aubergine aubergine, eggplant
Aumônière pancake drawn up into shape of beggar's purse
Auvergnate (à l') Auvergne style: with cabbage, sausage and bacon
Avocat avocado pear
Baba au rhum sponge dessert with rum syrup
Baguette long bread loaf
Baie berry
Baigné bathed or lying in
Banane banana
Bar sea-bass
Barbeau de mer red mullet
Barbue brill

Basilic basil
Basquaise (à la) Basque style: Bayonne ham, rice and peppers
Baudroie monkfish, anglerfish
Bavette skirt of beef
Béarnaise thick sauce with egg yolks, shallots, butter, white wine and tarragon vinegar
Béchamel creamy white sauce
Beignet fritter
Belle Hélène poached pear with ice cream and chocolate sauce
Berrichonne bordelaise sauce
Betterave beetroot
Beurre (Échiré) butter (finest butter from Poitou-Charentes)
Beurre blanc sauce with butter, shallots, wine vinegar and sometimes dry white wine
Beurre noir sauce with brown butter, vinegar, parsley
Bière à la pression beer on tap
Bière en bouteille bottled beer
Bifteck steak
Bigarade (à la) orange sauce
Bisque shellfish soup
Blanc (de volaille) white breast (of chicken); can also describe white fish fillet or white vegetables
Blanchaille whitebait
Blanquette white stew
Blé corn or wheat
Blettes swiss chard
Blinis small, thick pancakes
Boeuf à la mode beef braised in red wine
Boeuf Stroganoff beef, sour cream, onions, mushrooms
Bombe ice-cream
Bonne femme (à la) white wine sauce, shallots, mushrooms
Bordelaise (à la) Bordeaux style: brown sauce with shallots, red wine, beef bone marrow
Boudin blanc white coloured sausage-shaped mixture; pork and sometimes chicken
Boudin noir black pudding
Bouillabaise Mediterranean fish stew and soup
Bouillon broth, light consommé
Bouquet garni bunch of herbs used for flavouring
Bourguignonne (à la) Burgundy style: red wine, onions, bacon and mushrooms
Bourride creamy fish soup with aioli
Brandade de morue salt cod
Bretonne sauce with celery, leeks, beans and mushrooms
Brioche sweet yeast bread
Brochet pike
Brochette (de) meat or fish on a skewer
Brouillé scrambled
Brûlé(e) toasted
Bruxelloise sauce with asparagus, butter and eggs

Days of the week

Monday	lundi
Tuesday	mardi
Wednesday	mercredi
Thursday	jeudi
Friday	vendredi
Saturday	samedi
Sunday	dimanche

Colours

black	noir/noire
blue	bleu/bleue
brown	brun/brune
green	vert/verte
orange	orange
pink	rose
red	rouge
white	blanc/blanche
yellow	jaune

Numbers

enough	assez
zero	zéro
one; first	un/une; premier/première
two/second	deux/deuxième
three/third	trois/troisième
four/fourth	quatre/quatrième
five/fifth	cinq/cinquième
six/sixth	six/sixième
seven/seventh	sept/septième
eight/eighth	huit/huitième
nine/nineth	neuf/neuvième
ten/tenth etc	dix/dixième etc
eleven	onze
twelve	douze
thirteen	treize
fourteen	quatorze
fifteen	quinze
sixteen	seize
seventeen	dix-sept
eighteen	dix-huit
nineteen	dix-neuf
twenty	vingt
twenty-one	vingt-et-un
twenty-two/three etc	vingt-deux/trois etc.
thirty	trente
forty	quarante
fifty	cinquante
sixty	soixante
seventy	soixante-dix
eighty	quatre-vingts
ninety	quatre-vingt-dix
hundred	cent
thousand	mille

Shopping (also see 'Paying')

USEFUL SHOPPING VOCABULARY

I'd like to buy...	Je voudrais acheter...
Do you have...?	Avez-vous ...?
How much, please?	C'est combien, s'il vous plaît?
I'm just looking, thank you	Je regarde, merci.
It's for a gift	C'est pour un cadeau.

SHOPS

antique shop	le magasin d'antiquités
baker	la boulangerie
bank	la banque
book shop	la librairie
cake shop	la pâtisserie
cheese shop	la fromagerie
chemist/drugstore	la pharmacie
clothes shop	le magasin de vêtements
delicatessen	la charcuterie
department store	le grand magasin
gift shop	le magasin de cadeaux
the market	le marché
newsagent	le magasin de journaux
post office	la poste/le PTT
shoe shop	le magasin de chaussures
the shops	les boutiques/magasins
tobacconist	le tabac
travel agent	l'agence de voyages

expensive	cher
cheap	pas cher, bon marché
sales	les soldes
size (in clothes)	la taille
size (in shoes)	la pointure
too expensive	trop cher

TELEPHONING

telephone/phone booth	le téléphone/la cabine téléphonique
phone card	la carte téléphonique
post card	la carte postale
stamps	les timbres

Months of the year

January	janvier
February	février
March	mars
April	avril
May	mai
June	juin
July	juillet
August	août
September	septembre
October	octobre
November	novembre
December	décembre

a year	un an/une année
a month	un mois

blackberries	les mûres
blackcurrants	les cassis
cherries	les cerises
fresh fruit	le fruit frais
grapefruit	le pamplemousse
grapes	les raisins
lemon/lime	le citron/le citron vert
orange	l'orange
peach	la pêche
pear	la poire
plums	les prunes/les mirabelles (type of plum)
raspberries	les framboises
red/white currants	les groseilles
strawberries	les fraises

DESSERTS AND CHEESE

apple tart	la tarte aux pommes
cake	le gâteau
cheese	le fromage
cream	la crème fraîche
goat's cheese	le fromage de chèvre
ice cream	la glace

SUNDRIES

ashtray	un cendrier
bread	le pain
bread roll	le petit pain
butter	le beurre
crisps	les chips
mustard	la moutarde
napkin	la serviette
oil	l'huile
peanuts	les cacahuètes
salt/pepper	le sel/le poivre
toast	le toast
vinegar	le vinaigre

DRINKS

beer	la bière
a bottle of	une bouteille de
black coffee	un café noir
coffee	un café
with cream	un café-crème
with milk	un café au lait
a cup of	une tasse de
decaffeinated coffee	un café décaféiné/un déca
espresso coffee	un express
freshly-squeezed lemon/ orange juice	un citron pressé/une orange pressée
a glass of	un verre de
herbal tea	une tisane/infusion
with lime/verbena	au tilleul/à la verveine
with mint	à la menthe
with milk/lemon	au lait/au citron
milk	le lait
(some) mineral water	de l'eau minérale
orange juice	un jus d'orange
(some) tap water	de l'eau du robinet
(some) sugar	du sucre
tea	un thé
wine (red/white)	le vin (rouge/blanc)

frogs' legs	les cuisses de grenouilles
game	le gibier
ham	le jambon
kidneys	les rognons
lamb	l'agneau
meat	la viande
pork	le porc
rabbit	le lapin
salami style sausage (dry)	le saucisson-sec
sausage	la saucisse
snails	les escargots
steak	l'entrecôte/le steak/le bifteck
veal	le veau

FISH AND SEAFOOD

cod	le cabillaud/la morue
Dublin bay prawn/scampi	la langoustine
fish	le poisson
herring	le hareng
lobster	le homard
mullet	le rouget
mussels	les moules
oysters	les huîtres
pike	le brochet
prawns	les crevettes
salmon (smoked)	le saumon (fumé)
sea bass	le bar
seafood	les fruits de mer
skate	le raie
squid	le calmar
trout	la truite
tuna	le thon

VEGETABLES, PASTA AND RICE

cabbage	le chou
cauliflower	le chou-fleur
chips/french fries	les frites
garlic	l'ail
green beans	les haricots verts
leeks	les poireaux
onions	les oignons
pasta	les pâtes
peas	les petits pois
potatoes	les pommes-de-terre
rice	le riz
sauerkraut	la choucroute
spinach	les épinards
vegetables	les légumes

SALAD ITEMS

beetroot	la betterave
cucumber	le concombre
curly endive	la salade frisée
egg	un oeuf
green pepper/red pepper	le poivron/poivron rouge
green salad	la salade verte
lettuce	la laitue
tomato	la tomate

FRUIT

apple	la pomme
banana	la banane

(in) cash	(en) espèces
coin	le pièce de monnaie
money	l'argent
notes	les billets
price	le prix
travellers' cheques	les chèques de voyage

Eating out

••

If you are having trouble understanding the rather complicated-looking menu which is put before you, then turn to p.x for the menu decoder. In the meantime, the following phrases should be useful when you are trying to communicate with the waiter or waitress.

GENERAL

Do you have a table?	Avez-vous une table libre?
I would like to reserve a table	Je voudrais réserver une table.
I would like to eat.	Je voudrais manger.
I would like something to drink	Je voudrais boire quelque chose.
I would like to order, please	Je voudrais commander, s'il vous plait.
The bill, please.	L'addition, s'il vous plait.
I am a vegetarian.	Je suis végétarien (ne).

MEALS AND MEALTIMES

breakfast	le petit-déjeuner
cover charge	le couvert
dessert	le dessert
dinner	le dîner
dish of the day	le plat du jour
fixed price menu	la formule/le menu à prix fixe
fork	la fourchette
knife	le couteau
lunch	le déjeuner
main course	le plat principal
menu	le menu/la carte
(Is the) service included?	Est-ce que le service est compris?
soup	la soupe/le potage
spoon	la cuillère
starter	l'entrée/le hors-d'oeuvre
waiter	Monsieur
waitress	Madame, Mademoiselle
wine list	la carte des vins

COOKING STYLES

baked	cuit/cuite au four
boiled	bouilli/bouillie
fried	à la poêle
grilled	grillé/grillée
medium	à point
poached	poché/pochée
rare	saignant
steamed	à la vapeur
very rare	bleu
well done	bien cuit

MEAT, POULTRY, GAME AND OFFAL

bacon	le bacon
beef	le boeuf
chicken	le poulet
duck	le canard

bag/handbag	le sac/le sac-à-main
case	la valise
left luggage	la consigne
luggage	les bagages

DIRECTIONS

Is it far?	Est-ce que c'est loin?
How far is it to...?	Combien de kilomètres d'ici à ...?
Is it near?	Est-ce que c'est près d'ici?
here/there	ici/là
near/far	près/loin
left/right	gauche/droite
on the left/right	à gauche/à droite
straight on	tout droit
at the end of	au bout de
up	en haut
down	en bas
above (the shop)	au-dessus (du magasin)
below (the bed)	au-dessous (le lit)
opposite (the bank)	en face (de la banque)
next to (the window)	à côté (de la fenêtre)

DRIVING

Please fill the tank (car)	Le plein, s'il vous plaît
car hire	la location de voitures
driver's licence	le permis de conduire
petrol	l'essence
rent a car	louer une voiture
unleaded	sans plomb

In the hotel

I have a reservation	J'ai une réservation
for 2 nights	pour 2 nuits
I leave	Je pars .....
I'd like a room	Je voudrais une chambre
Is breakfast included?	le petit-déjeuner est inclus?
single room	une chambre à un lit
room with double bed	une chambre à lit double
twin room	une chambre à deux lits
room with bathroom	une chambre avec salle de bains
and toilet	et toilette/W.C.
a quiet room	une chambre calme
bath	le bain
shower	la douche
with air conditioning	avec climatisation

1st/2nd floor etc	premier/deuxième étage
breakfast	le petit-déjeuner
dining room	la salle à manger
ground floor	le rez-de-chaussée (RC)
key	la clef
lift/elevator	l'ascenseur

PAYING

How much?	C'est combien, s'il vous plaît?/ Quel est le prix?
Do you accept credit cards?	Est-ce que vous acceptez les cartes de crédit?
Do you have any change?	Avez-vous de la monnaie?

Time and space

••

PERIODS OF TIME

a minute	une minute
half an hour	une demie-heure
an hour	une heure
a week	une semaine
fortnight	une quinzaine
month	un mois
year	un an/une année
today	aujourd'hui
yesterday/tomorrow	hier/demain
morning	le matin
afternoon	l'après-midi
evening/night	e soir/la nuit
during (the night)	pendant (la nuit)
early/late	tôt/tard

TELLING THE TIME

What time is it?	Quelle heure est-il?
At what time?	A quelle heure?
(at) 1 0'clock/2 0'clock etc.	(à) une heure/deux heures etc.
half past one	une heure et demie
quarter past two	deux heures et quart
quarter to three	trois heures moins le quart
(at) midday	à midi
(at) midnight	à minuit

Getting around

••

by bicycle	à bicyclette/en vélo
by bus	en bus
by car	en voiture
by coach	en car
on foot	à pied
by plane	en avion
by taxi	en taxi
by train	en train

IN TOWN

map of the city	un plan de la ville
I am going to …	Je vais à…..
I want to go to….	Je voudrais aller à …
I want to get off at…	Je voudrais descendre à
platform	le quai
return ticket	un aller-retour
single ticket	un aller simple
ticket	le billet
timetable	l'horaire
airport	l'aéroport
bus/coach station	la gare routière
bus stop	l'arrêt de bus
district	le quartier/l'arrondissement
street	la rue
taxi rank	la station de taxi
tourist information office	l'office du tourisme
train station	la gare
underground	le métro

Good evening/night/Hello	Bonsoir (during the evening)
Hello/Goodbye (very informal)	Salut
Goodbye	Au revoir
See you soon.	bientôt
Excuse me	Excusez-moi
I am sorry	Je suis désolé(m)/désolée(f)
Pardon?	Comment?

Handy phrases

• •

Do you speak English?	Parlez-vous anglais?
I don't speak French	Je ne parle pas français
I don't understand	Je ne comprends pas
Could you speak more slowly please?	Pouvez-vous parler moins vite s'il vous plaît?
Could you repeat that, please?	Pouvez-vous répéter, s'il vous plaît?
again	encore
I am English/Scottish/ Welsh/Irish/American/ Canadian/Australian/ a New Zealander	Je suis anglais(e) /écossais(e)/ gallois(e)/ irlandais(e)/ américain(e)/ canadien(ne)/ australien(ne)/ néo-zélandais(e)
My name is ...	Je m'appelle ...
What is your name?	Comment vous appelez-vous?
How are you?	Comment allez-vous?
Very well, thank you.	Très bien, merci.
Pleased to meet you.	Enchanté(e).
Mr/Mrs	Monsieur/Madame
Miss/Ms	Mademoiselle/Madame
How?	Comment?
What?	Quel (m)/Quelle (f)?
When?	Quand?
Where (is/are)?	Où (est/sont)?
Which?	Quel (m)/Quelle (f)?
Who?	Qui?
Why?	Pourquoi?

Essential words

• •

good	bon/bonne
bad	mauvais/mauvaise
big	grand/grande
small	petit/petite
hot	chaud/chaude
cold	froid/froide
open	ouvert/ouverte
closed	fermé/fermée
toilets	les toilettes/les w.c.
women	dames
men	hommes
free (unoccupied)	libre
occupied	occupé/occupée
free (no charge)	gratuit/gratuite
entrance	l'entrée
exit	la sortie
prohibited	interdit/interdite
no smoking	défense de fumer

Handy words and phrases

Over the next few pages you'll find a selection of very basic French vocabulary and many apologies if the word you are looking for is missing. For those struggling with French menus, there is more help at the back of the book in the detailed menu decoder.

Let us begin, however, with a very basic guide to some French grammar: All French nouns are either masculine or feminine and gender is denoted as follows: 'the' singular is translated by le (m), la (f) or l' (in front of a word beginning with a vowel or mute 'h'; 'the' plural = les (whatever gender and in front of a vowel or mute 'h'). 'A' = un (m), une(f) (no exceptions for vowels or mute 'h').

There are two forms of the word 'you' – tu is 'you' in the singular, very informal and used with people you know, vous is 'you' in the singular but is used in formal situations and when you don't know the person, vous is also the plural form. Young people often address each other as 'tu' automatically, but when in doubt and to avoid offence, always use 'vous'.

Adjectives agree with the gender of the accompanying noun. For a singular masculine noun there is no change to the adjective, but to indicate the masculine plural, an 's' is added to the end of the adjective; an 'e' is usually added for a feminine noun and 'es' for the plural. If you are not very familiar with French don't worry too much about gender agreement when talking (unless you wish to perfect your pronunciation, as 'e' or 'es' usually makes the final consonant hard), we have used feminine versions where applicable simply to help with the understanding of written French. These are either written out in full or shown as '(e)'. Finally, if you do not know the right French word try using the English one with a French accent – it is surprising how often this works.

The verb 'to be'

I am	je suis
you are (informal/sing.)	tu es
he/she/it is	il(m)/elle(f)/il est*
we are	nous sommes
you are (formal/plural)	vous êtes
they are	ils(m)/elles(f) sont*

When you are in a hurry gender can complicate things – just say le or la, whichever comes into your head first and you will sometimes be right and usually be understood.

* The most common forms use the masculine: 'it is' = il est, 'they are'= ils sont. C'est = 'that is' or 'this is', and is not gender specific.

Essential vocabulary

Yes/No	Oui/Non
OK	D'accord
That's fine	C'est bon
Please	S'il vous plaît
Thank you	Merci
Good morning/Hello	Bonjour (during the day)

This guide was written by VALÉRIE PÉAN and SYLVIE BERTIER, with additional help from FRANÇOISE BOUILLÉ, PIERRE CHAVOT and LAETITIA GÉRARD.

Illustrations: F. LACHÈZE, p. 25 (top), p. 44 (b.) and RENAUD MARCA, P. 29 (top).

Illustrated maps: RENAUD MARCA

Cartography: © IDÉ INFOGRAPHIE (THOMAS GROLLIER)

Translation and adaptation: Y2K TRANSLATIONS (Email: info@y2ktranslations.com)

Additional design and editorial assistance: SOFI MOGENSEN and CHRISTINE BELL

Project manager: LIZ COGHILL

We have done our best to ensure the accuracy of the information contained in this guide. However, addresses, telephone numbers, opening times etc. inevitably do change from time to time, so if you find a discrepancy please do let us know. You can contact us at: hachetteuk@orionbooks.co.uk or write to us at Hachette UK, address below.

Hachette UK guides provide independent advice. The authors and compilers do not accept any remuneration for the inclusion of any addresses in these guides.

Please note that we cannot accept any responsibility for any loss, injury or inconvenience sustained by anyone as a result of any information or advice contained in this guide.

First published in the United Kingdom in 2001 by Hachette UK

Distributed in the United States of America by Sterling Publishing Co., Inc. 387 Park Avenue South, New York, NY 10016-8810

A CIP catalogue for this book is available from the British Library

ISBN 1 84202 098 6

Hachette UK, Cassell & Co., The Orion Publishing Group, Wellington House, 125 Strand, London WC2R 0BB

Printed in France by I.M.E. - 25110 Baume-les-Dames

there were around 20 craftsmen at work on the Aubrac plateau. From 1920 the handmade output from Laguiole declined in the face of competition from Thiers, and the craftsmen assemblers vanished.

A chic knife

In 1981 a handful of men who wished to revitalise the regional economy decided to relaunch the knife business at Laguiole. A local man, Jean-Louis Costes, the owner of brasseries in Paris, gathered a group of investors and turned to the famous designer Philippe Starck.

A massive success

Their company, Le Couteau de Laguiole, was set up in the 1980s, and became the sole workshop in France forging blades. Production growth was impressive: between 1990 and 1992, output rose from 80,000 to 140,000 knives, the workforce from 30 to 65. Since then, Laguiole has acquired a factory comprising a forge and numerous knife-assembly workshops, some of which can be visited all-year round.

A user's guide

Custom demands that when you use a Laguiole knife, you take it out before the meal, then clean it carefully after using it, closing it gently. Above all, you should never leave it on the table.

Top design award

In 1987 the famous designer Philippe Starck adapted the whole assembly process of the knife to modern industrial design methods. The result was a re-interpretation and improvement of the Laguiole knife using 20th-C. materials and the construction of an astonishing factory topped by a giant blade 60 ft (18 m) high, incorporating two sales outlets on site with distinctive

furniture, displays and packaging. The new look quickly boosted the image of the Laguiole knife and other stylists, such as Sonia Rykiel, Éric Raffy and Yann Pennor,

Grinding and polishing workshop

were drawn into the business, adding their own unique interpretations. Since then, the legendary knife has won award after award. The most recent was the European design award at the Seville Expo World Fair.

Knife designed by Philippe Starck

BEWARE OF IMITATIONS

The knives must possess two distinctive signs: a bull carved on the blade, proof that the knife was indeed made at Laguiole, and a bee on the back of the handle. The tip of the spring at the folding point is designed in the shape of a fly. This fly, typical of the Aubrac knife, must form part of the spring and not be superimposed. On top of this there is the rare quality of the materials: the handles are plated with real horn, the bolsters and rivets are made of brass, while the blade is always steel.

Fairs and markets

Foie gras, truffles, cep mushrooms, crafts, antiques... You will find all the traditional and specialised local products in the region's fairs and markets.

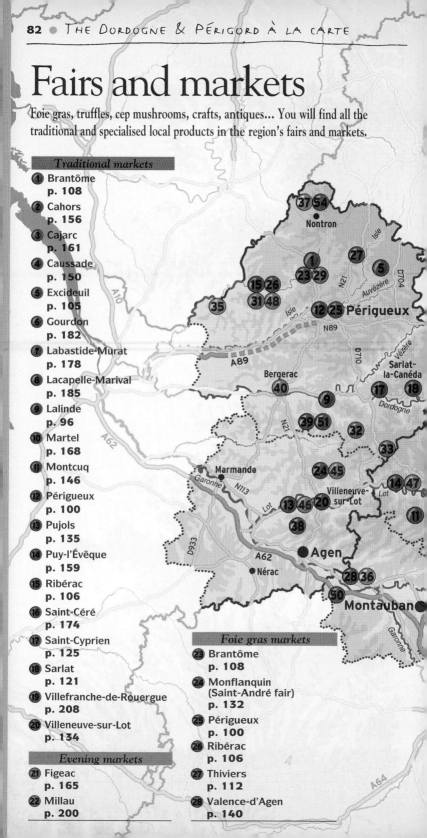

Traditional markets

1. **Brantôme**
   p. 108
2. **Cahors**
   p. 156
3. **Cajarc**
   p. 161
4. **Caussade**
   p. 150
5. **Excideuil**
   p. 105
6. **Gourdon**
   p. 182
7. **Labastide-Murat**
   p. 178
8. **Lacapelle-Marival**
   p. 185
9. **Lalinde**
   p. 96
10. **Martel**
    p. 168
11. **Montcuq**
    p. 146
12. **Périgueux**
    p. 100
13. **Pujols**
    p. 135
14. **Puy-l'Évêque**
    p. 159
15. **Ribérac**
    p. 106
16. **Saint-Céré**
    p. 174
17. **Saint-Cyprien**
    p. 125
18. **Sarlat**
    p. 121
19. **Villefranche-de-Rouergue**
    p. 208
20. **Villeneuve-sur-Lot**
    p. 134

Evening markets

21. **Figeac**
    p. 165
22. **Millau**
    p. 200

Foie gras markets

23. **Brantôme**
    p. 108
24. **Monflanquin**
    (Saint-André fair)
    p. 132
25. **Périgueux**
    p. 100
26. **Ribérac**
    p. 106
27. **Thiviers**
    p. 112
28. **Valence-d'Agen**
    p. 140

Truffle markets
29 Brantôme
p. 108
30 Lalbenque
p. 157

Walnut markets
31 Ribérac
p. 106

Cep markets
32 Monpazier
p. 128
33 Villefranche-du-Périgord
p. 129

Livestock markets and shows
34 Laissac: cattle and sheep
p. 189
35 Saint-Aulaye:
La Latière livestock fair
p. 107

Antiques/bric-a-brac
40 Bergerac
p. 94
41 Cajarc
p. 156
42 Caussade
p. 150
43 Figeac
p. 166
44 Labastide-Murat
p. 178
45 Monflanquin
p. 132
46 Pujols
p. 135
47 Puy-l'Évêque
p. 159
48 Ribérac
p. 106
49 Saint-Céré
p. 175

Craft markets
50 Auvillar: Pottery market
p. 142
51 Issigeac: Basketwork
fair
p. 93
52 Labastide-Murat
p. 178
53 Saint-Céré:
Pottery market
p. 175
54 Varaignes:
weavers' market
p. 111

Poultry fairs
36 Valence-d'Agen
p. 140
37 Varaignes (turkeys)
p. 111

Fruit and vegetable fairs
38 Prayssas: Fruit market
p. 136
39 Issigeac:
Pumpkin and gourd
fair
p. 93

0 10 20 30 miles
0 10 20 30 40 50 km

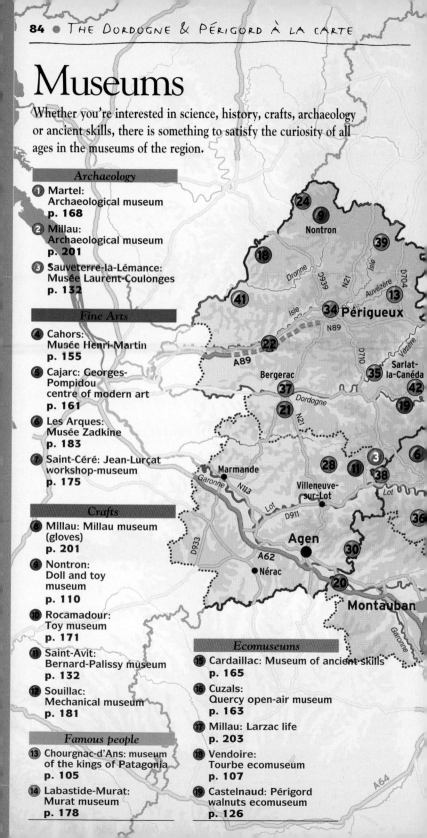

Museums

Whether you're interested in science, history, crafts, archaeology or ancient skills, there is something to satisfy the curiosity of all ages in the museums of the region.

Archaeology

① Martel:
Archaeological museum
p. 168

② Millau:
Archaeological museum
p. 201

③ Sauveterre-la-Lémance:
Musée Laurent-Coulonges
p. 132

Fine Arts

④ Cahors:
Musée Henri-Martin
p. 155

⑤ Cajarc: Georges-
Pompidou
centre of modern art
p. 161

⑥ Les Arques:
Musée Zadkine
p. 183

⑦ Saint-Céré: Jean-Lurçat
workshop-museum
p. 175

Crafts

⑧ Millau: Millau museum
(gloves)
p. 201

⑨ Nontron:
Doll and toy
museum
p. 110

⑩ Rocamadour:
Toy museum
p. 171

⑪ Saint-Avit:
Bernard-Palissy museum
p. 132

⑫ Souillac:
Mechanical museum
p. 181

Famous people

⑬ Chourgnac-d'Ans: museum
of the kings of Patagonia
p. 105

⑭ Labastide-Murat:
Murat museum
p. 178

Ecomuseums

⑮ Cardaillac: Museum of ancient skills
p. 165

⑯ Cuzals:
Quercy open-air museum
p. 163

⑰ Millau: Larzac life
p. 203

⑱ Vendoire:
Tourbe ecomuseum
p. 107

⑲ Castelnaud: Périgord
walnuts ecomuseum
p. 126

Traditional arts and trades

20 Donzac: Bygone crafts conservation centre **p. 141**

21 Monbazillac: Museum of local furniture/history **p. 92**

22 Mussidan: Périgord of yesteryear **p. 98**

23 Salles-la-Source: Museum of arts and crafts **p. 197**

24 Varaignes: Tisserand and Charentaise regional workshop-museum **p. 111**

Mining museums

25 Aubin **p. 210**

26 Decazeville **p. 230**

Science and technology

31 Carennac: Stills museum **p. 176**

32 Espalion: Musée Joseph-Vaylet **p. 188**

33 Figeac: Champollion **p. 164**

Prehistory

34 Périgueux: Périgord museum **p. 102**

35 Les Eyzies: National prehistory museum **p. 115**

36 Montcuq: Roland cave **p. 146**

Others

37 Bergerac: Tobacco **p. 94**

38 Bonaguil: Museum of ornithology **p. 133**

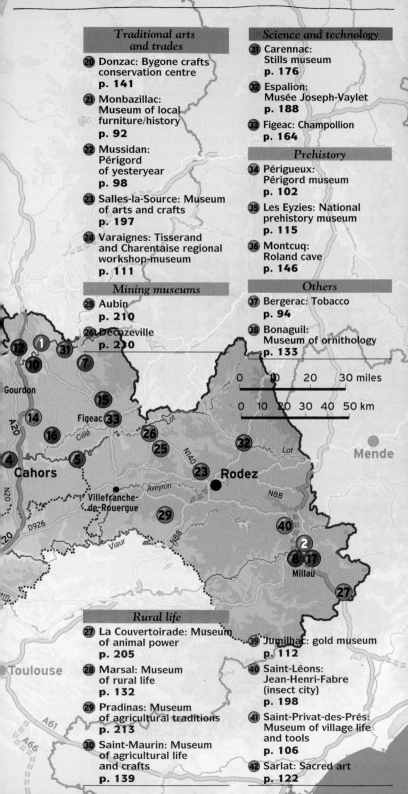

Rural life

27 La Couvertoirade: Museum of animal power **p. 205**

28 Marsal: Museum of rural life **p. 132**

29 Pradinas: Museum of agricultural traditions **p. 213**

30 Saint-Maurin: Museum of agricultural life and crafts **p. 139**

39 Jumilhac: gold museum **p. 112**

40 Saint-Léons: Jean-Henri-Fabre (insect city) **p. 198**

41 Saint-Privat-des-Prés: Museum of village life and tools **p. 106**

42 Sarlat: Sacred art **p. 122**

The Dordogne & Périgord in detail

Southern Quercy   146

Cahors and the wine trail   154

Down the Lot and Célé valleys   160

Causses de Quercy 168

Gardens of Quercy   180

Lot valley, Aubrac and Carladez   186

Rodez, Causse Comtal and Lévezou   196

Millau and the Grands Causses   200

Bastide country   208

Index   215

The Dordogne & Périgord in detail

On the following pages, you'll find all the information you need to visit the Dordogne and Périgord. For easy reference the region has been divided into zones. A colour code will enable you to find the area you are looking for at a glance.

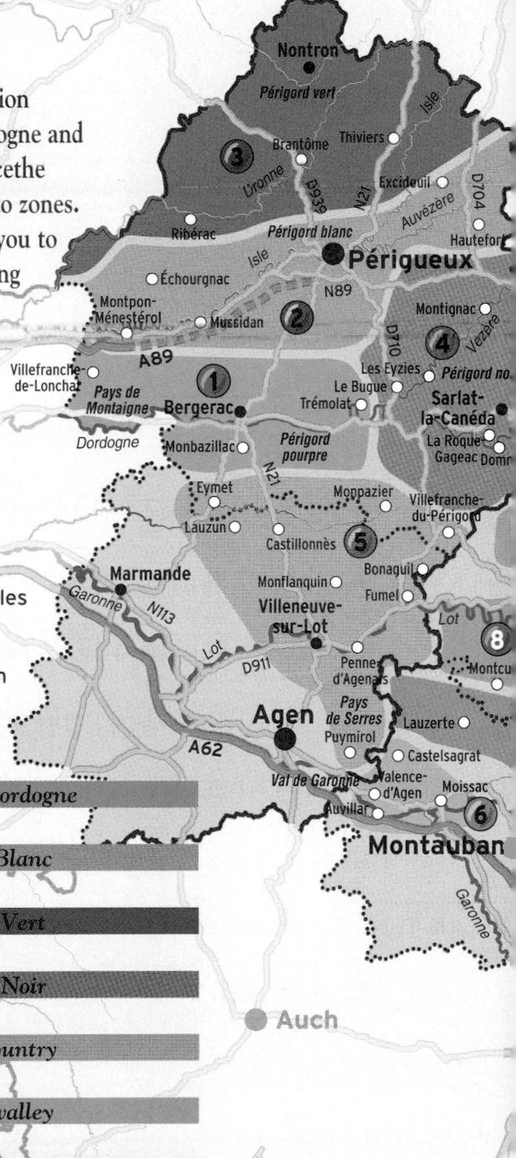

Bordeaux

Nontron
Périgord vert

Brantôme   Thiviers
Excideuil
Ribérac   *Périgord blanc*
Échourgnac   **Périgueux**
Montpon-Ménestérol   Mussidan   ②   N89   Montignac
Hautefor
Villefranche-de-Lonchat   *Pays de Montaigne*   ①   **Bergerac**   Les Eyzies   ④   *Périgord no*
Le Bugue   Sarlat-la-Canéda
Dordogne   Trémolat   La Roque-Gageac   Dom
Monbazillac   *Périgord pourpre*
Eymet   Moppazier   Villefranche-du-Périgord
Lauzun   Castillonnès   ⑤   Bonaguil
Monflanquin   Fumel
Marmande   Villeneuve-sur-Lot   *Lot*   ⑧
Penne-d'Agenais   Montcu
Agen   *Pays de Serres*   Lauzerte
Puymirol   Castelsagrat
Val de Garonne   Valence-d'Agen   Moissac
Auvillar   ⑥
Montauban

● **Auch**

0   10   20   30 miles

0   10   20   30   40   50 km

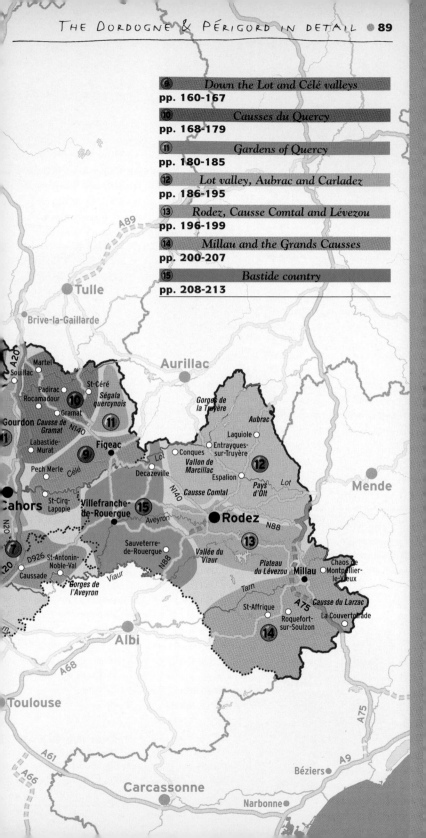

Montaigne country
half Périgord, half Gironde

Those who prefer to leave the beaten track will love the area around Montaigne, far from the main highways and tourist crowds. It stretches from the frontiers of La Double and western Le Landais to the slopes of the Libourne region and the Dordogne river. The present-day scenery is more or less as it was in the day of the great philosopher Montaigne. Apart from the Lac de Gurson, the lake leisure centre occupying 27 acres (11 ha), the countryside has scarcely changed at all.

Villefranche-de-Lonchat

Carsac-de-Gurson

Saint-Michel-de-Montaigne

Montazeau

Montcaret

Vélines

Vélines

21 miles (34 km)
W of Bergerac
Jardins de Sardy
☎ 05 53 27 51 45
Open daily July-Sept.,
weekends and public
holidays, Apr.-June and
Oct., 11am-7pm (during
week by appt).
Admission charge.

Jardins de Sardy

Created in the 1950s, this is an English garden that is a gem-like setting for an 18th-C. house and 17th-C. dovecote. The rockeries and leafy paths, refreshed by a double stone pond with darting goldfish, are perfect for a stroll. You can even order a quick meal (cold food at lunchtime), with a **view** of the Dordogne.

Montcaret

4 miles (6 km)
W of Vélines
**Gallo-Roman
luxury**
☎ 05 53 58 50 18
Open daily Apr.-Sept.
9am-noon and 2-6pm;
July-Aug. 9am-1pm and
2-7pm; Oct.-Mar.
10am-noon and 2-4pm.
Guided visit.
Admission charge.

This village preserves traces of its numerous occupants (Gauls, Visigoths and other barbarians). The remains of a Gallo-Roman villa and its baths built in the 1stC. AD are the principal attraction. You can admire the superb mosaics and remarkable heating system.

Pewter workshop
Le Bourg, Tête Noire
☎ 05 53 58 67 08
Open Mon.-Sat. 9am-
noon and 2-7pm.
Admission free.

ANIMAL CENTRE

Parc et Poterie de Montazeau
4 miles (6 km)
N of Vélines
☎ 05 53 61 29 84
Open daily 2-7pm.
Admission charge.
Your children will enjoy a walk in the park among animals of their own size – donkeys and dwarf goats, llamas, rheas (a type of ostrich), fallow deer and kangaroos. You can enter the enclosure and stroke the animals and there is a nursery for baby animals – who could resist those bundles of fur? Adults will want to explore the earthenware exhibition in the pottery studio (egg cup 35F, wine jug 150F, small gratin dish 135F).

A pewter craftsman born a few centuries ago would hardly feel out of place in Gérard Lasserre's workshop. In the corner of a room amply lit by the sunlight, located beside the main Bordeaux-Bergerac road, there is just space for a display of his copies of candlesticks, teapots, old dishes etc. (bottle stopper 90F, coaster 160F). You can even take objects here to be restored.

Saint-Michel-de-Montaigne
2.5 miles (4 km)
NW of Montcaret
Château de Montaigne
☎ 05 53 58 63 93
Open Wed.-Sun., Mar.-May and Nov.-Dec., 10am-noon and 2-5.30pm; June, Sept. and Oct., 10am-noon and 2-6.30pm; daily July-Aug., 10am-6.30pm.
Admission charge.
Périgord's most famous son, the essayist Michel de Montaigne (1533–1592), grew up in pretty countryside surrounded by vineyards. Badly damaged by fire in the 19thC., his house was rebuilt in Neo-Renaissance style. Fortunately the round tower, the writer's library and study escaped the catastrophe. Don't miss the neighbouring Château de Mathecoulon, owned by Montaigne's brother.

Villefranche-de-Lonchat
7.5 miles (12 km)
N of Saint-Michel-de-Montaigne
Bastide and lake
Musée d'Histoire locale
Open all year by appt (town hall).
Admission charge.
This bastide formerly guarded the route between the River Isle in the north, the River Dordogne in the south and the slopes of Castillon in the west. It still has the ruins of a 14th-C. château and also a museum of

Local History museum in Villefranche-de-Lonchat.

Spotcheck
B3

Dordogne

Things do to
Jardins de Sardy
Visit a pewter workshop

With children
Lac de Gurson outdoor leisure centre
Animal centre

Within easy reach
Landais and La Double (18 miles/30 km NE), p. 98
Bergerac (22 miles/35 km E), p. 94

Tourist offices
Carsac-de-Gurson: ☎ 05 53 80 78 88
Saint-Michel-de-Montaigne: ☎ 05 53 73 29 62
Villefranche-de-Lonchat: ☎ 05 53 80 77 25

local history. Close by is the 27-acre (11-ha) **Lac de Gurson**, an outdoor lake and leisure centre where you can swim in safety. For the younger ones, the special treat is a water chute 350 ft (108 m) long (Base de Loisirs de Gurson ☎ 05 53 80 77 57).

Carsac-de-Gurson
1.5 miles (2 km) E of Villefranche-de-Lonchat
The lion and the leopard
The superb Romanesque church that dominates the village is dedicated to Eleanor, duchess of Aquitaine and queen of England (1122-1204), hence the leopard of England and lion of Aquitaine on the facade. Don't miss the superb sculpted doorway and have a look at the small cemetery to the right of the church. Don't leave Carsac without going to **Grappe de Gurson**, a wine co-operative selling white, rosé and red wines over the counter (☎ 05 53 82 81 50).

Monbazillac,
the wine road

The wine road is lined with fine houses and ancient wineries. This is the region where England's medieval establishment obtained its wines, the home of 'claret' long before Bordeaux was thought of. The vineyards of Bergerac cover more than 25,000 acres (10,000 ha), concentrated along the Dordogne valley around the town of Bergerac. Notable names include Côtes-de-Montravel, Pécharmant and Monbazillac.

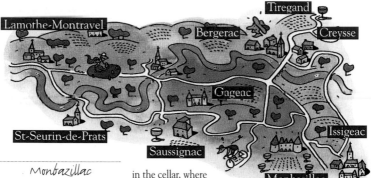

Monbazillac

4 miles (7 km)
S of Bergerac
Château
☎ 05 53 61 52 52
Open daily June-Sept.
10am-12.30pm and
2-7.30pm (10am-
7.30pm in July-Aug.).
Telephone out of season.
Admission charge.
The 16th-C. château, with its conical roofs and four large round towers, contains two museums: the **Musée des Arts et Traditions Populaires** (a collection of fine Périgord furniture and documents on the history of Protestantism) and a **Musée du Vin**, a small wine museum

in the cellar, where your visit ends in a tasting. From the terraces, you get a splendid view of the vineyards of Bergerac.

Saussignac and Gageac

9.5 miles (15 km)
SW of Bergerac
Hilltop castles
Saussignac is surrounded by a vineyard that produces white 'liquoreux' wines and full-bodied reds labelled Côtes-de-Saussignac. The château of the dukes of Lauzun faces the fine Château de Gageac. They are both private properties and can only be admired from the outside.

Lamothe-Montravel

25 miles (40 km)
W of Bergerac
Mellow slopes

The slopes around this small village are home to one of the best vineyards in the Dordogne valley (the 'crus' of Montravel are mellow whites). Montravel is also famous for the battle of Castillon in 1453, which took place only 2 miles from here and ended the Hundred Years War between France and England. If you want to follow the banks of the Dordogne, take the little road to Saint-Seurin-de-Prats.

Château de Monbazillac (16thC.)

Issigeac
*12 miles (19 km)
SE of Bergerac*
Pumpkin capital
This is a very pretty medieval town with stalls and fortified half-timbered or cob-built houses. Particularly noteworthy are the Maison des Dîmes (tithe house) and Maison des Têtes. The town, which prospered from the 14thC., became a retreat for the bishops of Sarlat. The impressive Château des Évêques (bishops' palace) was built for François de Salignac, bishop of Sarlat, in 1660. Watch out for the **pumpkin and cucurbit fair** in Noember., which is held in the vault of the Salles des Évêques (bishops' halls). July is the month of the **basketwork fair** (Foire de la Vannerie), when all the basketmakers converge on Issigeac, the osier capital.

Creysse
*5 miles (8 km)
E of Bergerac*
Ancient flints
☎ 05 53 23 20 45
Open daily June-Sept. 10am-7pm; out of season, weekends and public holidays 10am-6pm.
Admission charge.

The stone in this area was used as the raw material for numerous tools by prehistoric man and in Creysse, on the Barbas site, thousands of flints have been unearthed. An exhibition explains how the stone is worked. You can even pretend to be a caveman and rub flints together. Afterwards, board the **Rivière Esperance**, an ancient barge that will carry you peacefully along the banks of the Dordogne (information from the tourist office).

Pécharmant hill
Château de Tiregaud
☎ 05 53 23 21 08
Open Mon.-Sat., 8am-noon and 2-6pm.
Admission free.
Located northeast of Bergerac, Pécharmant hill ('pech' means 'peak') produces full-bodied red wines (1,230 acres/300 ha), which according to the experts resemble the red wines of Saint-Émilion. Take a break at the **Château de Tiregand** at Creysse to see its French gardens and its very fine 17th-C. wine cellars (visit by appointment, tasting and sales: 44F per bottle).

Spotcheck
BC3

Dordogne

Things to do
Wine road
Musée du Vin
Pumpkin fair at Issegeac

With children
Discovering flints
Barge trips on the Dordogne

Within easy reach
*Landais and La Double
(19 miles/30 km N), p. 98
Bergerac (6 miles/10 km
N), p. 94*

Tourist offices
Bergerac:
☎ 05 53 57 03 11
Creysse: ☎ 05 53 23 20 45

MONBAZILLAC
VINEYARDS

The vineyards cover about 7,400 acres (3,000 ha) in five communes, and produce a golden 'liquoreux' white wine that owes its high sugar content to the famous noble rot. Monbazillac is a stable wine that ages well. It goes well with foie gras and desserts. It is regaining its reputation thanks to the efforts of those in charge of the 'appellation', who would like to impose manual picking and lower yields.

Château d'Issigeac (17thC.)

Bergerac,
or the ghost
of Cyrano

Musée du Tabac, Place du Feu

Once the capital of Protestantism (16thC.), Bergerac's prosperity was based on the River Dordogne, with the ancient town built around the port. Today the little town at the gates of the Bordelais region is still busy, possessing two major advantages. It is the capital of the French tobacco industry and the heart of a wine region with prestigious 'appellations' such as Bergerac, Montravel, Pécharmant, Rosette, Saussignac and Monbazillac.

Tobacco flower

A town, a river
Musée ethno-graphique du vin, de la tonnellerie et de la batellerie
5, rue des Conférences
☎ **05 53 57 80 92**
Open Tues.-Sat., 10am-noon and 2-5.30pm; Sun., 2.30-6.30pm. Closed Sat. pm and Sun. from mid-Nov. to mid-Mar.
Admission charge.
Bergerac was one of the great French ports in the 18th-19thC. thanks to 'batellerie' (river transport), and its 'tonnellerie' (barrel-making), tobacco and wine industries. The museum occupies an 18th-C. half-timbered

building, and contains a wide range of objects relating to the town's industries, including models and ancient artefacts to take you back to the past.

River of history
Boat trips from the old port, Quai Salvette
☎ **05 53 24 58 80**
Open daily Easter to All Saints' Day (1 Nov.).
Admission charge.
Boarding a **pleasure boat** (*photo below*) on the Dordogne is one of the nicest ways to see Bergerac. The trip takes an hour, during which time you learn the history of river

transport and the great historic moments of the town. You are also taken to a nature reserve where you can spot herons, kites, cormorants and other feathery friends as well as terrapins.

Restaurant façade, Rue Pélissière

The ancient town: the tale of Cyrano

Tourist office
☎ 05 53 57 03 11
Organised visits (admission charge) at 11am in July-Aug.
The 16thC. was a period of great prosperity for the town, as is borne out by the

TOBACCO CAPITAL

Maison Peyrarède
Place du Feu
☎ 05 53 63 04 13
Open Tues.-Fri. 10am-noon and 2-6pm; Sat. 10am-noon and 2-5pm; Sun. 2.30-6.30pm.
Admission charge.
The Maison Peyrarède is a superb townhouse

constructed in 1604 that now houses the Musée du Tabac, which is unique in France. The museum presents the history of tobacco, which was imported from the New World and popularised in France by diplomat and scholar Jean Nicot (b. 1530). It was a far cry from the anti-nicotine campaigns of today. Tobacco was initially a cure for migraines. The exhibits include some fine collections of tobacco jars, snuffboxes and carved pipes.

Statue of Cyrano de Bergerac, Place de la Myrpe

corbelled and half-timbered buildings (Rue d'Albert, Rue Saint-James, Rue des Fontaines). Go down to the Dordogne via the beautifully restored Place Pélissière. The Église Saint-Jacques, a church completely rebuilt in the 17thC., is on the way to the Place de la Myrpe, where you will see a statue of the huge-nosed Cyrano de Bergerac. Though the irascible Cyrano was not native to Bergerac but just another Parisian, the Bergeracois don't mind.

Bergerac holy of holies

Maison des Vins
Rue des Récollets
☎ 05 53 63 57 55
Open daily May-June 10am-12.30pm and 1-6pm; June to mid-Oct. 10am-1pm and 2-7pm.
Admission free.
Home of the council of Bergerac wine industries, the Maison des Vins offers its visitors free wine-tastings and on-site sales. Besides an oenological laboratory, the house also contains the very pretty **Cloître des Récollets**, a 17th-C. cloister. Every Wednesday in summer jazz is played in the shady courtyard (concert at 6pm, admission free). Another must is the **antiques and crafts market** (marché à la brocante et aux

Spotcheck
BC3

Dordogne

Things to do

Jazz concerts
Antiques and crafts market
Tobacco museum

With children

Barge trips

Within easy reach

Landais and La Double (15.5 miles/25 km N), p. 98
Monbazillac (6 miles/10 km S), p. 92
Trémolat (22 miles/35 km E), p. 96

Tourist office

Bergerac: ☎ 05 53 57 03 11

métiers d'art) held all year in Rue des Récollets in front of the Maison des Vins (first Sunday of the month).

La Flambée

Route de Périgueux
☎ 05 53 57 52 33
Closed Sun. eves and Mon. out of season and Jan.-Mar.
Set menus 98-195F.
Located in a wooded park, this restaurant has a menu featuring the produce of the region. Don't miss the zander, to be sampled with a delicious white Bergerac.

Cloître des Récollets, cloister

Around Trémolat
the river in focus

Between Bergerac and Limeuil the countryside changes, but it is not an abrupt transition. The right bank of the Dordogne is steep and notable for the narrowness of the plain squeezed between the river and the slopes. The left bank opens up into a broad plain where tobacco and maize crops are grown. And upstream of Lalinde, the Dordogne is picturesque with its pebble banks and hairpin meanders called 'cingles'. Scattered châteaux remind us of the strategic importance of the river.

Trémolat
21 miles (34 km)
E of Bergerac
Film set
The main square may seem familiar. That's because it was a setting for Chabrol's 1969 film Le Boucher. Trémolat is equally famous for the view from the **Belvédère de Rocamadou**, a viewpoint overlooking one of the lovely river meanders, the **Cingle de Trémolat**. The panorama is magnificent.

Cingle de Trémolat (river meander)

Farm tour
Tues. July-Aug., meet at 3pm.
☎ **05 53 22 77 38**
Admission free.
This is an excellent idea for exploring rural life and the wide variety of farming skills. On summer Tuesdays, meet up (in your car) outside the 'grenier' (hayloft) in Trémolat, where Laurent Colet will be waiting. He will take you round a farm or goose breeder's or to meet a beehive basketmaker. To round off the visit, your guide invites you home to sample some succulent duck conserves.

Going down the Dordogne
Lalinde, the burning bastide
5.5 miles (9 km)
W of Trémolat
A large part of this 13th-C. English fortified town was destroyed in a disastrous fire in 1914. However, the Thursday **market** is very pleasant, as are the local activities, the 14th-C.

governor's house, the remains of the fortifications and the **garden,** which runs down to the water, opposite the main square.

Couze, the paper-makers' town
2 miles (3 km)
E of Lalinde
Ecomuseum, Rouzique paper mill
☎ **05 53 24 36 16**
Open mid-June to mid-Sept. 10am-noon and 2.30-6.30pm; Apr. to mid-June and mid-Sept. to mid-Oct. 2.30-6.30pm.
Admission charge.

Rouzique paper mill

Château de Lanquais

From the 16thC., papermakers set up shop in a dozen or so 'moulins' (mills) on the banks of the Couze. The reams of paper were shipped with the wines of Bergerac and Monbazillac and transported to Holland via Bordeaux. At the Moulin de la Rouzique you can buy sheets of water-colour paper from 20F, writing paper,

NATURE TRAIL

A two-hour walk (4 miles/7 km) along a nature trail is just the thing to enjoy the view of the Dordogne river and see the flora and fauna along its banks. You start from the port of **Mauzac**, by Lalinde (19 miles/30 km E of Bergerac). The path is signposted red, white and yellow. Green lizards, black kites and pretty flowers add to the pleasures of the walk along the cliffs, descending to the ruins of the castrum at Milhac (12th-15thC.).

envelopes etc. At the Musée du Filigrane (watermark museum), visitors can even make their own paper.

Larroque paper mill
☎ 05 53 61 01 75
Open Mon.-Fri. 9am-noon and 2-5.30pm.
Admission free.
The Moulin de Larroque is one of the few mills in France where paper is made by hand. The sheets are drawn one by one, then laid on felt before being pressed and dried. Papermaker Georges Duchêne's range on sale includes marbled papers, gold books, sketch pads etc. Visiting cards cost 90F, photo albums 80F, a water-colour pad 90F.

Lanquais, the spy's château
1 mile (2 km)
E of Couze
☎ 05 53 61 24 24
Open daily July-Aug. 10am-7pm; daily exc. Tues. Sept./June, 10.30am-noon and 2.30-6.30pm (Oct.-Apr. afternoons only).
Admission charge.
Medieval in layout but with a Renaissance wing, the Château de Lanquais is associated with Isabelle de Limeuil, Catherine de Medici's petticoated spy, who made the mistake of getting pregnant and having to live out her life in Lanquais, married to the banker Scipion Sardini.

Saint-Capraise-de-Lalinde, forest locks
2 miles (3 km)
NW of Lanquais
This village, lying between the Dordogne and the hillside, straddles the canal, the main road and the railway. Downstream at Tuilières, the lateral canal runs out in a series of locks. The lockkeepers' cottages (two remain) are cheerful and well preserved. Go up into the Fôret de Liorac to explore the forest village of Liorac-sur-Louvre and its fine 17th-C. houses.

Lockkeepers' cottage, Saint-Capraise-de-Lalinde

Landais and La Double

the Petite Sologne region

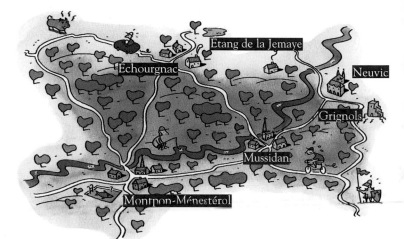

West of Périgord is a region called the Petite Sologne, an area shrouded in legend and once dreaded for the wolves and wild boars that roamed its forest. It still retains an atmosphere of mystery. In the heart of the lush verdure, Mussidan is a crossroads town that is ideal as a starting point to explore the many Landais châteaux.

Mussidan

15.5 miles (25 km) NW of Bergerac

Craft workshops and distillery

Musée des arts et traditions populaires
1-2, rue Raoul-Grassin
☎ 05 53 81 23 55
Open daily 1 June-15 Sept.; weekends and public holidays Oct.-Nov. and Mar.-May. Visits at 10am and 2.30pm.

Admission charge.
This museum of local trades and crafts, housed in a fine former **Périgord charterhouse**, displays the collections assembled by ardent local patriot Dr Voulgre. You can see inside a 19th-C. bourgeois home and old trades workshops (cooper, clog-maker and smithy). The barn contains a collection of agricultural implements and timber houses of La Double have been reconstructed in the park. Make a detour via **Villamlard** (10.5 miles/17 km E) to see visit the **Distillerie Reymond**. This old firm, established in 1834, sells fruit conserves in liqueur and wine spirits (eaux-de-vie). ☎ 05 53 81 90 01.

Neuvic

7.5 miles (12 km) NE of Mussidan

Château de Mellet
☎ 05 53 80 86 65
Open daily July-Aug., 1.30-7pm; Sept.-June, 1.30-6pm (6.30pm Sept.-Oct.).
Admission charge.
A listed historic monument, this 16th- to 18th-C. château contains rooms of different periods, including rooms with massive vaults, King Henry IV's bedroom with Renaissance frescoes, Diana's room, a large elegant drawing room, etc. Its 15-acre (6-ha) **botanical park** has 1,200 trees

and shrubs from all over the world. Its flowerbeds contain magical scarecrows created by children from the château's special needs institute.

Grignols
4 miles (6 km)
SE of Neuvic
A fortress
A masterpiece of Périgord military architecture, the medieval Forteresse de Grignols guarded

Grignols château

the road between Périgueux and Bordeaux. It was destroyed by the Prince of Condé's army in 1652. Its ramparts still overhang the village, but only the fortified 13th-C. château has been restored (not open to visitors). The village also contains a fine half-timbered house and an ancient covered market.

Chanterac
11 miles (18 km)
NW of Grignols
Local produce explained
Charriéras-Chanterac farm produce
☎ 05 53 82 61 23
Open daily Mon.-Sat., guided visits 8am-7pm.
Admission free.
Foies gras, truffle pâtés, duck breasts stuffed with duck liver... At the Ferme de Charriéras you can find out how these

The kitchen at Ferme de Charriéras

specialities are prepared, seasoned and cooked. If you visit the farm between 1 September and 15 June, you can watch the animals being force-fed. Tasting and sale of produce on site (duck foie gras 110F per 7 oz/200 g).

Jemaye lake
12 miles (19 km)
W of Chanterac
The Grand Étang de la Jemaye is a large natural lake with a beach in the middle of a forest. People swim here when it's hot, or watch the dragonflies. If you like, you can bring your fishing rod. But it's nice to follow up a dip with a ride in an open carriage along the wooded avenues. Farm and stables at Saint-Rémy-sur-Lidoire,
☎ 05 53 82 49 04.

Échourgnac
4 miles (7 km)
S of La Jemaye
La Double settlement
Ferme du Parcot
☎ 05 53 81 99 28
Open daily July-Aug. 2.30-5.30pm; Sun., May-June and Sept. 2.30-5.30pm.
Admission charge.
On the road out of Échourgnac, Parcot farm and its 125 acres (50 ha) display a traditional La Double farm environment: simple functional buildings most often built with materials from the local terrain.

La Latière
6 miles (10 km)
NW of Échourgnac
Cattle fair
There's usually nothing here, just a clearing in the woods beside the D38 (1.5 miles/2 km SE of Saint-Aulaye) with a few empty hangars with large girders in which, it's said, that bandits once hid. It all comes to life, however, between

Spotcheck
B2

Dordogne

Things to do
Carriage rides
Guided farm visits

With children
Swimming and fishing at Jemaye lake

Within easy reach
Montaigne country (19 miles/30 km SW), p. 90
Bergerac (15.5 miles/25 km SE), p. 94
Ribérac (15.5 miles/25 km N), p. 106

Tourist office
Mussidan: ☎ 05 53 81 73 87

30 April-1 May and the second weekend in Sept. during the famous Foire de la Latière. At this cattle fair, you can wander among the animals, drink or haggle amid a huge, noisy crowd of men and beasts. A rare sight.

THE STURGEON
This fish requires patience, because it only matures after 5-7 years. The males provide the flesh, the females the Périgord caviar, which has an excellent flavour. The texture is smaller than the Russian or Iranian version, but it is firm and separates well. It costs 5,400F per 200 g, but tins start at 30 g. Pisciculture Estudor: Montpon-Ménestérol
☎ 05 53 80 61 10.

Périgueux
capital of Périgord

*Cathédrale
Saint-Front*

Administrative capital of the Dordogne, Périgueux is a fine, well-restored town. A visit will take you back to different eras, ranging from the days of Gaul to the 20thC. The best way is to divide your visit into two: the Gallo-Roman city, then the medieval/Renaissance city. If you want just one thing to remember the Périgueux by, choose the market. Saturday morning is a ritual. The presence of market gardeners and small farmers brings out the patois, the local accent and the jokes.

The markets

Stalls in the Place du Coderc sell poultry, cheeses, vegetables and fruit fresh from local farms every day. If a good dandelion salad takes your fancy, a little legwork will take you to a stall selling it. The **foie gras market** takes place on Wednesday and Saturday mornings from November to March in the Place Saint-Louis. Truffle croppers are there too, but you'll have to be up at the crack of dawn.

STAMP CAPITAL

☎ 05 53 03 17 00
Visits Wed. 9-11.30am
by appt, all year exc.
July-Aug.
Admission free.
In 1970 the nation's stamp printers moved to Périgueux. They are responsible for printing all stamps for France and certain foreign countries. Craft, art and technology come together to create stamps that are sought after by collectors. Less poetically, all duty stamps are likewise manufactured here. Tax disks are also produced, but in small numbers only, as private individuals do not need to buy them anymore.

Gallo-Roman city
Vésone tower and Jardins des Arènes
Quartier de la Cité
Admission free.
When the Romans created the city on the right bank of the Isle, they gave it the name of one of their divinities, Vesunna. Her tower, the Tour de Vésone (90 ft/27 m high), was the sacred part of a temple dedicated to the city's tutelary goddess. Built in the 2ndC., it is still magnificent, and gives an idea of the Roman city, which featured splendid

Vésone tower

houses and an aqueduct. The Arènes gardens are found in the 1st-C. amphitheatre. It could once hold 20,000 people and was one of the largest in Gaul. If you want to know more about Roman times, take a visit to the Musée du Périgord (p. 102).

Saint-Étienne-de-la-Cité
Until 1669 this was Périgueux's cathedral. Elegant but very plain, it has suffered over the years, losing several domes and its bell tower. Have a look also at the nearby **Château Barrière**. The keep dates from the 12thC., while the house alongside is from the Renaissance.

Quartier du Puy-Saint-Front
A walk round this medieval quarter of the city enclosed by ramparts is a journey back in time. The **Tour Mataguerre** (15thC.) is the last of 28 towers that lined the mile-long (1.5 km) city walls. If you set off down the back alleys on foot, you will discover the charm of old Périgueux, the fine townhouses ('hôtels') of Rue Aubergerie and the pedestrianised Rue Limogeanne. If you open the door of the Hôtel de Lestrade at 1, Rue de la Sagesse, you will see some magnificent Renaissance staircases (visits organised by the tourist office). Have a drink on the

terrace of one of the cafés that line the small squares (Place Saint-Louis).

Quay houses
The quays of old Périgueux overflow with very pretty buildings, such as the Maison Lambert (16thC.), Hôtel de Lur (17thC.) and the Maison des Consuls (15thC., Boulevard Georges-Saumande). Further on, a little structure made of half-timbering and cob once overhung the river and bears, quite wrongly, the name

Street in old Périgueux

Vieux-Moulin (the old mill). This was originally a lodge for the lookout on the ramparts, which then became a barn for the monks of the chapter of Saint-Front.

Périgueux confectionery

Philippon-Lavaud
2, Rue Taillefer
☎ **05 53 53 40 48**
Open Mon. pm to Sat., 9am-noon and 2-7pm. Those with a sweet tooth will adore the fascinating confectionery shop of

Canal de Périgueux

Phillipon-Lavaud. A notable treat is a delicious sweet called the **croquant du Périgord**, containing two loops of nougat round a layer of chocolate, with a hint of Cognac and almonds. Reckon on 40F for around 3.5 oz (100 g). You will also find a classic selection

of the famous Périgord truffles, mushrooms and walnuts covered in chocolate (34F for 3.5 oz/100 g).

Canal walks

It was a dream as far back as the Middle Ages to make the Isle river navigable, but the branch canal was not opened until 1837. Nowadays walkers and joggers can follow the three circuits between the river and the canal (0.6-2.5 miles/1-4 km., information from the tourist office).

Cathédrale Saint-Front

The Saint-Front cathedral looms imposingly over the city. The style could be Périgordin Romanesque or Byzantine. In fact, it dates from the 11th-12thC. It is remarkable to see such

a visible oriental influence in the heart of Romanesque country. The Greek cross-ground plan and rounded domes are typical of Eastern churches. The cathedral we see now was almost entirely reconstructed in the 19thC. by the architect who would later design Sacré-Cœur in Montmartre. A pilgrim station on the road to Compostela, it has been a UNESCO world-heritage site since Sept. 1998.

Musée du Périgord

Cours Tourny
☎ **05 53 06 40 70**
Open Mon.-Fri., Apr.-Sept., 11am-6pm; weekends 1-6pm; rest of year by appt.
Admission charge.
The Périgord museum was originally set up to exhibit Gallo-Roman relics of ancient Vesunna. It has since become one of the most important museums of prehistory in France, having accumulated a large collection representative of the region's long history. It also has an interesting section on ethnographic art.

Mimos

International festival of mime
☎ **05 53 53 18 71**
First fortnight of Aug. (8 days).
Their faces are mournful, expressive, strained – but the performers never speak. This festival is something else. Its inspiration is the stage, life,

Cathédrale Saint-Front

the circus or the silent screen. The 'Festival Mimos' is the event of the language of gesture and expression. Rich and fascinating, it includes numerous events on stage and in the streets.

Boat trips
☎ 05 53 53 10 63 (tourist office)
Easter-Oct., departures daily/hourly 10am-6pm from Quai de l'Isle. Tickets on quay.
Admission charge.
Weigh anchor for an hour and sail down the Isle. It's very relaxing after being on your feet in the old city. Take the time to explore Périgueux from a boat drifting past its quays. The guided tour will show you the main monuments and history of the city from a different angle.

20, Rue Limeogeanne) has the wonderful aroma of freshly-cut wood. Near the Isle, a **basketmaker** tames his osiers into natural, strong but light objects such as cradles and tidy baskets (33, Boulevard Georges-Saumande ☎ 05 53 08 70 84).

Chancelade
4 miles (6.5 km)
NW of Périgueux
A magnificent abbey
The 12th-C. Abbaye de Chancelade lies in a magnificent setting. The buildings form a rectangle around the central courtyard and it contains a cellar where the monks once made wine. The abbey site as a whole, with its stables, the lodge (named De Bourdeilles, or the Abbot's House), the

PLAYING TRUANT

It only takes about 3 hours (8-9 miles/ 14 km) to escape the tourist crowds. Starting from Chancelade abbey, follow the signposted trail (two yellow arrows) to the village of Les Maines. You can reach Les Andrivaux (once a Templar base, 12th-14th C.) via the Fôret du Lac de Bétoux. From there, continue through the forest to the Château des Brunies. In the book *Les Misérables*, Jean Valjean has an adventure here. You are able to return to the abbey via Les Landes and Terrassonie.

as monsters and mythical beasts. The prior's house and graveyard lost in the forest undergrowth make this a somewhat moving place.

Abbaye de Chancelade

In search of yesteryear
The **woodturner** still makes chairs as they used to be made.

His workshop (you can enter at Place du Marché-au-Bois or

Romanesque church and delightful Chapelle Saint-Jean are certainly worth taking a detour.

Prieuré de Merlande
4 miles (6 km)
NW of Chancelade
The Merlande priory is a small house founded by the monks of Chancelade in the 12thC., hidden away in the gloomy depths of the Forêt de Feytaud. The chapel is fortified, and its carved capitals in the thick walls contain such surprising motifs

Prieuré de Merlande chapel

Restaurant de l'Oison
Avenue des Reynats
☎ 05 53 03 53 59
Closed 1 Feb.-15 Mar.
Set menus 135-380F.
The menu in this restaurant changes daily, depending on the season and produce available, but the cuisine is consistently outstanding, especially the fish.

Hautefort and the Auvézère valley
land of blacksmiths

Château de Hautefort

If you prefer countryside and views to culture and historic monuments, then the Auvézère is for you. This is world's end Dordogne, where building materials blend the light walls of Périgord with the dark roofs of Limousin. It was an area noted for its forges, because Périgord once provided more than 10% of France's iron. Some remain to preserve the memory of past activities, adding to the interest of the region.

Magnificent Hautefort
26 miles (42 km) NE of Périgueux
☎ **05 53 50 51 23**
Open daily Apr.-Oct. 9.30am-noon and 2-6pm; out of season, open Sun. Closed 15 Dec.-15 Jan.
Admission charge.
One of the finest châteaux (17thC.) of Périgord should have been lost. It suffered a terrible fire in 1968, but has fortunately been faithfully restored by its owner, with state help. Built on a limestone knoll 758 ft (231 m) above sea level, it is visible from far away. Some of the rooms still have their original furniture and 16th-17thC. Flemish tapestries. Don't leave without visiting the magnificent **Jardins à la**

Française (French gardens) and superb 100-acre (40-ha) **park** (admission charge).

Walks in the Auvézère gorges
Circuit 1: take the Auvézère circuit at Génis (7.5 miles/ 12 km N of Hautefort) to the **Moulin de Pervendoux.**

Pervendoux mill

This old mill stands next to a bridge leading to the gorges, and the trail enables you to explore the winding route of the river.
Circuit 2: the **Chutes de l'Auvézère** (Auvézère falls). Behind the church at Saint-Mesmin (13 miles/21 km NE of Hautefort), join the trail that goes down to the river, and for a quarter of an hour

you will be engulfed in the scent of box wood. Follow Trail GR646 to reach the waterfall, the **Cascade du Saut-Ruban**. A nature centre now occupies the old 17th-C. presbytery and caters for numerous sports such as mountain-biking, canoeing and rock-climbing (☎ 05 53 08 23 83 or 05 53 52 78 02).

Excideuil
9.5 miles (15 km) NW of Hautefort
The Thursday market

Thursday morning is very busy, being market day. The town contains a number of fine old houses (e.g. Rue des Cendres). A stroll round the ancient streets will bring you to Rue Jean-Jaurès,

where an antiques shop has a fine display of old coffee mills. Drop in at **Leroy** (Ave Gambetta) to nibble a macaroon, or **Conangle** (Place Bugeaud) for their cakes.

Château

The hilltop Forteresse des Vicomtes de Limoges (11thC.) suffered many attacks

due to its strategic location. Two impressive keeps and double walls bear witness to the château's warring past. The two peaceful lodging houses added in the 16thC. create a surprising image of a two-part château. Only the public rooms are open to visitors.

Tourtoirac
4 miles (6.5 km) W of Hautefort
The King of Patagonia

All set to become a country solicitor, young Périgordin Antoine de Touneins upset everything by deciding to become a king.

Alas, thrones being rare in the 1850s, he quit his native Dordogne to find his promised land in southern Chile and Argentina, where he had himself crowned king by the Indians. Orélie-Antoine I did not reign long in Patagonia. Booted out by the Chileans, he died at Tourtoirac in 1878. You can have a silent audience at his tomb in the village graveyard. At Chourgnac-d'Ans (4 miles/ 6.5 km S of Touroirac),

the family piously preserve the memory of the 'kings of Araucania' in the tiny **Musée des Rois d'Araucanie** (☎ 05 53 51 12 76; open daily except Tues., 10.30am-noon and 2.30-5.30pm).

Spotcheck
CD2

Things to do

Auvézère gorges
Mountain biking, canoeing and rock-climbing
Excideuil Thursday market

Within easy reach

Thiviers (15.5 miles/25 km NW), p. 112
Causses and Vézère (15.5 miles/25 km S), p. 118

Tourist office

Excideuil: ☎ 05 53 62 95 56

LACOSTE UMBRELLAS

Cherveix-Cubas
2 miles (3 km) N of Hautefort
☎ 05 53 50 42 60
Open Mon.-Sat. 2.30-6pm. Visits daily at 11am and 3pm in July-Aug.
Free guided visits to the workshop.
Lacoste are experts in the field of umbrellas. They have been making them in all colours and styles since 1930, bearing the familiar green crocodile trademark. Find the one of your dreams, and pay a factory price.

Château of the Vicomtes de Limoges, Excideuil

Ribérac and the Val de Dronne

churches on the defensive

Tourbières de Vendoire

Cherval

Saint-Martial-Viveyrols

Bourg-des-Maisons

Ribérac

Saint-Privat-des-Prés

Siorac

Saint-Aulaye

W est of Périgord, the area around Ribérac is a region of transition, anticipating Charente. Characterised by undulating valleys, irrigated by the lovely River Dronne, the area is remarkable for its numerous domed Romanesque churches.

British Ribérac and the local calendar

24 miles (39 km)
NW of Périgueux

The administrative capital of the region, Ribérac hosts a large British contingent, and on market days you hear more English spoken than patois. Visit the **traditional market** in the Place du Palais-de-Justice (every Thursday), the small **produce market** in the Place

de la Liberté (Tuesday morning, May-Sept.), the **foie gras market** (mid-Nov. to mid-Mar.) or the **walnut market** (Oct.- Nov.), Place J.-Débonnière. The third Saturday in August is traditionally reserved for **antiques and bric-a-brac**. July and August sees the **festival of music and lyrics** ('Musiques et Paroles en Ribéracois'), whose eclecticism (classical music, jazz, songs) is only matched by its quality.

Rendez-vous on the farm

Every Tues. in July-Aug. Meet up at the tourist office to be taken round one of the many farms in the area to see the calves, cows, pigs, horses and chickens. Afterwards, you can sample the produce. The

visit is free – you only pay for the (optional) samples. Beware, the portions are huge!

Domed churches

Domes are typical of the Romanesque churches in the Ribérac area. Some are almost fortresses, their crenellations and loopholes showing that they also acted as refuges for the locals (Saint-Martial-Viveyrols, Bourg-des-Maisons, Cherval or Siorac).

Round and about
Musée de l'Outil et de la Vie au Village

7 miles (11 km)
SW of Ribérac
Saint-Privat-des-Prés
☎ **05 53 91 22 87**
(town hall)

MUSÉE DU COGNAC ET DU VIN

Saint-Aulaye

11 miles (18 km) SW of Ribérac
☎ 05 53 90 81 33
Open daily exc. Mon., July-Aug. and Sat., Sept.-June, 3-5pm; closed in Feb.
Admission charge.

If traditional skills fascinate you and you like Cognac and wine, this museum, housed in an old chai barn, will make your mouth water. The work of the grower and cooper are explained, numerous utensils are on display plus a still and an 18th-C. press. The shop is well stocked and recreates the traditional wine-merchant's premises. An instructive journey through nostalgia.

Open daily exc. Mon. in July-Aug., 3-6pm; out of season phone for appt.
Admission charge.
This museum sets out to explore life in a village street, recreating all the small trades of the La Double region, such as glassmaking, barrel-making and wood-working. Other exhibits include planes, posters and prints.

Peat bogs of Vendoire

9.5 miles (15 km) N of Ribérac
Maison des Tourbières
☎ 05 53 90 79 56
Open daily exc. Mon., May-Sept., 10am-7pm; Sun., Apr.-Oct., 10am-6pm; out of season by appointment.
Admission free. Charge for guided tour.
Peat ('tourbe') is made of vegetable matter and water, and in the past was a common fuel. Nowadays the Tourbières de Vendoire are not quarried, but the two-hour guided tour will enable you to explore and understand the unique

environment of these peat bogs, with abundant fauna and flora both typical and rare. Take field glasses so you can spot the butterflies, dragonflies and birds that inhabit these extraordinary wetlands.

Château de Mareuil

17 miles (27 km) NE of Ribérac
☎ 05 53 60 74 13
Open daily July-Sept., 10am-noon and 2-6.30pm; out of season 2-6.30pm.
Admission charge.
This château defended one of the four baronies of Périgord. It was subsequently

Spotcheck
B2

Dordogne

Things to do

Markets
Music festival
Visit the peat bogs
Cognac and wine museum

With children

Rendezvous on the farm
Cluzeaux caves

Within easy reach

Le Landais and La Double regions (15.5 miles/25 km S), p. 98.
Brantôme (25 miles/40 km NE), p. 108.
Périgueux (19 miles/30 km SE), p. 100.

Tourist offices

Ribérac: ☎ 05 53 90 03 10
Mareuil: ☎ 05 53 60 99 85

transformed into a splendid Renaissance residence. You can also take a 25-mile (40-km) cycle tour of the 15 châteaux around Mareuil (info. from tourist office).

Cluzeaux caves

2 miles (3 km) from the Château de Mareuil
Saint-Pardoux-de-Mareuil
☎ 05 53 60 99 85
(tourist office)
Guided tours can be organised. These **caves** were hollowed out in limestone rock and inhabited in the Middle Ages. It is difficult to work out the logic of this underground habitat with its rooms, very low corridors (you'll have to crawl) and vertical shafts.

Château de Mareuil

Brantôme
the Venice of Périgord

The Dronne runs through a delightfully pretty and quiet valley. Mankind arrived here very early, as the caves and underground refuges bear out. You'll soon have the urge to follow the river's path. Give in – going by canoe will give you a greener and more intimate look at these richly historical landscapes.

Medieval Brantôme

17 miles (27 km)
NW of Périgueux

The Venice of Périgord is worth a detour. Dominated by a four-storey bell tower built on a 40-ft (12-m) rock, the town nestles in the Dronne valley. The Pont Coudé (crooked bridge), adjacent to a grand Renaissance building, strides across the river to the **Jardin des Moines** (monks' garden), with its 16th-C. wayside altars, the setting for a lovely walk. The tourist office

organises visits to the **troglodyte part of the abbey** all-year round (exc. third week in January).

The good life in Brantôme

There's no shortage of footbridges to cross the water into the town. A pleasant walk will take you past both Gothic and Renaissance houses, the remains of the city walls and antiques shops. Gourmets should head for the **local market** every Friday morning in winter or **produce market** in summer, and don't forget the famous **truffle and foie gras fairs** in winter.

Bourdeilles

5 miles (8 km)
SW of Brantôme
The elder brother's château

☎ 05 53 03 73 36

Open daily July-Aug. 10am-12.30pm and 1.30-5.30pm (7pm, Apr.-June and Sept.-Oct.). Closed 3-25 Jan. *Admission charge.*

This magnificent château was once the seat of one of the four barons of Périgord, André de Bourdeille. His birthright was the fortune, the estates, the honours and above

Crooked Bridge

Lying 5.5 miles (9 km) east of Brantôme, the Château de Puyguilhem dates from the 16th C.

all his beautiful, peerless wife. She designed the château, which was coveted by André's younger brother, Pierre (1540-1614). He, however, had to leave and seek his fortune at court. He was given the living of Brantôme abbey, and took the title of abbot.

Richemont
4 miles (7 km)
NW of Brantôme
The younger brother's château
☎ 05 53 05 72 81
Open daily July-Aug.
10am-noon and 2-6pm.
Admission charge.
Pierre de Bourdeille, the younger brother, returned at the age of 40. On a hilltop he built a country seat fit for a cultivated gentleman.

He had travelled and fought all over the world, for the king of Spain in Morocco, and for three kings of France, who appreciated his ability to spin a yarn. A fall from a horse, however, ended his military service. He had an easy manner and was cheerful and unaffected. He carried this over into his writing – memoirs, both fact and fiction, stories of beautiful women and brave captains. Thanks to these books, Brantôme is associated with him, the author of *Les Dames Galantes*, rather than his older brother. You can visit both the châteaux to decide once and for all whether you prefer to become a billionaire or a prize-winning author.

Villars
8 miles (13 km)
NE of Brantôme
Abbaye de Boschaud
Leave time to stop at Villars, where Boschaud abbey is a haven of peace. A long way from the major highways, it was founded in 1154 and became one of Périgord's four

Spotcheck
C2

Dordogne

Things to do

Fairs and markets at Brantôme

With children

Villars caves
River Dronne by canoe

Within easy reach

Nontron (14 miles/22 km N), p. 110,
Périgueux (14 miles/ 22 km S), p. 100,
Thiviers (16 miles/26 km NE), p. 112.

Tourist offices

Brantôme:
☎ 05 53 05 80 52

Cistercian houses. Today you can visit its ruins (some walls are being restored), found in a splendid **green setting**.

Painted caves
☎ 05 53 54 82 36
Open Apr., May and Oct.. 2-6pm; June and Sept. 10am-noon and 2-7pm.
Admission charge.
If prehistory is your thing, make a detour via the **Grottes de Villars**. In these caves (discovered in 1953) with

Villars caves

their limestone formations, distant ancestors left pictorial relics, especially drawings of horses, including a notable small blue galloping horse.

ALONG THE RIVER: THE DRONNE BY CANOE

This is an extremely pretty river for canoeing. Sportier types start at Saint-Pardoux, everyone else at Quinsac. The 9.5-mile (15-km) stretch towards Brantôme is a real joy, as you discover new countryside in total tranquillity. Arriving right in the middle of Brantôme is pure magic, with the village reflected in the water and its mullioned windows decorated with flowers. Continue downstream to the next stop at Bourdeilles. The cliff rears up, crowned by its château. The Dronne calms down again towards Tocane, so you'll have to do it again! Brantôme Canoës
☎ 05 53 05 77 24.
Allo Canoës
☎ 05 53 06 31 85.

Nontron
France's oldest knife

N ontron, far from the tourist crowds, gives the feeling that you are one of the few chosen to come here. Around every corner of aptly named Périgord Vert (Green Périgord) you will find a village, a bridge, a view, a château or a prehistoric cave. After a heavy rainfall, the forests draw crowds of visitors all looking for the prized cep mushrooms.

Toys of yesteryear
Museum of dolls and old toys
Avenue du Général Leclerc
☎ 05 53 56 20 80

Open daily exc. Tues., June and Sept., 10am-noon and 2-6pm; daily exc. Tues. 2-6.30pm, Mar.-May, Oct., and school holidays; daily 10am-7pm, July-Aug. *Admission charge.*
The town, with its ramparts and ancient streets, preserves a distinct charm from former times. If however you prefer to recall your own childhood, then the Musée des poupées et jouets d'Antan, housed in an 18th-C. château, is well worth a visit.

Boutique Hermès
Route de Piégut
☎ 05 53 60 86 21
Open Tues.-Fri. 8.30am-noon and 2-6pm (4pm Fri.); afternoons only Mon. and Sat.

This former Adidas shoe factory changed completely when the Hermès porcelain-decorating centre took it over, saving hundreds of jobs. Look out for bargains in the shop, where seconds are sold at 50% discount.

Nontron knives
33, Rue Carnot
☎ 05 53 56 01 55
Open daily, 9am-noon and 2-7pm, exc. Sun. pm. Closed Sun. and Mon. am out of season.
Nontron knives, instantly recognisable by their pale boxwood handles and black 'V', are what this town is famous for. The tradition of their manufacture dates back to the 15thC.

PÉRIGORD BY CARRIAGE

Start at Quinsac (8.5 miles/14 km NE of Nontron)
Beauvignère
☎ 05 53 35 50 24
(departmental tourism commission)

Get away for a week (4,500F in high season) or a weekend (from 1,300F in low season) and forget about beating the clock. Cover about 9.5 miles (15 km) each day and stay in post houses booked in advance by the centre manager. A unique opportunity to see Périgord Vert at a relaxed pace.

The skill of the Nontron craftsmen is legendary – the smallest knives can fit into a nutshell. The works is owned by the Laguiole company.

Glass workshop

Atelier Louis Martin
Rue de l'Église
☎ 05 53 56 16 98
Louis Martin, who created the Aquitaine regional logo that can be seen at the entrance to the Hôtel de Région de Bordeaux, has worked with other master glassmakers to create the Vitrail-Comparaison association, whose aim is to revive the art of glass-making in France. Come and see these craftsmen at work in the studio.

Teyjat
6 miles (10 km) NW of Nontron
Far back in time
☎ 05 53 06 90 80
Open Sat. July-Aug., 10am-5pm, booking essential.
Admission charge.

The **Grotte de la Mairie** has made this little village world-famous. A far cry from the busy, better-known prehistoric sites, this cave is home to about 40 splendid paintings dating from the Upper Magdalenian Period (about 10,000 BC). Visits can only be made in summer and on one day each week. If you prefer the 21stC., let off steam at the nearby **go-kart track**. École de Pilotage (driving school), ☎ 05 53 56 36 11.

Saint-Estèphe
4 miles (6 km) N of Nontron
Leisure centre
☎ 05 53 35 50 10
Admission free.
A great favourite with the young people of Nontron, this Base de Loisirs has a 57-acre (23-ha) lake which offers swimming, fishing, pedalos, windsurfing, and many other attractions to cool you down in summer. Nearby is a path leading to the Roc Branlant, a balancing rock that wobbles when pushed – a trick of the forces of erosion. Just below is a scattering of odd-shaped rocks, known as the Chapelet du Diable (devil's chapel).

Varaignes
9.5 miles (15 km) NW of Nontron
For lovers of tradition
This village boasts a feudal **château**, home to a **working**

Spotcheck
C1

Dordogne

Things to do

Visit a master glassmaker
Périgord by carriage

With children

Museum of dolls and old toys
Saint-Estèphe leisure centre
Go-kart track

Within easy reach

Brantôme (14 miles/ 22 km S), p. 108

Tourist office

Nontron:
☎ 05 53 56 25 50

museum of weaving and slipper-making (atelier-musée du tisserand et de la charentaise ☎ 05 53 56 35 76). It also has a **nut festival** (Fête de la Noix) and **mill trail** (Circuit des Moulins) in the last week of February, a **weavers' market** (marché des tisserands) in Whitsun week, and a **turkey fair** (Foire aux Dindons), held on 11 November.

Varaignes feudal château

Thiviers
truffles and foie gras

Shepherd's hut, Thiviers

The colours in Périgord are the stuff of landscape paintings and between Thiviers and Jumilhac you will see the real Périgord Vert, with its oak forests, chestnut groves and luxuriant green meadows. Then, carrying on towards Saint-Jean-de-Côle and Sorges, you come across another area altogether – Périgord blanc (White Périgord).

Force-feeding a goose

Musée de foie gras
Place Foch (next to tourist office
☎ **05 53 55 12 50)**
Open Mon.-Sat. 9am-6pm and Sun. 9am-noon in summer; 10am-noon and 3-6pm, the rest of the year.
Admission charge.
Jean-Paul Sartre's home town is also a major centre for foie gras, and its **foie gras markets** (marchés au gras) attract gourmets from far and wide

on winter Saturdays. The town is also home to a museum of foie gras, a must for lovers of this very French food.

Hopeful healing
Old beliefs are alive and well in Périgord, where several dozen faith healers practise. Their secret skills, which can cure warts, diseased joints and hundreds of other ailments, have been handed down through history. A 'prelate' (not recognised by the Catholic Church) has set up a practice between Thiviers and La Coquille, offering cures for both sick bodies and sick souls. The fact that the Church disapproves has not put people off – on the

contrary, it seems to have increased his popularity!

Nantheuil
0.5 mile (1 km) E of Thiviers
Raining stars
Fri. eves, end June-end Sept.
☎ **05 53 55 21 95 or 05 53 62 08 08**
Admission charge.
Come here in summer to enjoy the delights of starry nights. Thiviers' lay association brings together astronomers and keen amateurs alike from far and wide at the **Haut Périgord observatory** (Observatoire du Haut Périgord), at

Château de la Marthonie

Les Courtigeauds, to study the night sky through its 18-inch (450-mm) telescope.

Saint-Jean-de-Côle
4.5 miles (7 km)
W of Thiviers
Château de la Marthonie
☎ 05 53 62 30 25
Open 10am-noon and 2.30-6pm, July-Aug.
Admission charge.
This is one of Périgord's most attractive villages, with its ochre-coloured houses linked by roofs of brown lauze tiles. Located around the town square are a Romanesque church, a covered market, a Renaissance priory and the **Château de la Marthonie**, which dates from the 15th-16thC. Take a donkey ride across the bridge and enjoy a wonderful view of the church and its cloisters.

Saint-Paul-la-Roche
9 miles (15 km)
NE of Thiviers
Local produce
First house on the right before the turn for La Coquille
☎ 05 53 62 50 01
If you feel a little peckish, call on **Dominique Bost**, famed for his homemade apple juice (12F for 2 pints/1 litre) and goats-milk cheeses (7.50F each).

Sorges
9.5 miles (15 km)
S of Thiviers
Truffle capital
Musée de la Truffe
☎ 05 53 05 90 11
Open 9.30am-12.30pm and 2.30-6.30pm, July-Aug.; 10am-noon and 2-5pm, rest of the year. Closed Mon.
Admission charge.

Spotcheck
C1-2

Things to do
Musée du foie gras
Musée de la truffe

With children
Discover the stars
Jumilhac gold mine

Within easy reach
Brantôme (16 miles/26 km S), p. 108
Périgueux (21 miles/34 km W), p.100
Auvézère valley (15.5 miles/25 km SE), p. 104

Tourist office
Thiviers: ☎ 05 53 55 12 50

In the early 20thC. truffles were unearthed by the ton in Sorges (only a few hundred kg now). The truffle museum has a wealth of information on the celebrated fungus and tells you all there is to know about truffles, including how to buy and eat them (a list of restaurants skilled in truffle cuisine is available). Nearby, a 2-mile (3-km) **trail** takes you right into truffle country.

GOLD RUSH
Museum of gold
Château de Jumilhac
12 miles (19 km) NE of Thiviers
☎ 05 53 52 55 43 (tourist info. centre)
Open daily 10.30am-12.30pm and 2.30-6.30pm, mid-June to mid-Sept.; 3-6pm Sun. and public holidays, mid-Sept. to mid-Oct.
Admission charge.
Become a gold prospector! There's gold in the ground of Jumilhac. A working mine is open for visits by appointment (Mines du Bourneix ☎ 05 55 09 31 00) and half-day introductions to gold panning are organised each summer (information from the tourist office). Before making your fortune, find out more about the precious metal in the Musée de l'Or, in the cellars of the château.

Les Eyzies and the Vézère valley

the origins of man

Les Eyzies and the Vézère valley are home to almost 100 prehistoric sites and offer you a trip through 400,000 years of human adventure. To find your way around, it's best to start at the educational museum at Les Eyzies, the place where the earliest men took to the cliffs of the Vézère valley, using the caves and natural shelters to protect themselves against cold and ferocious animals. For this reason Les Eyzies-de-Tayac-Sireuil, in the heart of the 'Valley of Mankind', has become the world capital of prehistory.

Lascaux I
Lascaux II
La Madeleine
La Roque-Saint-Christophe
Commarque
Le Bugue
Les Eyzies-de-Tayac-Sireuil
Bara-Bahau
Grottes de Font-de-Gaume/ Combarelles
Village du Bournat
Proumeyssac

Les Eyzies-de-Tayac-Sireuil

28 miles (45 km) from Périgueux

Dawn of prehistory

The village of Les Eyzies is strung out along a cliff with caves halfway up, and became the birthplace of prehistoric science when excavations began here in 1863. Many thousands of tourists visit this centre in summer, but don't be put off by the crowds.

Font-de-Gaume cave

Just outside Les Eyzies, on the road to Sarlat
☎ 05 53 06 90 80
Open daily exc. Wed., 10am-noon and 2-5pm, Nov.-Feb.; 9.30am-noon and 2-5.30pm, Apr.-Sept.; 9am-noon and 2-6pm, Oct. and Mar. Maximum 200 visitors per day, please book several days in advance. *Admission charge.*
The corridor-shaped Grotte de Font-de-Gaume, nearly 400 ft (120 m) long, was home to Cro-Magnon man, who painted and engraved a remarkable frieze of bison and a fresco of very lifelike animals fighting and following each other. Our ancestors' artwork is now protected, and the number of visitors is strictly limited.

Combarelles cave

☎ 05 53 06 90 80
Opening hours as for Font-de-Gaume cave. Maximum 60 visitors per day.
Admission charge. Tickets sold at Font-de-Gaume.

The Grotte de Combarelles is an ancient natural art gallery showing mammoths, bison, reindeer, horses and ibex. At the back of the hollow, almost 300 figures are displayed over a stretch of 230 ft (70 m), including a number of human faces.

Musée National de la Préhistoire
Château de Tayac
☎ 05 53 06 45 45
Open daily exc. Tues., 9.30am-7pm, July-Aug.; 9.30am-noon and 2-6pm (5pm mid-Nov. to mid-Mar.), rest of the year.
Admission charge.
This museum of prehistory, situated in the 13th-C. former town fortress, is guarded by a statue of a primitive man who

Statue of Primitive man, entrance to the Musée National de la Préhistoire

will accompany you, so to speak, throughout your visit. The museum displays relics almost untouched by the ravages of time – a priceless collection making up the world's greatest prehistoric museum. It's an essential stop for every visitor to the 'Valley of Mankind'.

A modern-day restaurant
Le Centenaire
Rocher de la Penne
☎ 05 53 06 97 18
Closed Tues./Wed. lunchtime, and Nov.-Apr.
Set menus 300-600F.
This restaurant's original menu gives pride of place to local flavours, including cep mushrooms, conserves, broad beans and chestnuts, taking their tastes to new heights.

Commarque
4.5 miles (7 km)
from Les Eyzies
Walk among the ruins
If you like walking, especially in a romantic location, you will definitely enjoy the ruined 13th-C. **Château de Commarque**. The château once bristled with fortifications and now, although much reduced, are nevertheless still impressive. Opposite is the ornate 15th-16thC. **Château de Laussel**. The ancient Laussel rock-bed at the foot of the château was where the famous Vénus à la Corne figure was discovered.

Le Bugue
6 miles (10 km)
from Les Eyzies
Périgord Noir aquarium
☎ 05 53 07 10 74
Open daily 10am-5pm, Feb.-Mar. and Oct.; 10am-6pm, Apr., May and Sept.; 9am-7pm, June-Aug.

Dordogne

Things to do
Prehistoric caves and sites
Musée national de la préhistoire
Bournat historical village
Proumeyssac sinkhole
Vézère river by canoe

With children
Périgord Noir aquarium
Bournat historical village

Within easy reach
Sarlat (12.5 miles/20 km SE), p. 120
Trémolat (6 miles/10 km SW), p. 96

Tourist office
Les Eyzies-de-Tayac-Sireuil:
☎ 05 53 06 97 05

Admission charge.
The open-air Aquarium du Périgord Noir is a real spectacle. Walking through the glass tunnels gives you the impression of being surrounded by the thousands of fish that inhabit the rivers of Périgord, France and Europe. A breeding section has been developed in a glass-fronted laboratory.

Bournat historical village
☎ 05 53 08 41 99
Open all year exc. Jan.; 10am-7pm, May-Sept.; 10am-5pm, Oct.-Apr.
Admission charge.
Step into a time machine and discover the simple village life of Périgord 100 years ago.

All the old trades are realistically recreated, with demonstrations from craftsmen using traditional tools. Of special interest are the nut mill, the still and the bread oven.

RIVER VÉZÈRE
BY CANOE

FFCK Bases
Les Eyzies
(at the road bridge)
☎ 05 53 06 92 92
Loisirs Évasion
Les Eyzies,
15, Avenue du Cingle
☎ 05 53 06 92 64
Canoeing is very popular on the Vézère and with good reason: this is the best way to see the Valley of Mankind. The roads are hot and gliding along the river gives you an opportunity to relax between visits to attractions. Choose between a two-hour trip (60F), a half-day (160F) or a full day (130F). These prices are for two-seater canoes.

Bara-Bahau cave
Route de Bergerac
☎ 05 53 07 44 58
Open daily 9am-7pm, July-Aug.; 10am-noon and 2-5pm, Sept.-Dec.; 10am-noon and 2-5.30pm, Feb.-June.
Admission charge.
This strange name is derived from the ancient Occitan language, meaning 'falling' – as of a man or rock. The Grotte de Bara-Bahau, a wide gallery nearly 400 ft (120 m) long, was once used by hibernating cave bears, who have left their claw marks. The soft rock also allowed prehistoric man to carve pictures of animals, and odd symbols whose meaning remains a mystery.

Proumeyssac sinkhole

2 miles (3 km)
S of Le Bugue
☎ 05 53 07 27 47
Open daily 9am-7pm, July-Aug.; 9.30am-noon and 2-5.30pm, Sept.-Oct. and Mar.-May; 2-5pm, Dec. and Feb. Visits last 45 minutes.
Admission charge.
If you have a head for heights, let this two-seater cradle carry you down 170 ft (52 m) into the Gouffre de Proumeyssac (book in advance). The less daring can take the access

tunnel to the spectacular under ground dome, with its stalactites and stalagmites in shades of ochre and white.

La Roque-saint-Christophe

6 miles (10 km)
NE of Les Eyzies
Cave-dwellers' caverns
☎ 05 53 50 70 45
Open daily 10am-6.30pm in season (7pm in July-Aug.); 11am-7pm, rest of the year. Visits last 45 minutes.
Admission charge.
The Corniche des Troglodytes is Europe's largest cave centre, carved out in a towering 260-ft (80-m) cliff overlooking the Vézère valley. About a hundred caverns, spread over five separate levels, reveal traces of human occupation over many thousands of years. The cliff has been a refuge during many troubled times and once sheltered up to 3,000 people. Visitors can go up to the fourth level, 115 ft (35 m) above the river.

Tursac

3.5 miles (6 km)
NE of Les Eyzies
La Madeleine
☎ 05 53 06 92 49
Open daily 9.30am-7pm, July-Aug.; 10am-5pm in low season.

DISCOVERY OF LASCAUX II

Montignac-Lascaux
*15.5 miles (25 km)
NE of Les Eyzies*
☎ 05 53 51 96 23
Open daily exc. Mon.
10am-12.30pm and
2-6pm, end Jan.-Mar.
and Oct.-Dec.; daily
9am-7pm, Apr.-Sept.
Admission charge.
On 12 Sept. 1940 four
boys, out looking for
their dog, ventured into
a cave and discovered
an incredible series of
coloured rock paintings
more than 15,000
years old.
Montignac-
Lascaux cave
immediately became
known as the
'prehistoric Sistine
Chapel'. Despite the
precautions of air
conditioning and low
lighting, however, this
attraction has become
a victim of
its own
success; over
1 million
people visited the
cave between 1948
and 1963 and the
penetration of damp
and carbon dioxide into
the walls threatened to
ruin the paintings. The
cave is therefore
now closed to the
public, although two
rooms containing life-
size reproductions
of the
paintings can be visited.
Your ticket to these
rooms also allows
admission to Le Thot
prehistoric park.

*Chef Roland Mazère admires the
exhibits at the Musée National de
la Préhistoire, Les Eyzies*

make a unique menu. Only
recommended for those with
big appetites.

Le Thot
*14 miles (22 km)
NE of Les Eyzies*

Espace Cro-Magnon
☎ 05 53 50 70 44
Open daily 10am-7pm,
Apr.-Sept.; daily exc.
Mon. 10am-noon and
1.30-5.30pm, Oct.-2
Jan. and 25 Jan.-Mar.
Admission charge.
This Cro-Magnon centre
should be combined with the
visit to Lascaux, and a half-
day can easily be spent here.
Several exhibits display the
galleries that are not
reproduced at Lascaux II
and others show scenes from
prehistoric life. The centre
also has an animal park that
is home to the direct
descendants of prehistoric
animals: roe deer, fallow deer,
horses and bison.

Admission charge.
At the foot of this cliff, which
was home to cave dwellers
until the mid-20thC., is the
prehistoric deposit that gave
its name to a specific period,
the Upper Magdalenian,
which lasted from 15,000
to 10,000 BC. The objects
discovered here are on display
in Les Eyzies museum and
today's visitors can walk
along the discovery trail and
admire one of the cliff-side
shelters.

Préhisto-parc
☎ 05 53 50 73 19
Open Mar.-11 Nov.,
10am-6pm.
Admission charge.
If the caves get a little too
much, here is a chance to
relax with the family – but
still in a prehistoric setting.
Every area in this prehistoric
park is a reconstruction of life
in the time of Neanderthal
and Cro-Magnon man. The
locations, and life-like
recreations of animals and
people are based on the latest
discoveries by researchers and
experts – the park was
designed by a scientist
specialising in prehistory.

Ferme-Auberge de Layotte
Route de Périgueux
☎ 05 53 06 95 91
Closed Sun. eves
and Mon. in season
and in Jan.-Feb.
Open weekends only,
low season.
Prices from 130F.
Not simply an old farm in
the forest with a beautiful
arbour, but an inn with a
bewildering variety of local
dishes all combining to

Bison

Les Causses and the Vézère

the land of Jacquou le Croquant

Jacquou le Croquant is a legend and the hero of a French TV series. The story of this peasant, who revolted against the local lords, was set in the Fôret Barade and officiandos of the series can now make a 'pilgrimage' there. Pass through the depths of the forest to the Château de l'Herm, the home of Jacquou's enemy, the Count of Nansac.

Jacquou le Croquant

Salignac-Eyvigues
*12 miles (19 km)
NE of Sarlat*
Château fair
☎ 05 53 28 81 93
(tourist info. office)
Open daily exc. Tues.
10.30am-noon and
2-6pm, July-Aug.

Admission charge.
This château, built on a limestone outcrop, is the former fief of the Salignac family of Mothe-Fénelon. Very little is left of the first citadel, built in the 11thC., but the residence, rebuilt in the 15th-17thC., is superb. A great **traditional fair** (Fête à l'Ancienne) takes place each year at the beginning of August.

Jardins d'Eyrignac
*5 miles (8 km)
SW of Salignac-Eyvigues*
☎ 05 53 28 99 71
Open daily 10am-
12.30pm and 2-7pm,
Apr.-May; 9.30am-7pm,
June-Sept.; 10.30am-

Jardins d'Eyrignac

12.30pm and 2.30pm-
dusk, Oct.-Mar.
Admission charge.
These gardens, originally created in the 18thC., were long neglected and then restored to their former glory by the father of the present

CHÂTEAU DE L'HERM

Rouffignac
☎ 05 53 05 39 03
The Forêt Barade contains the ruin of the 16th-C. Château de l'Herm. Here, led by Jacquou, the tenant farmers revolted against the misery and injustice inflicted by the dreadful Count of Nansac and burned down his home. You will come across the tower and its monumental staircase. The château, currently being restored, is open in summer.

owner. There are a wealth of different influences – French in the borders in front of the manor (18thC.), Italian in the many different shapes, and English in the touch of fantasy.

Saint-Géniès
5 miles (8 km)
NW of Salignac-Eyvigues
Village and mill

This is a typical Périgord village with its château and lauze-roofed houses huddled around a Romanesque church with fortified bell tower. The Gothic chapel of Le Cheylard has a series of beautiful 14th-C. frescoes depicting the life of Christ and well-known saints. If you like old-style bread, visit the **Moulin La Coste** (1 mile/2 km north of Saint-Géniès). This is one of the last mills powered by the waters of the River Chironde, the wheat ground between stones of natural flint. On Friday and Saturday evenings you can purchase 100%-natural **organic** or **wholemeal** bread at 16-18F per kilo (☎ 05 53 28 96 64, mill open daily except Sunday).

Saint-Amand-de-Coly
6 miles (10 km)
N of Saint-Géniès
War church

This beautiful abbey church, which seems simply enormous compared to the village, is the most unusual religious building in Périgord. Is it a fortress or a place of prayer? The answer is both: the church was converted into a fortress in the 14thC., with the construction of the impressive tower and keep, which also contains a defence chamber. Now, however, the church is the venue for concerts of the

Périgord Noir music festival and is a magnet for music lovers from all over Europe.

Le Dinandier copper shop

Le Bourg
☎ 05 53 51 66 48
Open Mon.-Fri. 8am-noon and 2-6.30pm (7pm in high season). Such is the noise that comes from this workshop that everyone knows that **Alain Lagorse**, the coppersmith, is at work. He hammers the copper by hand, turning flat sheets into saucepans, frying pans, fish kettles and even jam bowls (saucepan 385F, 7-inch (18-cm) frying pan 510F).

Spotcheck
D2

Dordogne

Things to do

Fairs and festivals
Eyrignac Gardens
La Coste Mill
Visit of a Copper Shop

Within easy reach

Les Eyzies (25 miles/ 40 km S.-W.), p. 114
Hautefort (18 miles/30 km N.), p. 104

Tourist office

Salignac-Eyvigues:
☎ 05 53 28 81 93

He visits local trade fairs and also sells his wares at Sarlat market on Saturdays.

Thonac
Château de Losse

8 miles (13 km) SW of Saint-Amand-de-Coly
☎ 05 53 50 80 08
Open daily 10am-12.30pm, Apr., May and Sept.;
10am-7pm, June-Aug.
Admission charge.
This medieval fortress, built on a cliff overlooking the River Vézère, was transformed into a splendid private residence in the 16thC. A magnificent stone staircase leads to the Renaissance lodge, and the apartments are adorned with beautiful 16th-C. furniture. The château opens up its delightful setting for heritage days and for the **Montignac folk festival** (Festival de Folklore), held in July.

Château de Losse

Sarlat
a walk through the Middle Ages

The remarkable town of Sarlat is by far the greatest tourist attraction in Périgord – a medieval jewel that takes you back to the distant past with its sculpted gables, lauze roofs and white limestone walls, all classic examples of 15th and 17th-C. architecture. Previously surrounded by ramparts, Sarlat has retained its distinctive heart shape, cut across by the busy Rue de la République or 'Traverse'. The town is so popular that in summer the crowds can become a little too much.

Rue des Consuls

Place de la Liberté

Chapelle des Pénitents Blancs

Le présidial

Lanterne des Morts

Maison de La Boétie

Rue du Siège

Cathédrale St-Sacerdos

Tour du Bourreau

Maison de la Boétie

Opposite the former bishop's palace, three listed buildings face the magnificent Cathédrale Saint-Sacerdos. The most attractive of these is the Hôtel de la Boétie, birthplace in 1530 of Étienne de la Boétie, friend of Montaigne, and Sarlat's most famous citizen. Today, the house is used to host summer exhibitions.

'Lantern of the dead'

When you leave the Chapelle des Pénitents Bleus, remarkable for the chapel's pure

View of Sarlat roofs

'Lantern of the dead'

Romanesque style, pass through the Cour des Fontaines and Cour des Chanoises. An alley will then lead you into the Jardin des Enfeux, a garden watched over by the 'Lanterne des Morts'. This 12th-C. tower, crowned with a cone, is something of a mystery: it is unclear whether it was built to commemorate the visit of Saint Bernard in 1147 or constructed as a funeral chamber. The garden offers a fine view of the cathedral and the courtyards.

Around the Présidial

The houses at 2–4, Rue d'Albusse make up three lodges, which were the setting for the exploits of General Fournier-Sarlovèze, Count of the Empire (1773-1827). At the corner of Rue Salamandre is the Hôtel de Grezel, and at 6, Rue du Prédisial is the Hôtel de Génis. Next comes one of Sarlat's most beautiful buildings, the Présidial, a former courthouse built by King Henri II in 1522. Its two

loggia-shaped windows topped with a pinnacle and its façade covered with creepers are stunning. Today, the Présidial is home to an antique shop.

Place de la Liberté

This magnificent square is bounded on all sides by ancient houses with arcades

in between, now home to café terraces and shops selling local produce. The square has been the location for many different films and is now the setting for the **theatre festival** (Festival des Jeux du Théâtre); the 16th-C. Hôtel Chassaing is a compelling backdrop.

During the festival, held in late July and early August, many French classics are staged. Another place not to be missed is the Hôtel de Vienne, a Renaissance château, which houses the tourist office.

Truffles

The market: heart of the town

The square is the setting for the **market**, held on Wednesday morning and Saturday, where there is

Spotcheck
D3

Things to do

The market in Sarlat
'Truffle week-end'
The Tower mill

Within easy reach

Les Eyzies (env. 20 km
N.-O.), p. 114
La vallée de la Dordogne,
p. 124

Tourist office

Sarlat:
☎ 05 53 31 45 45

just as much chit-chat as there is buying. A victim of its own success, it becomes very crowded after 10am in summer – it's better to get up at the crack of dawn. In season, you can buy ceps, foie gras and truffles, but be careful – some unscrupulous traders take advantage of tourists' ignorance to sell products of dubious quality.

Rue des Consuls

This old main street contains the beautiful former residences of people of note. The most picturesque is certainly the 15th-C. **Hôtel de Vassal** at 9, **Place des Oies**, followed by the **Hôtel de Plamon**. Just opposite are the Fontaine Sainte-Marie and the 15th-C.

Geese by sculptor Lalanne

Hôtel de Mirandol. When you pass the **Hôtel Tapinois-de-Betou**, take time to admire the wooden staircase.

Salamander

This little lizard, the 'Salamandre', is the symbol of Sarlat, and can be found in many different places in the town. Historically, the lizard was the symbol of King François I (1515-1547). In the 15th C., the seal of Sarlat was a letter 'S' crowned with three fleur-de-lis, but the lizard replaced the 'S' on the town coat of arms in 1523, as a mark of the town's allegiance to the king.

Rue du Siège

This is a long street full of ancient houses. At the

junction with Rue des Trois-Conils, stop to admire the 17th-C. Hôtel de Cerval before rejoining the ramparts with the Tour du Bourreau towering overhead. For those interested in history, 2, Rue des Trois-Conils was once a brothel or, as the French put it, a 'maison close' ('closed house'). Of greater interest today is the Hôtel de Marsac, whose 15th-C. tower conceals

a spiral staircase. Before coming back onto the Traverse, walk down to Place Liarsou.

Pénitents Blancs chapel

The whole of Rue des Armes seems to be occupied by a huge 15th-C. half-timbered house. From here, walk down Rue de la Charité and you will come to Rue Jean-Jacques Rousseau, passing, on the way, the Chapelle des Pénitents Blancs, which is home to a **museum of sacred art** (Musée d'Art Sacré) with a 17th-C. portal. After passing the 17th-C. Hôtel Monmeja and the Sainte-Claire convent with its corbelled tower, walk along Rue la Boétie and view the attractive gardens at the junction of the two streets.

Jardin du Plantier
Above Place de la Grande-Rigaudie

This garden is well worth a visit, especially for its cool, pleasant atmosphere and commanding view of Sarlat's rooftops.

Sainte-Nathalène
5.5 miles (9 km) NE of Sarlat
Tower mill
☎ 05 53 59 22 08
Workshop open Fri. 9am-noon and 2-6.30pm, Oct.-Mar.; Wed. and Fri.,

Apr.-June and Sept.; Mon., Wed., Fri. and Sat. am, July-Aug. (same opening hours).
Admission charge.

The workshop at the Moulin de la Tour is one of the last specialising in walnut-oil production. In their 16th-C. mill, Jean-Pierre Bordier and his wife continue to make the oil in the style of the old craftsmen. A bottle of **walnut**, **hazelnut** or **almond oil** adds a

Jardin du Plantier

distinctive taste to salads and ready-made meals, and aids digestion.

Saint-André-d'Allas

3 miles (5 km) W of Sarlat

Breuil shepherds' huts

On the road to Les Eyzies, the hamlet of Breuil boasts the largest collection of dry-stone shepherds' huts (known as 'cabanes' or 'bories') in Périgord; it is a French listed site. Several dozen of these remarkable circular huts, with their layered roofs, stand together in groups of two or three. Excellently preserved, these huts evoke the atmosphere of a bygone pastoral age and also have an air of mystery – their origin is unknown.

Puymartin

3.5 miles (6 km) NW of Sarlat

Haunted château

☎ 05 53 59 29 97

Open daily 10am-noon and 2-6.30pm, Apr.-Oct. *Admission charge.*

This is one of Périgord's haunted 15th and 16th-C. châteaux, where some people claim to have seen the ghost of a woman, whose jealous husband imprisoned her in the château long ago, walking along the ramparts. Rest assured, however, that if you visit the château during the day you'll be able to enjoy in peace the beautiful furniture and a little bedroom with walls entirely covered in paintings depicting myths (17thC.).

Old house, Sarlat

Dordogne valley
fortified châteaux

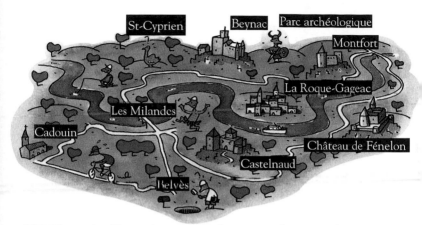

St-Cyprien   Beynac   Parc archéologique

Montfort

La Roque-Gageac

Les Milandes

Cadouin

Château de Fénelon

Castelnaud

Belvès

The south of Périgord is an area rich in rivers, châteaux and panoramic views. All you need to do is look upwards: the cliffs on both sides of the river are dotted with châteaux, all using their lofty location as an effective means of defence. There is history in these stones – the fortified châteaux have witnessed many displays of pomp and decadence.

Cadouin

22.5 miles (36 km) W of Bergerac
Abbey and covered market
☎ 05 53 63 36 28
Open daily 10am-7pm, July-Aug.; daily exc. Tues. 10am-12.30pm and 1.30-7pm, Apr.-June and Sept.; 10am-noon and 2-5pm, Feb.-Mar. and Nov.-Dec.

Cadouin market place

Admission charge.
This village is well known for its Cistercian abbey, founded in the 12thC., and the 15th-C. cloisters, a remarkable piece of flamboyant Gothic architecture. The abbey, supposed to contain a relic of the holy shroud, is a major centre for pilgrimages. The convent, somewhat surprisingly, is home to a museum of bicycles (Musée du vélocipède). Finally, do not leave Cadouin without visiting the covered **market place**, with its impressive stone pillars.

Holy shroud
The shroud is kept in a vase beside a spear, alleged to be the one that pierced Jesus' side, brought back to France during the first crusade (1096-1099). The sacred shroud was brought to Cadouin in the 16thC., and for many hundreds of years pilgrims have gathered before it. In 1933, however, a scientific examination revealed the harsh reality – this is not the shroud in which the body of Christ was wrapped. What's more, the shroud bears 11th-C. inscriptions that are, in fact, Islamic prayers!

Belvès

7.5 miles (12 km) SE of Cadouin
Cave dwellings
☎ 05 53 29 10 20
Open daily 10.30am-noon and 3-6pm, 15 June-15 Sept.; in low season, guided tours (booking advised) at 11am, 3pm and 5pm daily.

Cave dwelling in Belvès

Spotcheck
CD3

Admission charge.
This attractive village, with its abundance of Gothic and Renaissance houses and flower displays, is built on a rocky outcrop above a series of caves. These caves were used as dwellings in the Middle Ages, and seven of the chambers have been restored.

Saint-Cyprien
8.5 miles (14 km) NE of Belvès
Kingdom of the goose
This is a village built in the style of Sarlat, with ancient houses and a lively Sunday-morning **market**. Just under 1 mile (1.5 km) from the village is a goose farm run by Marc and Marcelle Boureau. In spring and autumn, at 2pm or 8.30pm, you can

participate in the **force-feeding** ('gavage'). Mme Boureau also makes her own conserves: 147F for a pot of goose foie gras and 70F for a pot of stuffed goose neck (Ferme de Campagnac, ☎ 05 53 29 26 03).

Castelnaud-la-Chapelle
8 miles (13 km) SE of Saint-Cyprien

Château des Milandes
☎ 05 53 59 31 21
Open daily 9am-7pm, June-Aug.; 10am-6pm, Apr.-May and Sept.; 10am-noon and 2-5pm, rest of the year.
Admission charge.
It was in this 15th and 19th-C. château, back in the 1950s, that Josephine Baker set up her 'world village' for her adopted children of various nationalities. The 17.5-acre (7-ha) park, with gardens kept in the French style, runs down to the Dordogne river. Part of the château has been given over to the artist's work and also contains a museum of falconry which puts on demonstration flights and displays.

Things to do
Campagnac goose farm
Périgord nut ecomuseum
Dordogne fishing

With children
Cave dwellings
Gaulish ancestors

Within easy reach
*Fortified towns of Périgord, p. 128
Les Eyzies, p. 114
Trémolat, p. 96*

Tourist office
Beynac: ☎ 05 53 29 43 08

Château de Castelnaud
☎ 05 53 31 30 00
Open daily 10am-6pm, Mar., Apr., Oct. to mid-Nov. and school holidays; 10am-7pm, May-June and Sept.; 9am-8pm, July-Aug.; 2-5pm, mid-Nov to Feb. (exc. Sat.).
Admission charge.
This magnificent château directly overlooks the Dordogne and offers one of the best panoramic views of

Château in Castelnaud, seen from the Dordogne

the valley. The view stretches all the way to the rival château at Beynac (*see below*). A museum relates the story of the battles between these two châteaux in the Middle Ages. In summer, visitors can train in handling weapons in the afternoon and historical shows in the evening.

L'écomusée de la noix du Périgord
Ferme de Vielcroze
☎ 05 53 59 69 63
Open daily 10am-7pm, Easter-1 Nov.
Admission charge.
Probably very few people know that a 'tricot' is a tiny hammer used to open nut shells. A one-hour guided tour of the Écomusée de la noix du Périgord will tell you all there is to know about nuts,

the art of growing them, their many varieties and the craft of making walnut furniture. Périgord speckled nuts, walnut oil and cakes are on sale.

Beynac
2 miles (3 km) N of Castelnaud-la-Chapelle
Ochre château
☎ 05 53 29 50 40
Open daily 10am-5pm (6.30pm in summer) 15 Mar.-15 Nov; 11.30am-4.30pm, Dec-14 Mar.
Admission charge.

RIVER BARGES
Beynac
☎ 05 53 28 51 15
Departures 10am-6pm, every 30 mins Apr.-Oct., every hour other months.
Admission charge. (Except 12 in the morning)
Board by foot, from the car park, and enjoy a 50-minute guided tour of the river. The 'gabares' (barges) sail up the Dordogne to Castelnaud-la-Chapelle and allow you to see the valley from a different point of view.

The magnificent 12th-C. Château de Beynac sits comfortably on the clifftop, dominating the whole valley. Leave the car in the car park and enjoy a walk through the narrow streets of the village. Take time to admire the rich ochre colour of the château, and its superb views, taking in the **Château de Feyrac** opposite and the **Château de Castelnaud** behind.

Gaulish ancestors
Parc Archéologique
☎ 05 53 29 51 28
Open 10am-7pm, Sun.-Fri., July-15 Sept.
Admission charge.
Travel back in time to a few hundred years BC and enter the world of the ancient Gauls. See wooden and cob-walled houses, billhooks and sickles, ancient crockery, the forge and the barns. Everything is reproduced life-size and it's much more interesting than a school history book!

Vézac
1 mile (2 km) SE of Beynac
Classical gardens
☎ 05 53 31 36 36
Open daily 10am-7pm, May-June and Sept.;

Château de Beynac

9am-8pm, July-Aug.; 10am-6pm, Oct. to mid-Nov. and mid-Feb. to Apr.; 2-5pm, mid-Nov. to mid-Feb.
Admission charge.
Situated opposite Castelnaud-la-Chapelle, the **Château de Marqueyssac** enjoys one of the best locations in Périgord Noir. Dominating the road along the Dordogne valley, the magnificent 15th-C. tower and 17th-C. lodge blend well together, and are surrounded by luxuriant parkland designed by a pupil of 'Le Nôtre'. Although the Château is closed to the public, the 55-acre (22-ha) park contains nearly 4 miles (6 km) of paths and offers panoramic views of the valley.

La Roque-Gageac
2.5 miles (4 km)
SE of Vézac
Exotic gardens
☎ **05 53 29 17 01**
(tourist info. office)
Guided tours.
Its houses hug the river in the shadow of the steep cliff, but at sunrise and sunset this village is flooded with light and the stone walls shine a rich orange-yellow. Along the clifftop is a most unexpected sight – an exotic garden with 12 varieties of palm, bay, cactus and orange trees, all of which grow outside thanks to the unusual

La Roque-Gageac

microclimate enjoyed here. It's best in summer, when the bays are in flower.

Montfort
5.5 miles (9 km) NE of La Roque-Gageac
Château walk
☎ **05 53 28 33 11**
(town hall)
Visits to park and ramparts daily 10am-7pm, July-Aug.; 10am-noon and 2-6pm, June-Oct.
Admission charge.
The Château de Montfort has been destroyed and rebuilt several times and owes its present condition to a 19th-C. restoration effort. The Montfort meander is one of the best known in the

Château de Montfort

Dordogne valley and the view from the lookout point on Route de Carsac is stunning.

Sainte-Mondane
7.5 miles (12 km)
E of Montfort
Château de Fénelon
☎ **05 53 29 81 45**
Open daily 9.30am-7pm, June-Sept.; 10am-noon and 2-6pm rest of year.
Admission charge.
Built in the 14thC. and finished in the 17thC., this château combines the severe appearance of a medieval fortress, with its double enclosure, and the gentle colours of a Renaissance lodge. Its layered roof is superb.

DORDOGNE FISHING
Dordogne fishing and aquatic environment protection federation
2, Rue Antoine-Gadaud, Périgueux
☎ **05 53 53 44 21**
Périgord is a fisher-man's paradise, with two major rivers, the Dordogne and the Vézère, 2,500 miles (4,000 km) of waterways and no less than eight lakes. It's best to go fishing at the crack of dawn, as in summer the sheer numbers of canoeists out on the river can disturb the balance of river life. But remember, you must buy a fishing permit (183F from fishing tackle shops) and you're not allowed to sell your fish, or you could be fined up to 10,000F.

PÊCHE
carte en vente au musée

Bastides of Périgord

a turbulent past

T he 'bastides' (fortified towns) were created by the kings as new towns intended to oversee and exploit areas not fully under the crown's control. Built in a chequered pattern, with a galleried 'place

Monpazier

centrale' (main square) and church-fortress, they were surrounded by ramparts and gates. Nowadays, the focus of the towns is not the church but the main square, where the market is held.

Eymet

12.5 miles (20 km)
S of Bergerac
An English bastide?

This attractive bastide was created in the 13thC. to counterbalance the many regional bastides then controlled by the English crown. However, thanks to a quirk of history, it is now truly an English colony. Maybe it was the attractiveness of the town or the low property prices that attracted settlers from England, but this place is as English as they come, with cricket clubs and public-school accents. A highlight of the year is the **bric-a-brac market**, held on the third Sunday in July.

Monpazier

29 miles (46 km)
E of Eymet
A fully-preserved bastide
Information from the tourist office
Open daily 10.30am-5pm, June-Sept.; by appt Oct.-May.
This bastide was founded in 1284 by Edward I of England, to colonise the areas between Agenais and Périgord. Everything – the covered market, the Saint Dominique church, the entrance gates and its 32 historic monuments – is worth seeing. In late July and early August, the area hosts the **Périgord Poupre music festival**

(Festival de Musique du Périgord Pourpre), with its classical, jazz and other styles. The **cep mushroom market**, at 3pm every day in August and September, is fascinating.

Biron

5 miles (8 km)
S of Monpazier
Château de Biron
☎ 05 53 63 13 39
Open daily 10am-7pm, July-Aug.; 10am-12.30pm and 1.30-5.30pm, rest of the year (7pm, Apr.-June and Sept.-1 Nov.).
Closed 3-25 Jan.

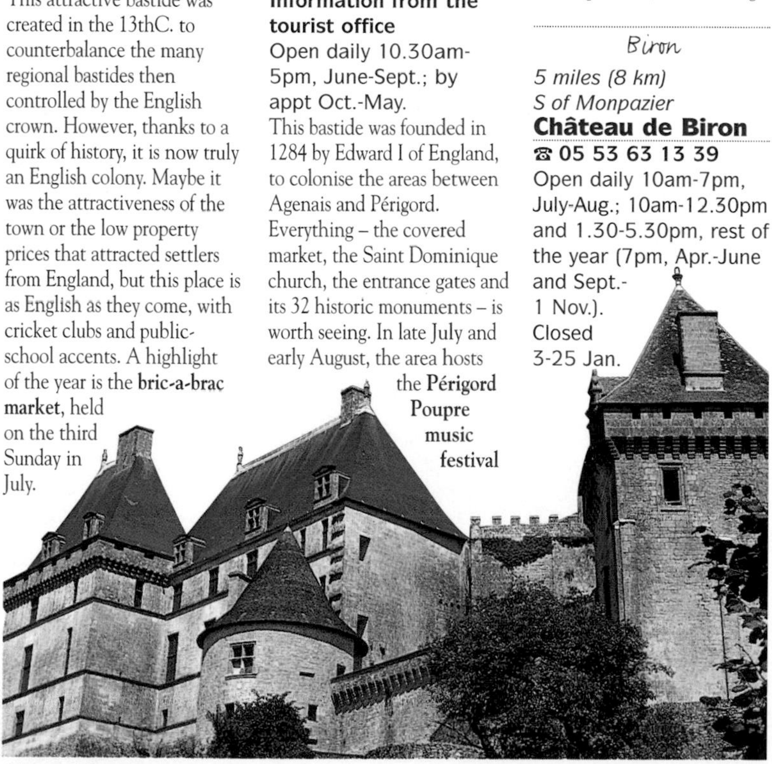

Château de Biron

Admission charge.
You cannot visit Biron without seeing the château. Building work on this magnificent edifice began in the 12thC. and went on for hundreds of years. It is in fact several buildings of different styles, put together by 14 generations of the Gontaut-Biron family. The village that surrounds the château boasts many fine Renaissance houses.

Villefranche-du-Périgord

12.5 miles (20 km) SE of Monpazier

Chestnuts and mushrooms

☎ 05 53 29 98 37
In season, open daily exc. Sun. and Mon. pm, 9.30am-12.30pm and 3-6.30pm, June-Oct.; out of season, open daily exc. Sun., Mon. pm and Wed. 9.30am-noon and 3-6pm.
Admission charge for museum.
This bastide is known for its

MUSHROOMING WEEKEND
Villefranche-du-Périgord
If you enjoy searching for mushrooms in the wild, experience the 'mushroom discovery' ('Connaissance des Champignons') weekend organised by the departmental tourism commission (☎ 05 53 35 50 05). Held in summer and autumn, in the woods around Villefranche-du-Périgord. 1,300F (inc. transport and accommodation in a rural guesthouse).

cep market (marché aux cèpes, Aug.-Oct. in the covered market). It is also home to a **museum of chestnuts** (Musée du Châtaignier), which tells the many uses of the fruit and wood of the chestnut tree, as well as the history of ceps.

Domme
21 miles (34 km) NE of Villefranche-du-Périgord

The Périgord acropolis
This bastide was built on a cliff by Philippe le Hardi in 1281. Its narrow streets are lined with **beautiful**, **ochre houses** (Maison des Gouverneurs, Place de la Halle). A walk along the ramparts will reveal the Del-Bos, Combe and Tours gates, used as a prison by the Knights Templar. From the Terrace de la Barre, beyond the church, there is a **superb view** from Beynac to Castelnaud.

Domme caves
Place de la Halle
☎ 05 53 31 71 00
The Domme caves are open daily exc. Sun. am and Mon. am, 9.30am-12.30pm and 3-6.30pm, in season; daily exc. Wed., Sun. am and Mon. am, 9.30am-12.30pm and 3-6pm, out of season.
Admission charge.
The Grottes de Domme provide a golden opportunity to seek refuge from the summer heat – among the

Spotcheck
BCD3

Things to do
Music festival
Cep mushroom market
Eymet bric-a-brac market
Museum of chestnuts
Mushroom weekend
Domme caves

Within easy reach
Sarlat, p. 120
Dordogne valley, p. 124

Tourist office
Monpazier:
☎ 05 53 22 68 59

View of the Dordogne valley from Domme

stalactites. A panoramic lift affords a **spectacular view** of the valley. At the exit of the caves, the **Jubilé clifftop walk** (Promenade du Jubilé) is very dramatic.

L'Esplanade
Rue Pont-Carrat
☎ 05 53 28 31 41
Closed Mon. lunchtime and Nov.-Feb.
Set menus 160-350F.
Discover the delightful combination of freshly caught and cooked sole with cep mushrooms at this restaurant, famed for its traditional Périgord produce, views of the Domme and typically warm welcome.

Bastides and châteaux in the Agen region

strongholds of the Middle Ages

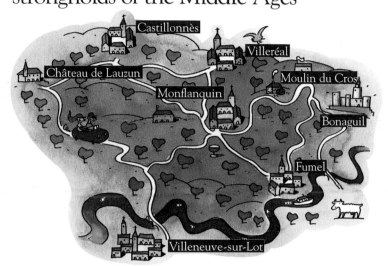

Lauzun

Unchanged for centuries, the bastides of Agen evoke the atmosphere of a time when this area was the site of constant battles between France and England. Founded principally by Alphonse de Poitiers, the Counts of Toulouse and the Kings of England, these magnificent and remarkably well-preserved bastides now have a gentleness that is echoed in their plum trees and the excellent local wine.

Lauzun

17.5 miles (28 km) N of Bergerac

The noble Gascon

☎ 05 53 94 18 89

Open daily 10am-noon and 2-6pm, 12 July-22 Aug. *Admission charge.*
This village has a place in history thanks to a military man from Gascony, a courtier of Louis XIV, who became a maréchal of France and eventually a duke. Only the Renaissance wing of the château is open to the public.

Douzains

6 miles (10 km) E of Lauzun

Pinseguerre donkey sanctuary

☎ 05 53 36 92 35

Visits by appt.
Everyone knows that donkeys are stubborn, but it's part of their inimitable charm. Come and see the donkeys at the Asinerie de Pinseguerre breeding centre and see the surrounding area from a donkey-drawn carriage. These willing animals can pull the

RIVER BARGES

The flat-bottomed 'gabare' barge, the forerunner of today's canal boat, was used for transporting goods by river. It was most popular in the 17thC., when Colbert, King Louis XIV's minister, commissioned major engineering works on the River Lot. This river, which crosses the Quercy area via Cahors, was an ideal natural transport route, but its dangerous shallow depths were only navigable by the gabares (see p. 30-31).

The old hall in Villeréal

Spotcheck
BC3

Lot-et-Garonne

Things to do

Villeréal nature museum
Trip to plum-land
Fairs, festivals and medieval days
Cros mill and bakery
Haut Agenais wines

With children

Donkey rides
P'Arc-En-Ciel

Within easy reach

Villeneuve-sur-Lot, p. 134

Tourist office

Monflanquin:
☎ 05 53 36 40 19

heaviest of loads and children can even ride on their backs.

Castillonnès

*3 miles (5 km)
NE of Douzains*
Guardian of the Dropt valley
This bastide overlooks the Dropt valley, and its ancient streets and central square with corner-towers have a distinct charm. The ramparts are open to walkers and the **Promenade de la Mouthe** offers a superb **view** right across the valley.

Villeréal

*8 miles (13 km)
E of Castillonnès*
Bastide and nature museum
☎ 05 53 36 09 65
Open 10am-noon and 2-5pm Mon.-Fri. (by appt). Admission charge for a guided tour of the bastide, which can be combined with a visit to the nature museum.
Villeréal has a fortified church and a 14th-C. market place with noble wooden pillars where grapes, plums and cereal

crops are still sold. The **nature museum** in Place Jean-Moulin (Maison de la Campagne ☎ 05 53 36 65 14) shows the flora and fauna that give the town its nickname 'ville nature' (nature town). The **Lac de Brayssou**, 2.5 miles (4 km) away, is a haven for migrating birds, with a hide and a scenic 4-mile (6.5-km) **walk** right round the lake.

Lac de Brayssou

Monflanquin

*8 miles (13 km)
S of Villeréal*
A taste of Tuscany
The most attractive bastide in Lot-et-Garonne was founded in 1256 on a hill, and enjoys a **superb view**. Although its ramparts and covered market have disappeared, the Place Centrale and its adjoining houses, and the impressive

Bric-a-brac fair

Maison du Prince Noir, still remain. There is always something happening in Monflanquin: the **bric-a-brac fair** (Foire à la Brocante, 13-14 July), the **Guyenne music festival** (Festival Musique en Guyenne, second fortnight in July), the **festival of tragedy** (Festival de la Tragédie, August), medieval days (Journées Médiévales, August) and the biggest event of all, **Saint-André fair** (Foire de Saint-André, December). The tourist office has information on all events.

Sept-Monts wine cellar
ZAC Mondésir Abattoir
☎ 05 53 36 33 40
Open Mon. pm-Sat. 9am-12.30pm and 3-6.30pm.
Admission free.
The first vines were developed way back in Gallo-Roman times in the hills of the Haut Agenais. The Cave des Sept-Monts ('Seven-Hills cellar' – the seven hills

being Monflanquin, Monségur, Montagnac, Montaut, Monsempron, Monbahus and Monmarès) has given the red wines of Agen their very distinctive, sought-after taste. These wines are best drunk young – less than four to six years old.

Marsal
2.5 miles (4 km) S of Monflanquin
Musée de la Vie Rurale
☎ 05 53 41 90 19
Open daily 3-7pm, July-Aug.; Sat. and Sun. June-Sept.
Admission charge.

This is prune country and at the museum of rural life you can see the traditional preparation methods. Visit the 'fournil', the workshop where the plums were dried in stoves, stop at the tile production shop, visit the orchard with over 120 trees, and discover the flora and fauna of the nearby river.

Montagnac-sur-Lède
4.5 miles (7 km) E of Monflanquin
Cros mill and bakery
☎ 05 53 36 44 78
Open Tues. and Thurs. 3-6pm, July-Aug.; Mon., Wed. and Fri. for groups by appt.
Admission charge.
The 16th-C. Moulin du Cros has been home to six

generations of millers and bakers from the Caumières family since 1933. The highlights of this **traditional bakery** visit are the two restored grain mills and a **tasting** session; enjoy bread flavoured with nuts, bacon, Gruyere cheese and poppy (10F for around 9 oz/250 g).

Saint-Avit
6 miles (10 km) NE of Montagnac-sur-Lède
Musée Bernard-Palissy
☎ 05 53 40 98 22
Open daily June-Oct., rest of the year by appt.
This museum commemorates Bernard Palissy, who burnt his own furniture in his efforts to discover the secret of firing ceramics. For many years this man was an official symbol in French schoolbooks, as an example of French dogged determination.

Lacapelle-Biron
1 mile (2 km) NE of Saint-Avit
P'Arc-En-Ciel
☎ 05 53 71 84 58
Open daily 10am-7pm, Apr.-Nov.; school holidays Nov.-Mar.
Admission charge.
This park, aimed mainly at children aged 3-14, has pretty much everything – animals, gardens, a play area and even a 'Noah's Farm' (Ferme de Noé). In July and Aug., find relief from the summer heat in the water of **Lougratte lake** (Plan d'Eau de Lougratte, between Castillonnès and Cancon on the N21).

Sauveterre-la-Lémance

7.5 miles (12 km)
SE of Lacapelle-Biron

Musée Laurent-Coulonges

☎ 05 53 40 68 81
(town hall)
Open July-Aug., Mon.
8.30am-12.30pm,
Tues.-Fri. 8.30am-
12.30pm and 2.30-
6.30pm (6pm Fri.).
Admission free.
This attractive village, at the
gateway to Périgord and
Quercy, is home to several
prehistoric sites belonging to
a recently discovered culture,
now known as 'Sauveterrian'.
The town hall houses a small
museum with displays of the
archaeological finds.

Bonaguil

4.5 miles (7 km) SE of
Sauveterre-la-Lémance

La Sentinelle

☎ 05 53 71 90 33
Guided tours daily 1
0am-6pm, July-Aug.;
10.30am-noon and 2.30-
5pm, Feb.-May and Sept.-
Nov. Illuminations until
midnight, every evening
1 June-30 Sept.
Admission charge.
This huge fortress, 1,150 ft
(350 m) around its 13 towers,
was the last of France's
châteaux forts. It was built
comparatively late, at the end
of the 15thC., by Baron
Béranger de Roquefeuil,

in order to keep out both
English and French crowns.
Neither rose to the challenge
– the château was never
besieged. Just 0.5 mile (1 km)
away, the **ornithological
museum** (Musée Ornitho-
logique) is home to some very
exotic birds (☎ 05 53 71 30 45,
open daily 2.30-6pm, June-
Sept., 10am-7pm, July-Aug.,
admission charge).

Fumel

5 miles (8 km)
SW of Bonaguil

All aboard

Fuméloise river barge
☎ 05 53 71 13 70
Guided tours daily May-
Sept., low season by appt.
Admission charge.
The first stage of your trip on
the Fuméloise gabare takes in
the Fumel barrage and the old

Grey heron

industrial port of Condat. The
barge then cruises past the
Cahors vineyards,
eventually arriving

A MOST WONDERFUL CAKE

Odette Salesse
Bonaguil
*1 mile (1.5 km) from
the château (signposted
'Tourtières').*
☎ 05 53 40 63 13
Demonstrations daily
July-Aug.; Thurs. and
Fri. in winter. Closed
Jan.-Feb.
**The tourtière, once
the favourite dessert of
regional kings and
lords, is made from a
combination of pastry,
apples and spirits, and
is traditionally eaten
during carnival time,
like Brittany pancakes.
In summer, the
tourtière fairs attract
visitors from all over
the region and the local
patisseries open their
doors to everyone.
Follow the advice of the
locals: 'a good foie
gras, a good tourtière
and a good white wine'.
Prices from 50F.**

at the foundry and Château de
Fumel. You may see giant carp
nearly 5 ft (1.5 m)
long, or a grey
heron or two.

Château de Bonaguil

Villeneuve-sur-Lot
the centre of the prune industry

Although Villeneuve-sur-Lot is best known for its prunes, the Lot-et-Garonne region also grows top-quality nuts. A walk through the modern orchards gives the lie to this peaceful town's turbulent past; during the war between England and France, Villeneuve, built by the brother of Saint Louis, was one of the most powerful bastides (fortified towns) in southwest France.

Place Lafayette
This square, which really is square, is surrounded by 17th- and 18th-C. timbered houses. It's best visited on **market** days (Tuesday and Saturday, with an organic produce market on Wednesday). The stalls reflect the local people's pride in the quality and variety of their fruit and vegetables.

Église Saint-Catherine
The old church, which was in danger of collapsing, has been replaced by a new church in the Romanesque-Byzantine style, begun in 1898 and as impressive as it is original.

The 23 beautiful old stained-glass windows (15th and 16thC.), unique in Aquitaine, have been preserved in the side chapels.

Tour de Paris
The Tour de Paris is one of the four gates of the bastide, which compensated for its position on a plain by having a number of lofty vantage points. The interior (the old guardroom and prison) is now an exhibition centre, open to the public. The pedestrian streets, such as Rue de Paris, are worth a visit.

Boutique du Pruneau
11, Porte de Paris
☎ 05 53 70 02 75
Open 9am-12.30pm and 2-7.30pm, Mon.-Sun. am.
There are shops selling prune goodies everywhere, but Boutique du Pruneau, run in the traditional style, offers every kind of plum confectionery imaginable. The best offers are pruneaux fourrés (filled prunes) at 14F for 3.5 oz (100 g), and old vintage Armagnac from 196F per bottle.

National stud
Rue de Bordeaux
☎ 05 53 70 00 91
Open 2-4.30pm, Mon. to Fri.
Admission free.
There are almost 40 stallions, both draught horses and bloodstock, at the Villeneuve

Place Lafayette

Haras National. There are also racing aristocrats, percherons and provincial horses from Brittany and Franche-Comté, working in harness teams. Why not pay them an afternoon visit?

Villeneuve Jazz festival

☎ 05 53 36 70 16
Admission charge.
Around 14 July, Villeneuve takes on the atmosphere of Louisiana. With the black music of the bayous and the white music of the Cajuns, it's New-Orleans-sur-Lot for four days!

(10 kph). Power boats can be hired on the banks of the Lot at Ponton l'Aviron.

Trips on the River Lot

☎ 05 53 36 17 30
No rowing, water-skiing or river racing; simply a gentle family trip down the river for 4-5 people, free of danger and travelling at a leisurely 6 mph

Spotcheck
C4

Lot-et-Garonne

Things to do

Plum markets and products
Villeneuve Jazz festival
Pujols bric-a-brac fair
Visit a nut farm

With children

Lot river trips
Visit to a stud farm

Within easy reach

Bastides and châteaux of Agen, p. 130

Tourist office

Villeneuve-sur-Lot:
☎ 05 53 36 17 30

In summer, many artists come to exhibit and there are plenty of opportunities to hunt for antiques at the **bric-a-brac fair** (Foire à la Brocante, second fortnight in July).

Hazelnut farm
Ferme de Vidalou

1.5 miles (2.5 km) from Pujols, towards Bias
☎ 05 53 70 21 55
 The speciality there is nuts, from which oil is produced. One drop of the oil is enough to add extra flavour to grilled fish or cheese, or to season salad (48F for 0.5 pt/25 cl).

Pujols
2 miles (3 km)
S of Villeneuve-sur-Lot

Art and bric-a-brac

This very attractive medieval village dominates the Lot valley. The old wooden covered **market** is still home to a market, held on Sunday morning, March-November.

> #### GASCON SALAD
> Choose from a wide range of leaves (endive, curly endive, radicchio lettuce or dandelion). Add a thin slice of duck's heart conserve and gizzard, with fried aiguillette and dried or smoked fillet of duck breast. Then add a few cubes of toast. Season with hazelnut oil, the juice from half a lemon, salt, and pepper.

Pujols

Serres country
a taste of the land

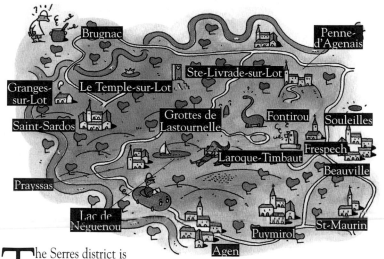

Brugnac

Penne-d'Agenais

Granges-sur-Lot

Le Temple-sur-Lot

Ste-Livrade-sur-Lot

Saint-Sardos

Grottes de Lastournelle

Fontirou

Souleilles

Frespech

Laroque-Timbaut

Beauville

Prayssas

Lac de Néguenou

St-Maurin

Puymirol

Agen

T he Serres district is believed to have got its name because the land is shaped like the foot of a bird of prey ('serre' meaning 'talon'), or derived from the ancient Occitan language, the *langue d'oc*. Numerous abbeys and churches are testimony to the devout faith of the local people.

Prayssas
11 miles (18 km)
NW of Agen
Fruit capital

The capital of Serres is an attractive bastide and a major **fruit centre**. Its sunny slopes are famous for their peaches, apples, plums and grapes, and are celebrated in late August and early September at the fruit fair.

Lac de Néguenou
2.5 miles (4 km)
E of Prayssas
☎ 05 53 95 00 67

Open May-Sept.
Admission charge.
Summer visitors flock to this lake to spend a day on the beach and enjoy slides, pedalos, water-bikes, fishing, mountain biking or walking. The little valley of the Masse (the river that feeds the 17-acre/7-ha lake) has kept its traditional charm,and has banks lined with poplars.

Saint-Sardos
5.5 miles (9 km)
NW of Prayssas
A corner of history
This place saw the beginning

of the Hundred Years War, when the English invaded and destroyed the bastide, founded in 1323 by the monks of Saint-Sardos. The governor of the bastide, who represented the king of France, was hanged, and Charles IV reacted by stepping up the battle against the English in 1324.

Granges-sur-Lot
3 miles (5 km)
NW of Saint-Sardos
**From a plum
to a prune**
**Musée du Pruneau
gourmand**
☎ 05 53 84 00 69
Open all year Mon.-Sat.
9am-noon and 2-7pm;
3-7pm Sun. and public
holidays.

After a fascinating explanation of how a plum is transformed into a prune, enjoy a taste of these traditional prunes – dried in the oven, soaked in Armagnac or brandy, stuffed, or coated in chocolate. The **museum shop** offers prunes in brandy (73F for 1.2 pt/0.7 litre) and stuffed prunes (61F for 10.5 oz/300 g).

Brugnac
9.5 miles (15 km)
N of Granges-sur-Lot
The magic cauldron
☎ 05 53 88 80 77
Open daily 10am-noon and 3-6pm (from 3pm Sun.), July-Aug.; open daily from 3pm in low season.
Admission charge.
The 'Chaudron Magique' is not a witches cauldron and there is no danger of falling in. It is, in fact, the huge vat in

which the wool from the 250 angora goats, kept on the adjoining farm, is dyed. The farm is also home to angora rabbits, and there are many opportunities to feed the goat kids, milk goats and make your own cheese. The shop, open daily 10am-7pm, sells pullovers, socks and other garments – all in mohair, of course. Just 5.5 miles (9 km) east is the little bastide of **Monclar**, 613 ft (187 m) above sea level – well worth a detour if only for its spectacular viewpoint.

Angora goats

Sainte-Livrade-sur-Lot
5.5 miles (9 km)
SE of Monclar
Richard the Lionheart country
This peaceful little town on the banks of the Lot is another **plum-growing centre**, as important as Villeneuve in that respect. Its church has a remarkable Romanesque stone

chevet. The Tour Richard Coeur de Lion is an imposing brick tower – all that remains of the old fortifications.

Sainte-Colombe-de-Villeneuve
7.5 miles (12 km) SE of Sainte-Livrade-sur-Lot
Lastournelle caves
☎ 05 53 40 08 09
Open daily 10am-noon and 2-7pm, July-Aug.; Sun. by appointment, rest of the year.
Admission charge.

Spotcheck
C4

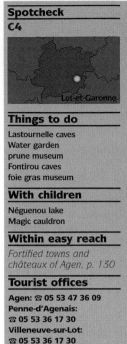

Lot-et-Garonne

Things to do

Lastournelle caves
Water garden
prune museum
Fontirou caves
foie gras museum

With children

Néguenou lake
Magic cauldron

Within easy reach

Fortified towns and châteaux of Agen, p. 130

Tourist offices

Agen: ☎ 05 53 47 36 09
Penne-d'Agenais:
☎ 05 53 36 17 30
Villeneuve-sur-Lot:
☎ 05 53 36 17 30

Lastournelle caves

WATER GARDEN

Latour-Marliac, Le Temple-Sur-Lot
10 miles (16 km) W of Villeneuve-sur-Lot
☎ 05 53 01 08 05
Shop open 9am-6pm, 15 Mar.-31 Oct. Visits
May-Sept.
Admission charge.

This Jardin Aquatique, the 'cradle of water-lilies', is a real family story. In 1870 the grandfather of the current owner, Joseph Latour-Marliac, assembled a collection of water-lilies from all over the world and created what is now the world's oldest nursery. Lovers of flowers will be fascinated by the 140 different varieties of lily.

The display of stalagmites and stalactites at the Grottes de Lastournelle has taken 25 million years to prepare, and is a spectacular demonstration of what can be achieved with time and a little water. Seven chambers are open to the public, including the magnificent Salle des Colonnes.

In the heat of summer, the coolness of the Grottes de Fontirou is very welcome indeed. Seven chambers have been opened, with panoramas of stalactites and stalagmites tinted ochre by particles of clay. In one chamber, bones of animals from the Tertiary period can still be seen.

Castella
*8 miles (13 km)
SE of Sainte-Colombe-de-Villeneuve*
Fontirou caves
☎ 05 53 41 73 97
Open daily 10am-12.30pm and 2-6pm,
July-Aug.; 2-5.30pm
Apr.-May and 1-15 Sept.
Open Sun. Oct. and
All Saints' Day, weather permitting.
Admission charge.

Penne-d'Agenais
*13 miles (21 km)
NE of Castella*
Art village
Previously known as Penne-la-Sanglante ('Penne the bloody') because of the massacres that once occurred here, this high-lying medieval village now attracts tourists with its narrow streets and their corbelled and half-timbered houses (Rue de Ferracap, Place Paul-Froment).

Many artists live in this village, which is itself a work of art.

Laroque-Timbaut
*8.5 miles (14 km)
NE of Penne-d'Agenais*
Miracle water
Legend has it that the water from the fountain in this village, located deep in the Vallon Saint-Germain, cured the sickness that struck the army of the famous knight, Roland. Since then, the water has been drunk at many tables in the village and the chapel, in the church beside the fountain, is visited by pilgrims every year on 28 May. The 12th-C. covered market and the tiny Rue du Lô are also worth visiting.

Beauville

Frespech and Beauville
*5 miles (8 km)
NE of Laroque-Timbaut*
Fortified town and village
The fortified village of Frespech still retains traces of its enclosures and old gates. The church, with its lauze-covered apse, dates from the 11thC., and the old houses have turrets and mullioned windows. The imposing bastide of Beauville, 5.5 miles (9 km) southeast of Frespech, dominates the valley of the

TOURTIÈRE FAIR

Penne-d'Agenais
Second weekend in July
Each year, the tourtière association (Confrérie de la Tourtière) meets at Penne-d'Agenais for the Foire à la Tourtière, in honour of this famous Basque country cake. Traditional Occitan dances and a ball are staged on Saturday night, and on Sunday the jury meets to award the prize for the best tourtière and elects the 'Lucky One'. The ceremony ends with a spectacular procession through the village streets and a show.

Petit-Séoune. A walking trail offers insights into the colourful past of this bastide.

Foie gras
Musée du Foie gras
Souleilles (near Frespech)
☎ 05 53 41 23 24
Open daily mid-June to mid-Sept., 10am-7pm; 3-7pm in low season. Closed Jan.
Admission charge.

This museum will teach you all there is to know about foie gras: its history from ancient times to the present day, and the process by which an unfortunate duck becomes a delectable dish. The museum also has a truffle-oak plantation, a duck-breeding centre and slaughter rooms. The resulting foie gras, duck-conserve cassoulet flambéed in Armagnac and duck conserve with ceps must be tasted to be believed. Be prepared to leave with your hands full as well as your stomach: semi-cooked foie gras, 160F for 6.5 oz/180 g.

Saint-Maurin
8.5 miles (14 km)
S of Beauville
Museum of rural life and crafts
☎ 05 53 95 31 25
Open daily exc. Tues., 3-7pm, July-Aug.; by appt in low season.
Admission charge.

This attractive village, nestling in a little valley next to a lake, has a charming Place Centrale with half-timbered houses, a well, a market place and the remains of a Clunisian abbey. The abbey is the ideal location for the Musée de la Vie Agricole et Artisanale, created by the local residents. Everything connected with village life can be found here, including a workshop, wood-turning lathe and cart-making.

Puymirol
7 miles (11 km)
SW of Saint-Maurin
An impregnable bastide
This fortified town, founded in 1246 by the Counts of Toulouse, was reputed to be impregnable. Today, the best way to discover it is to walk along Rue Royale, where you find the Église Notre-Dame-de-Grand-Castel, a church with a 13th-C. porch. The main square is surrounded by towers and still has its ancient well. The 1-mile (2-km) walk along the ramparts offers commanding views and a number of medieval treasures.

Frespech

Val de Garonne,
a taste of Tuscany

Southwest of Cahors, between Moissac and Valence-d'Agen, the River Garonne crosses a narrow plain. The Brulhois wine-producing area lies on the southern slopes, while Serres country is to the north. The roundness of the hills, the gentle colours of the countryside and the brick and stone houses combine to give this area an atmosphere more reminiscent of Tuscany than France.

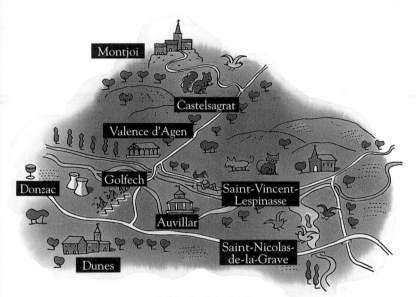

Montjoi

Castelsagrat

Valence d'Agen

Donzac

Golfech

Saint-Vincent-Lespinasse

Auvillar

Dunes

Saint-Nicolas-de-la-Grave

Valence-d'Agen
15 miles (24 km)
SE of Agen
Washhouses
This fortified town, founded by King Edward I of England in 1283, has three ancient 'lavoirs' (washhouses), among the finest in the Midi-Pyrénées region.

Built in the 18th-19thC., they are unfortunately all that remain of the old village.

Birds in the hand
Every Tuesday, the **poultry market** (marché à la volaille) in Halle Dumon brings together breeders from throughout the region to sell free-range chickens, turkeys, ducks, pigeons, rabbits and guinea-fowl, against a background of unbelievable noise. For fresh fruit or conserve, head for the town centre,

where the market gardeners and producers meet. From November to March, gourmets come to enjoy the **gras market** (marché au gras).

Golfech
2 miles (3 km)
SW of Valence d'Agen
Hydroelectric and nuclear power stations
☎ 05 63 29 39 06
Admission free
(by appt only).
This is a must if you want to understand the mysteries of the atom and the story of nuclear power. However, the

Centrales Hydraulique et Nucléaire are only open to those aged 10 and over, and booking must be made by telephone several days in advance. Near to the viewpoint that overlooks the power station, a 'lift', unique in Europe, helps the salmon on their migration up the River Garonne.

Donzac
3 miles (5 km)
SW of Golfech
'Black wine' cellar
Route de Dunes
☎ 05 63 39 91 92
Open daily 8am-noon and 2-6pm, exc. Sun. and Mon. am.
The Garonne valley produces very special wines, a rich ruby red that produces most notably blackcurrant and gooseberry aromas as it

matures in oak barrels. The Côtes-de-Brulhois, the 'vins noirs' ('black wines'), carry the VDQS trademark. At the Caves des Vins Noirs, in Donzac, you can enjoy a **free tasting** of red and rosé wines, together with a visit to the barrel vaults and the bottling centre. And you might come away with a few bottles, such as 1996 vintage at 20F and 1995 barrel-matured Château-Grand-Chêne at 34F.

Bygone-crafts conservation centre
☎ 05 63 29 21 96
Open daily 9.30am-noon

and 2-7pm, July-Aug.; 2-6pm, rest of the year. Closed Jan.
Admission charge.
The Conservatoire des Métiers d'Autrefois has a surprisingly large collection, comprising over 10,000 items from the cultural and craft heritage of this area. Of particular interest is the **museum of vines and wines** (Musée de la Vigne et du Vin), with a huge, 17th-C., large-wheeled squirrel-press, unique in France.

Dunes
3.5 miles (6 km)
SW of Donzac
Queen Margot's village
Despite this impressive title, Dunes is in fact a very small bastide, located in the depths of the country; but what it lacks in size, it makes up for in character. Stroll around the central square with its remarkable houses, and dwell upon Queen Margot, who

Spotcheck
C4

Tarn-et-Garonne

Things to do

Valence-d'Agen poultry market
Wine-tasting at Donzac

With children

Angora goat farm
Tarn and Garonne boat trips

Within easy reach

Moissac (10.5 miles/ 17 km E), p. 144

Tourist offices

Valence-d'Agen:
☎ 05 63 39 52 52
Auvillar:
☎ 05 63 39 89 82

once stayed here. The **Église Sainte-Madeleine** has a magnificent reredos and one

of the most beautiful Gothic church naves in the region.

Pottery workshop
Rue Basse
☎ 05 63 39 97 76
Open daily 9am-6pm.
Nicole and Alain Morellini, who have lived in Dunes since 1981, specialise in **glazed earthenware** and **stoneware**. In the workshop,

their expert hands transform simple earth into fascinating art forms with beautiful round shapes and bright colours (bowls from 35F, jugs from 110F, dishes 150-500F).

Auvillar

8 miles (13 km)
SE of Dunes

A stroll beneath the arches

Auvillar, which overlooks the Garonne river, is one of the finest villages in Tarn-et-Garonne, with its perfectly round **covered market** and main square, surrounded by old, galleried houses with lattice work and brick-piling; it also offers exceptional views of the river and the old port. In the clock tower (Tour de l'Horloge), a permanent **exhibition of river transport** evokes the grand old days of river commerce.

Museum of old Auvillar

Rue du Château
☎ 05 63 29 05 79
Open daily exc. Tues. 2.30-6.30pm (5.30pm out of season).

Admission charge (ticket includes admission to river-transport exhibition).
The main attractions of the Musée du Vieil-Auvillar are the **earthenware collection** (18th and 19thC.), and the **rustic pottery**, together with a few moving **commemorative plaques** of Garonne sailors. The **pottery market**, held every October in the covered market, carries on the old traditions of the earthenware producers; about 40 of whom come from all over France to display their work.

COUNTRYSIDE WALKS

Info. from Auvillar tourist office
This area is crisscrossed by about a dozen signposted walking trails, which are accessible to all and may be followed on foot, bicycle or horseback. The Valence-d'Agen route, which runs along an ancient Roman road, rises up the slopes and affords a splendid view back across the Garonne valley. At Auvillar, two trails wander down to the riverbank and the old port before climbing the ridge.

Ferme du Cap-de-Pech

☎ 05 63 39 08 34
Open daily 2-6pm.
Admission charge.
Marie-Josée Joly's pretty, curly-haired goats are not reared for milk but for soft, light mohair wool. In this visit to Cap-de-Pech farm, which lasts a little under an hour, you will find out how this special fibre is made into garments and how the goats are reared. Buy yourself a ball of wool (38-42F) or, for the winter, a pair of gloves or socks (65-90F) or a scarf (from 165F), in any colour. As a bonus, there is a chance to taste farm goat cheese.

Saint-Vincent-Lespinasse
10.5 miles (17 km)
N of Le Pin
Ceramic cats
☎ 05 63 04 93 42
Visits by appt
(telephone in advance).
Cat-lover and renowned
ceramic artist Christian
Pradier lives surrounded
by impressive
toms and graceful
queens all made
of ceramic, and
his workshop is
also home

Place Centrale and galleries, Castelsagrat

Montjoi
3 miles (5 km)
NW of Castelsagrat
Heritage village
A great place for a stroll.
This small village is a real
delight, from its arched
entrance gate to its timbered
and corbelled houses, and
its covered passage, well,
squares and streets.
From its lofty location,

Montjoi affords a compelling
view across the Séoune
valley. The village itself is so
pretty, that it is actually listed
by the French government.

Montjoi

to garden sculptures and
fountains. The selection is
varied, from the unique and
very expensive to the
affordable (prices from 150
to 3,000F and over). These
remarkable art forms are
regularly exhibited abroad.

Castelsagrat
7 miles (11 km)
N of Saint-Vincent-Lespinasse
Church carvings
This typical medieval bastide
has a large Place Centrale
surrounded by houses with
irregular, covered galleries,
as well as beautiful stone –
and wood-sectioned houses.
The magnificent **church
reredos**, with painted and
gold-leafed wood, is a must;
the tall columns depict
squirrels and birds at play
among vine branches.

LEISURELY THRILLS
Lou Malaousenc
Quai Blanc, Malause
5 miles (8 km) SE of Valence-d'Agen
☎ 05 63 39 55 78
Every Sun. 3-5pm, Apr.-Sept.
Admission charge.
Take a trip along the river on the Lou Malaousenc.
The 90-minute ride (adults 40F, children aged
5-15 20F) takes you along either the Tarn or the
Garonne. You will see the canal and its locks,
cross the great lake at Saint-Nicolas-de-le-Grave
and visit bird island (Île aux Oiseaux), home to
a huge colony of mallards, sandpipers, gulls
and coots.

Moissac
fine art on the water

W hether you prefer nature or culture, Moissac will fascinate you. From the sculptures in its Roman cloisters to the workshops and its many summer concerts, art can be found everywhere. To escape to nature, simply walk along the banks of the canal, the meanders of the Garonne and the shores of the Tarn. The luxuriant banks are home to colonies of herons, gulls and mallards.

Cloister of the Abbatiale Saint-Pierre

Place Delthil
☎ 05 63 04 01 85.
Open daily 9am-7pm, July-Aug.; 9am-noon and 2-6pm, 15 Mar.-June and Sept.-Oct.; 9am-noon and 2-5pm, 15 Oct.-15 Mar. Closed 25 Dec. and 1 Jan.
Admission charge.
This is the oldest, largest and most beautiful of the **Romanesque cloisters**; its capitals are adorned with sculptures and the large **portal** of the abbey church, with its finely chiselled tympanum, is famed the world over. All this magnificence, of course, comes at a price – it's a magnet for the crowds so, if you want to enjoy the spectacle in relative peace and quiet, get here early.

Artisan street

Rue Moura
Workshops open daily exc. Mon.
About 10 artists have opened their workshops to the public in this street, including a glass-blower, lace-maker, potter, carver, painter and porcelain restorer. Take a family walk and discover these various crafts together; Saturday is the best day. On summer evenings, round the trip off with a **free concert** in the cloisters square.

Viewpoints

Starting behind the former Carmelite convent (Couvent des Carmélites), climb up to **Point de Vue de la Vierge** for a great view of the Tarn and the canal. On the way down you'll pass through a pine wood that is home to France's largest **reserve of night herons**. The other magnificent view for which Moissac is justly famous is the panorama of the confluence of the Tarn and Garonne, visible from **Point de Vue de Boudou**, 2.5 miles (4 km) from Moissac on the Valence-d'Agen road.

River Tarn canal bridge

The unusual Pont-Canal, 1,168 ft (356 m) in length, allows the canal running alongside the Garonne to cross the River Tarn. This makes a good location for a

River Tarn canal bridge

walk; the floral displays around the canal locks are magnificent. A walk starting from the Uvarium takes you to the bridge.

Ciboulette
Route de Toulouse
☎ **05 63 32 23 09**
Open daily exc. Sun. am, 8.30am-1pm and 3-7pm.
This shop is really more like a garden, with its fresh fruit and organic vegetables, wines and homemade cheeses and jams (15F for 11.5 oz/ 330 g). Goose conserve (100F), semi-cooked foie gras (120F for 6.5 oz/180 g), honey (15-35F for 9 oz/ 250 g), eggs and hams are also available, as are flowers and aromatic plants. Perhaps Ciboulette's greatest attraction is that the producers sell all their farm products here, straight from basket to table.

Voice festival
Early July.
☎ **05 63 04 32 69**
Moissac is home to the 'Vibrations de la Voix' festival, which combines gospel, song and humour. The shows are held on the banks of the Tarn, in the Abbatiale Saint-Pierre or its cloisters. There is also a 'fringe' festival, with Jazz groups performing nightly on the café and restaurant terraces.

Saint-Nicolas-de-la-Grave
5 miles (8 km) SW of Moissac
Lakeside leisure centre
Base de loisirs
☎ **05 63 95 50 00**
Open daily 8am-noon and 2-5.30pm, Apr.-Sept.
Admission charge.
This 1000-acre (400-ha) Base de Loisirs is a delight for lovers of water sports. You can hire windsurfing boards (50F per half-day), catamarans (165F per half-day),

pedalos (50F per hour) and boats, sailing dinghies and canoes. On hot days, cool off in the swimming pool or hire a bike and head for the shade. The lake is also home to large numbers of migrating birds.

Spotcheck
C4

Tarn-et-Garonne

Things to do
River Tarn canal bridge

With children
Visit the artisans' workshops
Lakeside leisure centre

Within easy reach
Valence-d'Agen (7.5 miles/12 km W), p. 140

Tourist office
Moissac:
☎ **05 63 04 01 85**

OFF-COLOUR? TRY GRAPE JUICE
During the 1930s, Moissac was a famous resort where high-society people came to try grape-juice therapy. The Kiosque de l'Uvarium (05 63 04 53 16) carries on the tradition: from May to September, top-quality fresh fruit and chasselas grape juices (18F per glass) are on offer on the splendid terrace overlooking the Tarn. The kiosk has kept its magnificent wall frescoes and Belle-Époque distillery decor.

Quercy blanc
chalk-white
and lavender blue

Belmontet

La grotte de Roland

Montaigu-de-Quercy

Valprionde

Montcuq

Castelnau-Montratier

Saint-Nazaire-
de-Valentane

Brassac

Southwest of Cahors is a dry, chalky upland area cut across by a number of waterways in narrow valleys, known as 'serres'. On the plateau, the sun lights up the pinkish roof tiles, the green cypress trees, the mauve of the lavender fields and the white of the chalk, giving a taste of Provence.

of chance and skill will keep the children busy. With all that, plus the sun farm, cart rides, donkey rides and the acrobatics area, there isn't time to be bored.

Castelnau-Montratier
23.5 miles (38 km)
S of Cahors
It's playtime!
Le Maillol recreation area
☎ 05 65 21 90 88
Open daily Easter-1 Nov., 10.30am-7.30pm.
Admission charge
(free for under 4s).
This 7.5-acre (3-ha) space, in the shade of an oak forest and by a lake, is full of weird and wonderful games. Two walking trails that really test the senses and another filled with games

Montcuq
12.5 miles (20 km) NW of Castelnau-Montratier
Montcuq
This peaceful, picturesque, sunlit village, with its brick and cob houses, is located in a

The Sunday-morning market at Montcuq

natural amphitheatre on a hill overlooking the chasselas vineyards. The **traditional market** on Sunday morning is the highlight of the busy village life.

Roland's cave
2.5 miles (4 km)
N of Montcuq
☎ 05 65 22 99 90
Open daily 10am-noon and 2-7pm, 15 June-11 Sept.; 2-5pm weekends, Apr.-15 June and 12 Sept.-1 Nov. Please telephone during school holidays.
The Grotte de Roland is the only cave in Quercy blanc developed for visitors. A 1,345-ft (410-m) gallery leads to an underground lake, which is surrounded by varied and highly unusual rock

formations, which resemble ancient fortresses or strange animals. The visit, which lasts about one hour, ends in an interesting little **Musée Préhistorique**.

Montaigu-de-Quercy

16 miles (26 km)
W of Montcuq
Chênes lake
**Information from
tourist office**
Open 15 June-15 Sept.
Admission charge.
A floating octopus, water slides, trampolines and diving-boards make this the ideal place to cool off in the heat of the summer. Have fun in the water or enjoy a lazy, relaxed time on the 330-ft (100-m) sandy beach. There's a picnic area and pedalos are available for hire.

Brassac

18.5 miles (30 km)
SW of Montcuq
**Château
de Brassac**
☎ 05 63 94 23 82
Open daily exc. Tues.
10am-noon and 2-7pm,
15 June-15 Sept.
Open Sun. and public holidays, 2-7pm,
rest of the year.
Admission charge.
Surrounded by ancient cedars and fir trees, this imposing château, which dominates the Séoune valley, dates back to at least the 12thC. and has always belonged to the same family. One member of this family, Hector de Galard de Brassac, is commemor-ated in the design of a playing card – the jack of diamonds. He fought alongside Joan of Arc and was honoured by King Louis XI.

Saint-Nazaire-de-Valentane

4.5 miles (7 km)
NE of Brassac
**Ferme des
Caouelles**
☎ 05 63 94 21 33
Open daily.

Spotcheck
D4

Things to do

Montcuq market
Château de Brassac
Servat lavender distillery

With children

Le Maillol recreation area
Roland's cave
Chênes lake

Within easy reach

Cahors (17 miles/27 km NE), p. 154
Lauzerte (8 miles/13 km SW), p. 148
Moissac (23 miles/37 km S), p. 144

Tourist offices

Montaigu-de-Quercy:
☎ 05 63 94 48 50
Montcuq:
☎ 05 65 22 94 04

Forget about the diet for a while and enjoy the rich flavour of canard (duck). At Caouelles farm, Jean-Louis Raynal offers only the best: the unmissable foie gras de canard (semi-cooked or raw), fillet of duck breast, conserves, stuffed necks and duck scratchings.

LAVENDER STILL

Distillerie de Lavande de Servat
*Between Belmontet and Valprionde, 3 miles (5 km)
NW of Montcuq*
☎ 05 65 31 90 17
Open Wed., 9am-noon and 2-7pm, July-Aug.;
by appt out of season.
Admission free.
Maryse and Dominique Thévenet carry on the tradition of distilling lavender. After cutting and drying, the flowers are placed in a huge tank surrounded with water-filled pipes. This water, when heated, produces steam that passes over the flowers, captures their aroma and is then cooled and finally trapped for conver-sion into their essential oils. The liquid is not only used in embalming, but is well known for its antiseptic and soothing effect on insect bites and minor wounds, helps colds and congestion, and repels clothes mites as well.

Lauzerte
Quercy's Toledo

Place des Cornières

The so-called 'Toledo of Quercy' is one of the region's most attractive bastides, founded in the 13thC. and now offering a delightful diversion with its timbered houses and arches. Perched on an outcrop, it is surrounded by wide valleys with soft chalky soil, ideal for growing all kinds of fruit, the most famous of which is undoubtedly the chasselas grape.

Square humour

The **market place** (Place des Cornières) is delightful, with its irregular arches, white-stone houses in a muddle of styles and, in addition, the wicked humour of the modern artwork by Jacques Bucholtz,

Jardin du Pèlerin and view from the Barbacane

in which a corner of the paved square is raised like the page of a book. **Rue de la Mairie** and **Rue de la Gendarmerie** have magnificently restored old houses and the **Barbacane** and **Promenade de l'Éveillé** offer

commanding views. Finish the walk with a visit to the **Église Saint-Barthélémy** and the **Église des Carmes**, and admire the 17th-C. reredos in these churches. The lower houses of the town have become the haunts of artists and craftsmen.

Lauzerte macaroons
M.J. Bonnefous, caterer
On the way into Lauzerte from Moissac
☎ 05 63 94 66 44
Open daily.
You really shouldn't miss this delicatessen, the home of the true Lauzerte macaroon, whose age-old recipe was once so renowned that

Raimond IV, the celebrated Count of Toulouse who was a chef for the First Crusade, had macaroons delivered every day. This delicacy is still made in a cottage industry and its recipe is a closely guarded secret even today.

Belvèze
7.5 miles (12 km) NW of Lauzerte
Jougla farm centre
☎ 05 63 94 41 42
Open daily 10am-7pm, 16 June-5 Sept., weekends and public holidays out of season. Closed Oct.-Easter. *Admission charge.* The Fermeraie du Jougla is not to be missed: a wide range of organised routes allow both young and old to discover over 400 different animal species.

But this is not a zoo. Children can feed, care for and cuddle the animals, explore the farm or pick vegetables while learning about the secrets of seeds. Vegetables and melons are on sale.

Cazes-Mondenard
3.5 miles (6 km)
E of Lauzerte

Take a ride on a donkey

Cazillac
☎ 05 63 95 84 61

Why not hire a donkey? It will make your journey much easier, carrying your bags or your children if they get tired. Brahmâne recommends a walk along the **Quercy footpaths**

(Sentiers de Quercy) or along the pilgrim route to Santiago de Compostela.

Chasselas tour

Information from the Moissac chasselas association
☎ 05 63 04 01 78

The exposed slopes around Lauzerte are home to the prized chasselas grape, whose quality has earned it an AOC trademark. Its cradle, so to speak, is Cazes-Mondenard, which marks the start of a signposted trail that snakes its way through the vineyards and the orchards from Cazes to Moissac.

HEARSE MUSEUM

Grange Minguet
Cazes-Mondenard
5 miles (8 km) SE of Lauzerte
☎ 05 63 95 84 02
Open daily 9am-8pm, July-Aug.
Closed rest of the year.

Yvan Quercy, who is not lacking in humour or grace despite his extraordinary hobby, will receive you warmly in period costume, offer you tasting sessions of local produce, and then show you to his barn, home to some 50 hearses – padded or simple, with fringes or feathers, or with columns or friezes. These 'resurrected' hearses, dating from the 18th to the early 20thC., stand together with barouches, harnesses, yokes and old agricultural machinery.

Bouloc
3 miles (5 km)
N of Lauzerte

Parachuting school

École Régionale de Parachutisme
☎ 05 63 94 30 48

This is one of the best parachuting schools in the Midi-Pyrénées region and a must for adrenaline junkies.

The programme includes a 6,500-ft (2,000-m) free-fall jump and, for beginners, jumps in tandem attached to an instructor (about 1,000F). The sensation that the jump brings should be experienced at least once in a lifetime.

Caussade and the surrounding area
round hills and round hats

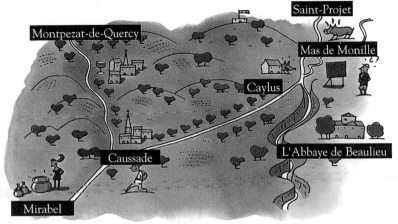

T his little town, with its white-stone houses, owes its fame to the manufacture of straw hats. These days, its greatest attraction is the Monday market, where conserves and foie gras abound. The slopes around the town are covered in orchards and market gardens, with apples, pears, peaches, plums, grapes and melons.

A stroll in Caussade

You'll admire the beautiful 17th-C. houses, the red-brick clock tower and the Récollets convent (Couvent des Récollets). Caussade market is a must: every Monday there is a festival of local produce where the poulet noir ('black chicken'), whose exquisite taste is said to resemble a partridge, is a speciality. A memorable bric-a-brac fair is also held each year on 15 August.

Église Notre-Dame clock tower

Mirabel
9.5 miles (15 km)
W of Caussade
Raymond Cabos' prunes
Pradié
☎ 05 63 31 04 16
Open Mon.-Fri.
Admission free.
Visit the only Agen-prune production site in the locality and enjoy the taste of prune cream, stuffed prunes or prunes with chocolate.

Montpezat-de-Quercy
7.5 miles (12 km)
NW of Caussade
The tapestries of Montpezat
Collégiale
Saint-Martin
☎ 05 63 02 05 55
Open daily 8.30am-7pm,

July-Aug., 8.30am-5pm, rest of the year.
Admission free.
Although this hilltop village has a pretty covered market and many medieval houses, it is best known for the remarkable series of 16th-C. Flanders tapestries that recall the life of Saint Martin in 16 separate scenes.

A real local wine
Some wines from the hills of Quercy are a rich dark red with the full flavour of mature fruit, while others are the colour of the local roof-tiles, with a more subtle flavour.

Maison du Vin du Quercy,
Montpezat

They all await you at the
Maison du Vin du Quercy in
Montpezat, next to the tourist
office (Boulevard des Fossés
☎ 05 63 02 05 55). Several
producers from around the
village have been honoured at
the agricultural show in Paris,
among them Guy Cammas
(**Domaine du Gabachou**
☎ 05 63 02 07 44) and the
Vignerons du Quercy co-
operative (☎ 05 63 02 03 50).
At Bernard Bouyssou's estate,
the Domaine de Lafage, you
can taste his organic red wines
(☎ 05 63 02 06 91/07 09).

Caylus

14.5 miles
(23 km) NE of
Caussade
Village walk

Stop for a while in this
picturesque village,
located at the foot of
the Causses. The **Église
Saint-Jean-Baptiste** has
a magnificent chancel
with tall windows and
Christ Monumental, a
1954 sculpture by Ossip
Zadkine, carved from an
elm tree. The village has
many medieval houses,
including the 13th-C. 'house
of wolves' (Maison des Loups),
with its odd-looking
gargoyles.

Caylus

Le mas de Monille

6 miles (10 km)
N of Caylus
**Spit-roasted
wild boar**

Between Loze and
Saint-Projet
☎ 05 63 65 76 85
Open July-Aug., visits
at 3.30pm and 5.30pm
(3.30pm only out of
season).
Admission free.
This unusual breeding farm
offers the opportunity to eat
wild boar straight from the
spit, enjoy the taste of unusual
conserves, and see a slide show
tracing the history of geese
and the life of the wild boar.

Ginals

18 miles (29 km)
NE of Caussade
Abbaye de Beaulieu
☎ 05 63 24 50 10
Open daily 10am-noon
and 2-6pm, July-Aug.;
closed Tues., 1 Sept.-1
Nov. Closed 2 Nov-1 Apr.
Admission charge.
This Gothic abbey has
impressive doors and a
magnificent rose window.
Its **modern-art centre**

Spotcheck
D4

Tarn-et-Garonne

Things to do

Caussade markets and fairs
Wine-tasting
Montpezat's Flanders
tapestries
Hat workshops
Beaulieu modern-art centre

With children

Prune production
Spit-roasted wild boar

Within easy reach

Cahors (23 miles/37 km
N), p. 154
Saint-Antonin-Noble-Val
(12.5 miles/20 km SW),
p. 152

Tourist offices

Caussade: ☎ 05 63 26 04 04
Caylus: ☎ 05 63 67 00 28

(Centre d'Art Contemporain)
has a wealth of works by
artists such as Dubuffet, Henri
Michaux and Mathieu. From
June to Sept., it stages several
interesting exhibitions of
contemporary art.

HAT WORKSHOPS

Société Willy's Paris
63, Avenue du Général Leclerc
☎ 05 63 93 09 96
Pétronille Cantecor, who
invented the straw
hat in 1789,
set up his
workshop in
Caussade, which
soon became the
hat capital along
with the neighbouring town
of Septfonds. In the early 20thC., over 30 factories
produced this distinctive form of headgear,
employing 2,000 people. Nowadays, Caussade also
produces caps, boaters and hats for the great
couturiers of Paris. Discover how they are made
at the Willy's Paris workshops or the summer hat
festival, held in August.

Aveyron gorges
a river of medieval villages

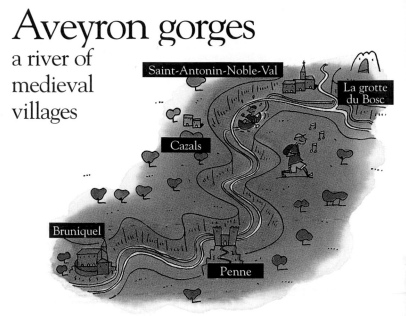

Saint-Antonin-Noble-Val

La grotte du Bosc

Cazals

Bruniquel

Penne

I n this part of Tarn-et-Garonne and on the edges of Rouergue, the River Aveyron has carved out caves and sculpted the chalk cliffs into deep gorges with stunning scenery. The route winds its way between medieval villages and venerable old castles which overlook the river.

Detail from the Maison de l'Amour

Saint-Antonin-Noble-Val
12 miles (19 km)
E of Caussade
A citadel between rock and river
This ancient white-walled citadel, situated under the Roc d'Anglars in the valley between the Aveyron and Bonnette rivers, alternated between Protestant, English and French control as the medieval wars progressed. In its long, winding streets you'll find a hotchpotch of old houses, the museum of the old town (Musée du Vieux Saint-Antonin), the covered market square (Place de la Halle), the splendid Maison de l'Amour on Rue Droite, and the Place du Berssarel, with its **walnut-oil mill** (Moulin à Huile de Noix, visits ☎ 05 63 30 63 47).

Bosc cave
2 miles (3 km) NE of Saint-Antonin-Noble-Val
☎ 05 63 30 62 91 (in season) or 05 63 56 03 12 (out of season)
Open daily 10am-noon and 2-6pm, July-Aug.
Admission charge.

The gallery of the Grotte du Bosc, 650 ft (200 m) long, once the site of an underground river, now houses a display of fascinating formations of varying colours. An exhibition of minerals from all over the world rounds off the visit, which lasts about 40 minutes. It's best to take something warm, as the temperature in the cave is a fresh 14°C (57°F).

Trips galore
Ask at the tourist office for a guide to short walks ('sentiers de petite randonnée').
☎ 05 63 30 63 47
Starting from Saint-Antoine-Noble-Val, about 10 different **circuit walks**, all clearly signposted, offer the chance to enjoy the splendid scenery of the Aveyron gorge. The best is

the walk to Roc d'Anglars, which rises to 650 ft (200 m), while slightly longer walks will take you to the interlocking stones of Le Pech, near to the Bône amphitheatre and restored by a CNRS researcher.

Penne

About 10.5 miles (17 km) SW of Saint-Antonin-Noble-Val

A stunning location

The French call this the 'citadel of vertigo'. The town is overlooked by the imposing

Penne

medieval fortress, whose walls, built on the very top of the rock, appear to defy gravity. From Penne, a number of walks take you into the cool woodlands of the private Forêt de Grésigne estate. Don't miss the spectacular sound and light show ('son et lumière', Wednesday and Saturday, 7 July to mid-Sept.).

Monsieur Sorin's goats

3 miles (5 km) S of Penne

Ferme de Valeyres
☎ 05 63 33 11 87
Open daily 10am-noon and 2-6pm.
Admission free.

These Angora goats, with their soft, curly fleece, will delight the children. M. Sorin, in a guided tour of the farm lasting about an hour, will tell you how the goats are bred and how their fleeces are transformed from mohair wool into finished products such as sweaters and rugs.

Angora goat

Spotcheck
DE4

Tarn-et-Garonne

Things to do

Museum of old Saint-Antonin
Visit to a walnut-oil mill
Bosc cave
Canoeing the river gorges
Penne light and sound show

With children

Angora goat farm

Within easy reach

Caussade (15.5 miles/ 25 km W), p. 150

Tourist offices

Saint-Antonin-Noble-Val:
☎ 05 63 30 63 47
Bruniquel:
☎ 05 63 67 29 84
Penne: ☎ 05 63 56 36 68

Porte Méjane, Bruniquel

Bruniquel

4 miles (6 km) SW of Penne

The Queen of Bruniquel
☎ 05 63 67 27 67
Château open school and public holidays, 10am-12.30pm and 2-7pm, Easter-1 Nov.

This hilltop village is a veritable history book. Its château, one of the most remarkable feudal buildings in the area, with a mix of styles from the 12th to the 19thC. and panoramic view of the valley, evokes the memory of the Visigoth Queen Brunehaut.

ADVENTURE DAY ON THE WATER

Découvertes
15, Boulevard des Thermes, Saint-Antonin-Noble-Val
☎ 05 63 68 22 46

Paddling down the Aveyron in a canoe might be tricky, but the reward for persistence is a truly different way to see the great beauty of the countryside. You can paddle the 5 miles (8 km) from Saint-Antonin-Noble-Val to Cazals in half a day, or take a full-day for the 10 mile (16 km) trip to Penne. The return journey, in a shuttle boat, is included in the price.

Cahors
a journey through time

Valentré bridge

At once Gallo-Roman, medieval and very modern, Cahors, the capital of Quercy, brings all these periods of history together. On its island, protected by the surrounding River Lot and the Cévennes amphitheatre, the town enjoys both a well-preserved historical heritage and a fascinating cultural life. The town is also famous for two other attractions – the Lot valley, one of the most beautiful in France, and the renowned Cahors wine.

The Valentré bridge

The Pont Valentré is the very emblem of Cahors. With its three tall, square towers and six majestic arches, the bridge is a splendid example of medieval defence; so imposing is its appearance, in fact, that it was never attacked. Straddling the Lot to the southwest of the town, it is open only to pedestrians, who can walk across the impregnable fortification and visit its central tower, once used as a lookout post.

Old Cahors

Leave your car in Place François-Mitterrand and walk along Boulevard Gambetta to enter old Cahors, with its narrow streets and wooded areas. Rue de la Daurade has magnificent Renaissance houses, including Maison Roaldès, on Place Henri-IV,

Maison Roaldès

Cloister of the Saint-Étienne Cathedral

Spotcheck
D4

Things to do

Festivals and Henri-Martin museum
Markets and fairs
Water-skiing on the Lot
Terracotta workshop
Château de Roussillon
Discover the secrets of truffles

With children

Rail and waterway trip
Archipel de Cahors water park

Within easy reach

*Cahors wine trail (7.5 miles/12 km NW), p. 158
Lalbenque and the Causse de Limogne (8.5 miles/ 14 km SE), p. 157
Caussade (23 miles/ 37 km S), p. 150*

Tourist office

Cahors: ☎ 05 65 53 20 74

where the French king once stayed. A 40-minute mini-rail journey will take you all around the old town (departs

Old houses, place Saint-Urcisse

Allée des Soupirs, daily 10am-noon and 2-7pm, Easter to September.
☎ 05 65 30 16 55).

Cathédrale Saint-Étienne

The cathedral is located right in the heart of the old district, but its clock tower, keep and remarkable slate-covered cupolas can be seen from a great distance. The fortress-like appearance of the cathedral gives it an impressive feeling of power and simplicity that is echoed in the interior.

Dine on the terrace
Le Bistrot de Cahors
46, Rue de la Daurade
☎ **05 65 53 10 55**
Closed Tues.

CAHORS: 'C' IS FOR CULTURE

Info. from the Cahors department of culture
☎ **05 65 20 37 37**
The city of Gambetta, former home of the poet Clément Marot, is a cultural centre and hosts a number of different shows. The internationally famous 'Printemps de Cahors' festival, held in June, transforms the whole town into a giant display of contemporary photographs and visual arts. Summer is the time for the 'Cahors Blues Festival', with its inviting concerts. In winter, the streets come alive with the 'Chaînon Manquant' – the festival's 60 or so live shows include theatre, dance and music. In addition, there are 'musical Mondays' all-year round, as well as the plastic-arts exhibitions of the musée Henri-Martin (Rue Émile-Zola ☎ 05 65 30 15 13).

On the Quai Champolion, the terrace of this small restaurant, housed in a medieval house, is a delightful shady area that has become very popular. The cuisine is straightforward and the hospitality warm. Depending on when you go, you can try hare, wild boar or belly of veal, all at very affordable prices.

Markets galore

Despite its town atmosphere, Cahors has not forgotten the richness of the surrounding countryside – the covered

markets at Place Chapou overflow with Quercy specialities from Tuesday to Saturday. The gras market (marché de gras) is on Saturday morning, November-March, and the fair, every first and third Saturday of the month, covers the whole of Place François-Mittérrand. There is also a bric-a-brac market on the last Sunday of every month, at Place Rousseau.

Wine hall

Atrium
Route de Toulouse
☎ **05 65 20 80 80**
Open Mon.-Sun. am, 7.30am-8pm, mid-July to Aug.; Mon.-Sat. exc. public holidays, 7.30am-12.30pm and 2-7.30pm, Sept.-early July.
This huge area at the entrance to the town is dedicated to the famous Cahors AOC. In bottles, casks, wooden cases or bulk, many varieties are offered, including Châteaux de Haute-Serre, Mercuès and Pech de Jammes (highlands of Cahors) as well as young spring vintages that will delight lovers of fruity wines.

Rail and waterways

Quercyrail/Safaraid
☎ **05 65 35 98 88**
Open Tues. and Wed. July-Aug. By request out of season.
Adults 150F, under-12s half price. Free for under-3s.

A novel way of discovering the Lot valley. From Cahors station, the little red and white Quercyrail tourist train takes a two-hour journey along the Lot valley up to the cliffs of Saint-Cirq-Lapopie (*see* p. 160), passing through Vers on the way.
After a stop for lunch, the journey continues on the Valentré pleasure boat, which will bring you back to Quai Valentré in Cahors in two-three hours. The journey can also be made in the opposite direction if you prefer. All aboard!

You've never been water-skiing?

Cahors Sport Nautique
Quai de Regourd
☎ **05 65 30 08 02**
Every pm July-Aug.; Wed., Sat. and Sun. pm, June and Sept.

Water-skiers, from beginners to experts, descend on the smooth waters of the Lot to the east of the town as soon as summer comes. If the excitement is too fierce for you, you could opt for a canoe instead.

Water park
Archipel de Cahors
Quai Ludo-Rollès
☎ 05 65 35 31 38
Open daily 10am-
7.30pm, mid-June
to mid-Sept.
Admission charge.
On the Île de Cabessut, on the Lot east of Cahors, this water park is the ideal place to have a splash. Its 4,300-sq-ft (400-sq-m) swimming pool, paddling pool, slides, jacuzzis,

games and water spectacles will delight both children and adults alike.

Mechmont
11 miles (18 km)
N of Cahors
Mylène's miniatures
Mylène Cros
☎ 05 65 36 80 17
Open daily 8am-noon and 2-6.30pm. By appt out of season.
Mylène Cros makes terracotta miniatures that are faithful reproductions of Quercy architecture: shepherds' huts, villages, country houses, mills and pigeon lofts. Her workshop is a real Quercy in miniature, in fact. Items to suit all budgets.

Saint-Pierre-Lafeuille
5 miles (8 km)
N of Cahors
Château de Roussillon
☎ 05 65 36 87 05
Visits by appt.
Admission charge.
With its moats (now dry), drawbridge and keep, this château had one purpose only – to defend Cahors against the English. Despite the ravages of time, it retains several well-restored remains and is well worth a look.

Lalbenque
13 miles (21 km)
SE of Cahors
A market in 'black gold'
Situated in the dry, bare country of the Causse de Limogne, Lalbenque is home to one of the region's most important truffle markets. Every Tuesday from Nov. to June the stallholders gather on the Grand Rue and at 2.30pm sharp, when the village policeman blows his whistle, the cloths are whipped off the baskets and the haggling begins. With prices reaching 2,500F a kilo, negotiations between producers and buyers can be fierce, and although this battle of words is really for traders only, it's worth a detour just to see it.

THE SECRET OF TRUFFLES
Le Montat
7.5 miles (12 km)
S of Cahors
☎ 05 65 21 07 56
Open daily by appt.
Go looking for truffles, with a friendly Labrador dog as your guide. As the location of these fungi is one of Quercy's most jealously guarded secrets, the public has never had the chance to discover them before. Now, however, at the Le Montat test centre you can take a course on the mysteries of the black gem, followed by a walk that is more like an initiation, and a local wine-tasting session. Although truffles can be found almost all the year round, the species harvested vary from one season to another (see p. 52).

On the Cahors wine trail
between the Lot and the slopes

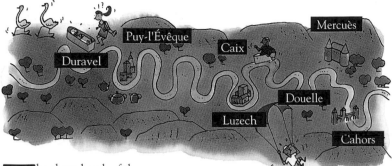

The sharp bends of the River Lot between Cahors and Soturac were formerly the route for the barges carrying wines to Bordeaux. Around these meanders, where charming villages huddle on narrow necks of land, are some 10,400 acres (4,200 ha) of vineyards growing the grapes for the wine that carries the Cahors AOC trademark.

Mercuès

7.5 miles (12 km)
N of Cahors
Château de Mercuès
Hôtel-restaurant
☎ 05 65 20 00 01
Open daily, Easter-1 Nov.
Restaurant closed Mon.
and Tues. lunchtime.

The 13th-C. château towers majestically over the surrounding forest and valley. This listed site, the former residence of the counts and bishops of Cahors, is home to one of the Lot's best restaurants (Set menus 250-360F)

Château storehouses

and dominates the large surrounding vineyard. Visit the storehouses with their Romanesque arches and enjoy the vintage wine with its full, fruity flavour that lingers.

Douelle

2.5 miles (4 km)
SW of Mercuès
Come fly with me...
Spirale paragliding school
☎ 05 65 30 78 20
Open all year.
This school offers the chance to discover the countryside from a hang-glider or paraglider. Two-seater flights and introductory courses allow everyone to enjoy being a birdman in total safety.

Luzech

3.5 miles (6 km)
W of Douelle

A stroll in the old town

Situated on the two slopes of a rocky isthmus and centred on a 13th-C. square keep, this town, which has been besieged several times, most notably by Richard the Lionheart, is noted for its medieval buildings,

OSTRICHES IN QUERCY

Quercy Autruche
Duravel (access signposted)
☎ 05 65 36 47 32
Open daily 4-7pm, July-Aug.; Wed. and Sun. 3-5pm, Apr.-June; Sun. only 3-5pm, Sept.-Mar.
Admission charge (free for under-6s).
On this very unusual farm, the traditional yard is home to ostriches, emus and rheas. After your one-hour visit, you will know all about the life and origin of these exotic birds. The farm shop, meanwhile, holds a few more surprises: eggs, feathers, pastes, lean and special-diet meat, and ostrich hide, which is much sought after for its flexibility and pearly appearance. This is a unique farm that children will love.

Gemelled windows of the Maison des Consuls, Luzech

including the Maison des Consuls, which houses the tourist office. Starting from the keep, a signposted walk takes you to the **Oppidum** (2 miles/ 3 km round-trip). The view from these 2,000-year-old Roman ruins is superb.

Caix

1 mile (2 km) N of Luzech

Water and wine

Navilot water-sports centre
☎ 05 65 20 18 19
Open 1 May-30 Sept.
This village is dominated by the Château of the Prince of Denmark, which produces an excellent Cahors wine offered at a tasting session (☎ 05 65 20 13 22). At the Base Nautique Navilot, situated by a 200-acre (80-ha) lake, you can enjoy swimming, fishing, water-skiing or canoeing, or join a barge or motorboat trip.

Puy-l'Évêque

9 miles (14 km)
W of Luzech

Puy-l'Évêque, pretty and vibrant

Sitting on a promontory overlooking the river, the town seems to be showing off its white buildings and episcopal château. The 13th-C. keep, the **Église Saint-Sauveur** church and medieval houses are all worth seeing. Near to the railway station is the workshop of **Porcelaines Virebent** (admission free ☎ 05 65 21 30 01), which has been making and exhibiting earthenware, porcelain and stoneware since 1924. Every Tuesday morning, Puy is home

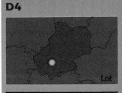

Spotcheck

D4

Things to do

Mercuès wine-tasting
Spirale paragliding
Luzech walks
Puy-l'Évêque tours and fairs
Duravel Romanesque church

With children

Quercy ostrich farm
Caix water-sports centre

Within easy reach

Cahors (11 miles/18 km E), p. 154
Montcuq (15 miles/24 km S), p. 146

Tourist offices

Puy-l'Évêque:
☎ 05 65 21 37 63
Luzech: ☎ 05 65 20 17 27

to a lively market, and also hosts a bric-a-brac fair on the first weekend in July.

Duravel

2 miles (3 km)
W of Puy-l'Évêque

Duravel church

This ancient Gallo-Roman town is home to one of the most attractive 11th-12th-C. churches in the Romanesque style. Its Merovingian crypt, the sculpted columns of the apse and the sarcophagi of three Eastern saints, placed carefully behind the altar and opened to the public every five years, are all well worth visiting. The most recent opening of the mummified remains was in October 2000.

Saint-Cirq-Lapopie in the Lot gorges
an invitation to poetry

I n this area, the River Lot meanders between imposing cliffs of grey and ochre, worn down over time. The best way to travel here is by river, with 40 miles (64 km) navigable from April to November Let the boat do the work and enjoy the spectacular views of the green vegetation, blue river and white chalk cliffs for which Saint-Cirq-Lapopie is justly famous.

Saint-Cirq-Lapopie, view from Popie rock

Saint-Cirq-Lapopie
18.5 miles (30 km)
E of Cahors

First things first...
Leave your car in the car park at the edge of the village (10F per day). Not far away is **Popie rock** (Rocher de la Popie), the remains of an ancient medieval château, with one of the most dramatic views in all of France. The pretty village perfectly offsets the great rock escarpment that towers above it.

Home to the founder of surrealism
This place will enchant you, as it did André Breton, who lived in the old Auberge des Mariniers, noted for its square tower. The shady streets are lined with narrow wood-panelled or stone houses and craft shops and galleries with painted signs, preserving such traditional skills as copper-beating, leather-work and wood-turning.

A house of wood-turning
Maison de la Fourdonne
☎ 05 65 31 21 51
In the heart of the village, this Renaissance house is home to the time-honoured art of wood-turning. There are work-shops, turning demonstrations, restoration, miniatures, an exhibition showing the history of Saint-Cirq-Lapopie and an open-air theatre that welcomes dance troupes, story-tellers, orchestras and film shows in summer.

A walk along the towpath

Down below the village, a path runs alongside the River Lot up to Ganil, the site of Aulanac mill (Moulin d'Aulanac) and a lock-keeper's cottage. This is the starting point for a towpath that leads to the railway bridge and Bouziès lake (Plan d'Eau de Bouziès). Running along the cliff face, this is one of the most dramatic walking trails in the valley.

Cénevières
3.5 miles (6 km)
E of Saint-Cirq-Lapopie
Château de Cénevières
☎ 05 65 31 27 33
Open Easter-1 Nov., 12am-noon and 2-6pm

Château in Cénevières

(2-5pm and mornings by appt only in Oct.).
Admission charge.
In 1580 the future king, Henri IV, visited Antoine de Gourdon, who had just transformed this château into an Italianate Renaissance palace. The gallery, with its Tuscan columns, and the small alchemist's room, are interesting. The Braquilanges family, who have lived here for the past 200 years, will show you round the château with justifiable pride.

Cajarc
15.5 miles (25 km)
E of Saint-Cirq-Lapopie
A veritable feast of culture
Georges Pompidou modern-art centre
☎ 05 65 40 78 19
Open daily Mar.-June and 1 Sept.-15 Nov. exc. Tues. (and Sun. am May-Oct.),10am-noon and 2-6pm; 10am-noon and 3-7pm, July-Aug.
Admission free for under-18s.

Spotcheck
D4

Things to do
Lot gorges, by boat or train
Towpath walk
Wood-turning workshop
Château de Cénevières
Market and bric-a-brac fair
Modern-art centre

With children
Cajarc lake

Within easy reach
Célé valley (9.5 miles/ 15 km N), p. 162
Cahors (18.5 miles/ 30 km W), p. 154

Tourist office
Saint-Cirq-Lapopie:
☎ 05 65 31 29 06

Far from being content to rely on its glorious past, this bastide town has become a renowned centre for modern art. The visit begins in Maison de l'Hébrardie, a remnant of the old château, and carries on along the attractive narrow streets to the fascinating Centre d'Art Contemporain Georges-Pompidou.

Something for everyone...
With its Saturday-afternoon market, bric-a-brac market (Sunday after 14 July) and huge **water-sports centre** on the Lot (follow Rue de Faubourg, opposite the town hall, 550 yds/150 m to the lake), Cajarc has something for everyone. To the east, 4.5 miles (7 km) along the D127, is the **Saut de la Mounine** (*see* p. 74), with its magnificent **viewpoint** that overlooks the Montbrun meander.

BY FOOT, TRAIN OR BOAT
Information from Cahors, Cajarc or Saint-Cirq-Lapopie tourist offices.
From Cahors to Cajarc, passing through the Vers valley, the Lot valley can be discovered by mini-rail or 1950s railcar. But you can also head off on foot from Saint-Cirq-Lapopie, or discover the delights of the river on a gabare (barge) or a houseboat that doesn't require a permit.

Célé valley
for thrills

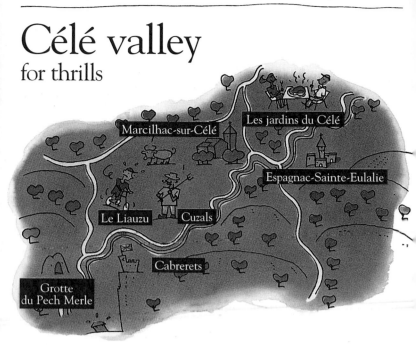

Here the River Célé – from the Latin 'celer', meaning 'fast' – races towards the Lot through steep-sided, richly coloured canyons housing a fine collection of prehistoric caves. Not surprisingly, this is ideal climbing, caving and canoeing territory.

Cabrerets

Cabrerets

18.5 miles (30 km) E of Cahors
Châteaux de Cabrerets
Information from the tourist office
Upstream, the Château des Anglais (a common name in the area) is a medieval fortification carved into the cliff to act as a lookout over the rivers and paths. Downstream, the 14th- to 15th-C. Château de Gontaut-Biron is recognisable by its angled tower and balustraded terrace, perched 80 ft (25 m) above the road.

Cave of pearls
Pech Merle caves
☎ **05 65 31 27 05**
Open daily 9.30am-noon and 1.30-5pm, Palm Sunday-1 Nov. Groups by appt out of season.

The Grotte du Pech Merle has some of the best of all examples of Palaeolithic art. The seven chambers all contain wall-paintings: mammoths standing on their hind legs, women with the attributes of bison, wounded human figures, and even traces of a child's footsteps. All this against a rich background of 'draperies' (calcite deposits that look like hanging sheets) and cave pearls (grains of sand covered by calcite).

Château des Anglais

Le Liauzu

3 miles (5 km)
NE of Cabrerets

Célé river sports

Les Amis du Célé
☎ 05 65 31 26 73
Open Apr.-Nov.

If you want to go climbing,
mountain biking, canoeing or
caving, then note the name of
this sports club. The centre,
built on the river's edge and
surrounded by cliffs, is accessible
only via a footbridge across
the Célé. It has all the facilities
and equipment necessary
for enjoying these exciting
activities in complete safety.

Cuzals

1 mile (2 km)
NE of Le Liauzu

Quercy open-air museum

Musée de Plein Air de Quercy
☎ 05 65 22 58 63
Open daily 2-6pm, Apr.,
May, Sept. and Oct.;
10am-7pm, June-Aug.;
closed Sat. exc. for public
holidays. Groups by appt
out of season.
Admission charge.

This museum, with its
interesting blend of humour
and ethnological genius, allows
both adults and children to
take part in medieval and
19th-C. rural life. Set in 124
acres (50 ha) of land around
the Château de Cuzals, it
boasts 5,000 individual objects,
30 themed exhibitions and
numerous play activities.
There's something to interest
everyone, with old-fashioned
agriculture, reconstruction of
traditional farms, pie-making
in a bakery, bee-keeping, and
medicinal and aromatic plants.

Marcilhac-sur-Célé

8.5 miles (14 km)
NE of Cuzals

A ship-wrecked abbey

Information from tourist office

The remarkable remains of
this 12th-C. **Romanesque
Benedictine abbey** tower
above the nearby lake like a
shipwreck. Visit the fortified
site, wandering along the
maze of narrow streets that
lead you through time, from
the Romanesque part (which
contains France's oldest
Romanesque door)
to the Gothic part.

Espagnac-Sainte-Eulalie

9.5 miles (15 km)
NE of Marcillac-sur-Célé

The belltower of Paradise

Information from the town hall:

> **JARDINS DU CÉLÉ**
> **Espagnac-Sainte-Eulalie**
> **Bookings**
> ☎ 05 65 40 08 34
> Set menus from 80F,
> 45F for under-12s.
> Under the arches of the
> presbytery, discover the
> organic delights of a real country table (Quercy
> lamb, vegetable gratin, and game from the nearby
> farm, which is open for visits). From April to
> September the teas (water-ices, pancakes and fruit
> juices from the 35 different types of fruit grown
> here) are a real delight.

Spotcheck
DE3

Things to do

Pech Merle prehistoric cave
Climbing, mountain biking,
canoeing and caving

With children

Cuzals open-air museum

Within easy reach

*Causse de Gramat (12.5
miles/20 km N), p. 178
Lot gorges (6-9.5
miles/10-15 km S), p. 160
Cahors (18.5 miles/30 km
W), p. 154
Figeac (31 miles/50 km
E), p. 164*

Tourist offices

Cabrerets:
☎ 05 65 31 27 12
Marcilhac-sur-Célé:
☎ 05 65 40 68 44

☎ 05 65 40 09 17

Surrounded by towering grey
cliffs, the pointed roofs of the
village, whose location is
known as 'paradise valley'
(Val-Paradis), cluster around a
13th-C. Augustinian priory.
The church has a magnificent
belltower, 50 ft (15 m) high –
the bell dates from 1518.

House of Pierre de Cisteron

Figeac
medieval and …
Egyptian!

This town, built around an abbey founded in 838, quickly became very prosperous on the wealth of its great merchants. Sitting on the banks of the River Célé, it is now home to a quite remarkable architectural heritage, with arches, narrow streets, timbered homes and opulent hôtels particuliers (townhouses). This historic and artistic town is justifiably proud of its most famous native, the Egyptologist Jean-François Champollion.

Old house, Place Champollion

and red sandstone buildings. Take time to appreciate the layout of arches, façades, soleios (which are covered first-floor galleries) and medieval alleys. The tourist office's discovery tours enable you to explore 1,000 years of history on foot or by car, with themes such as 'Figeac merchants in the Middle Ages' and 'The era of Louis XIV in Figeac'. The night visits, with torches, are particularly exciting.

Hôtel de la Monnaie
Tourist office
Place Vival
☎ 05 65 34 06 25
Open daily May-June (exc. Sun. pm); 10am-1pm and 2-7pm, 1 July-15 Sept.; 10am-noon and 2.30-6pm, 16 Sept.-30 Apr. Closed Sun.
Enter Figeac by Place Vival, where there's a car park. First, visit the Hôtel de la Monnaie, one of France's most celebrated medieval houses. Built in the 13thC., this merchant's residence has been restored and is now home to the tourist office and the old-town museum (Musée du Vieux Figeac). On the ground floor, ask to see the Sully room, whose lock is cleverly hidden by a lion's tongue.

Torch-light tours
From Place Vival, go on to the old town, with its rich ochre

Supported windows, Hôtel de la Monnaie

Musée Champollion
4, Rue des Frères Champollion
☎ 05 65 50 31 08
Open Tues.-Sun. (daily July-Aug.) Mar.-Oct, 10am-noon and 2.30-6.30pm; 2-6pm Nov-Feb. Open Mon. from Easter to Whitsun. Closed 1 Jan, 1 May and 25 Dec.
Right in the heart of the old town, the birthplace of Jean-François Champollion, who first decoded hieroglyphics, is now a museum. Two floors are devoted to displays of papyrus, steles, mummies, sarcophagi

Replica of the Rosetta Stone

and other objects from the days of the Pharaohs. At the end of Rue des Frères-Champollion, pause to admire the huge replica of the Rosetta Stone, enlarged 200 times, designed by contemporary artist Joseph Kosuth. This area is known as Place des Écritures.

Artisans street
Rue Émile Zola, next to Place Champollion and one of Figeac's oldest streets, is a favourite haunt of artists. The most interesting sight is the

Place des Écritures

earthenware workshop of **Nadine Miniot** at no. 47; her demonstration of how she paints her lace designs, using just a very fine brush, is fascinating. The artwork and earthenware are of the very highest quality.

A mix of markets
Every Saturday morning, the covered market in Place Carnot fills up with all kinds of stalls. On selected Thursday nights in July and August there is a **market of local products**, from 6pm until midnight, with shows and tasting sessions. Antique hunters will head for the great **bric-a-brac fair** (Foire à la Brocante), which takes place during the second fortnight in August.

An aptly-named restaurant
La Cuisine du Marché
15, Rue Clermont
☎ 05 65 50 18 55
Closed Sun.

In the centre of old Figeac, Joël Centeno offers light and richly flavoured cuisine

Spotcheck
E3

Things to do
Hot-air ballooning
Musée Champollion
Earthenware art visit
Bric-a-brac and evening markets
Horse and pony rides
Gourmet stop
Château Jazz festival

With children
Surgié leisure park
Seyrignac mill
Capdenac-le-Haut miniature port
Cardaillac open museum

Within easy reach
Célé valley (18.5 miles/30 km W), p. 162
Villefranche-de-Rouergue (22 miles/35 km S), p. 208

Tourist offices
Figeac: ☎ 05 65 34 06 25
Capdenac: ☎ 05 65 64 74 87

CARDAILLAC MUSEUM
9.5 miles (15 km) NW of Figeac
☎ 05 65 40 10 63
Open 3-6pm, July-Aug. By appt out of season. *Admission charge.*
At the Musée Éclaté de Cardaillac, children can discover and take part in early 20th-C. life. This museum re-creates and preserves an entire district of an early-20thC. village, complete with village school, prune-drying workshops, old craft shops, an oil-mill with its press, and many other places full of interest and nostalgia.

An early 20th C. school

prepared using local market produce. He is also one of the few truly great fish chefs. The atmosphere is warm and welcoming. Set menus around 70-230F.

Surgié leisure park

☎ 05 65 34 59 00
Open daily 11am-10pm, July-Aug. Open 2-7pm Wed., Sun. and public holidays, during term time.

Near to the town centre, the Parc de Loisirs du Surgié, on the banks of the Célé, includes a 35-acre (14-ha) lake with a beach, and a water centre offering wave pools, slides, jacuzzis and paddling pools. Children will love the play area, with its trampolines, bouncy castles and floating island. In addition, swimming, fishing and canoe and pedalo hire are available, and there are several different types of show.

Place Carnot

Trot or gallop?

Figeac horse and pony club

Avenue Neyrac
☎ 05 65 34 70 57
Open all year.

On horses or ponies, with rides lasting an hour or a day or accompanied rides lasting several days – at the Club Figeacois du Cheval et du Poney, beginners and experienced riders, young and old alike, can saddle-up in complete safety.

··

Fons

6 miles (10 km)
NW of Figeac

Gourmet stop

Les Sols de Fons

☎ 05 65 40 11 54
Open Wed., July-Aug., or by request.
Admission free.

Fancy a Quercy gastronomic treat? This conserve centre will welcome you and introduce you to local cuisine and the preparation of foie gras. There are menu ideas and, once your appetite is whetted, there are tasting sessions to help you appreciate the delightful dishes.

And, as if that were not enough, Fons itself is truely a charming little village.

··

Loupiac
7.5 miles (12 km)
S of Figeac

Hot-air ballooning in Olt country

Ballon Libre en Vallée d'Olt

Le Mas du Causse
☎ 05 65 64 63 50

THE GREAT CHÂTEAU

Château d'Assier
16 miles (26 km) NW of Figeac
☎ 05 65 40 40 99
Open all-year round, 9.30am-12.30pm
and 2-6.45pm (exc. Tues.).
This jewel of the Renaissance, situated on the edge of the Causse de Gramat, is every bit as splendid as the royal residences. It reflects the mad lust for power of Lord Galiot de Genouillac (1465-1546), the chief equerry to King François I. Although only part of the château now remains, its interior decoration, inspired by Chambord and Blois, has all the refinement of the Loire châteaux. The church, which contains Galiot's tomb, is also well worth a detour because of its magnificent frieze. Floodlit in summer, the château stages a number of concerts; probably the most notable is the garden Jazz festival ('Jardin dans Tous ses États') in early August, with a mixture of modern music, visual arts, dance and theatre. ☎ 05 65 40 42 42.

Claudine and Patrick Legendre, both professional pilots, will take you over the most attractive villages in Rouergue in a multi-coloured balloon. This is an unforgettable introduction to hot-air ballooning, but it's not cheap – 800F per person for a 1-hour flight. Flights available 7am-7pm.

Capdenac-le-Haut
4.5 miles (7 km)
SE of Figeac
**Like the prow
of a ship**
Situated on a promontory, this pretty village, whose name means 'ship's head', dominates a peninsula formed by a loop in the River Lot. This much-sought-after defence site was once the ancient settlement of Uxellodunum, the last city in Gaul to be conquered by Julius Caesar. Often besieged, the fortress, which is right on the departmental boundary between Lot and Aveyron, is surrounded by 13th-C. ramparts; its gate is flanked by a square keep, barbicans and watchtowers.

**Children's
miniature port**
☎ 05 65 64 74 87
You can pilot a channel ferry, a trawler or a tug, even if you're only three feet tall! At the foot of Capdenac-le-Haut, the Plan d'Eau des Berges du Lot water park has a miniature port, in which children can steer miniature reproductions of real boats. It is also combined with a recreation area, offering mini-golf, canoes, kayaks, pedalos and mountain bikes.

Lunan
3.5 miles (6 km)
E of Figeac
**Seyrignac,
Lord of Art**
Seyrignac mill
☎ 05 65 34 48 32
Visits by appt.
This is one of just four windmills still operational in Quercy, and certainly one of the prettiest. Bought 15 years ago by two enthusiasts who now live there, the Moulin de Seyrignac, which dates from the 15th C., has been painstakingly restored. However little wind there is, this stone giant can grind flour due to its 40-ft (12-m) height and 860 sq feet (80 sq m) of canvas.

Causse de Martel
and the town of the seven towers

The smallest of the Causses du Quercy, a mere 980 ft (300 m) above sea level, is also the least arid, the least remote, and the most hospitable; but strangely enough, it is also the least visited. A pity, as its capital, Martel, is so full of history it could be called 'museum town'.

Cavagnac

Puy d'Issolud

Martel

Creysse

Martel
13.5 miles (22 km) N of Rocamadour

Town of seven towers

Some are wide, some are slender; they include a bell tower, a clock tower, a house turret and a watch tower. Together, these seven towers dominate the town of Martel. In summer, the town comes alive with the **Tondailles wool fair** (Foire à la Laine), on 23 July, the **comics festival** (Festival de BD) on the last Sunday in July, and the Haut Quercy **classical music festival** (Festival de Musique Classsique) in July and August.

A covered market, palace and church

The town centre is dominated by the Place des Consuls, boasting an 18th-C. market place with a wooden roof resting on huge stone pillars (market held Wednesday and Saturday mornings). Nearby,

Palais de la Raymondie, built in the 13th and 14thC., is flanked by watch towers and a crenellated bell tower, and is home to a little **archaeological museum** (Musée Archéologique) showing the Gaulish excavations at **Puy d'Issolud** (8.5 miles/14 km northeast of Martel). Not far away is the 13th-14th-C. Gothic Église Saint-Maur, with its 160-ft (48-m) clock tower.

Get lost!
Labyrinthus
Parc des Labyrinthes
3 miles (5 km) S of Martel on the N140, towards Gluges and Creysse
☎ 05 65 32 20 30

Palais de la Raymondie

Open daily 10.30am-7.30pm July-Aug. Allow a full day. *Admission charge.*

Getting lost is a real delight in this huge maze with its towering hedges. As you enter, clowns leap out from the hedges and drag you into the labyrinth, populated with figures from Ancient Egypt.

In the centre is a blue and gold mask of Tutankhamen, made from flowers and fragments of minerals. The elevated lookout has a panoramic view of the maze.

A nutty story
Moulin de Martel
On the D703, towards Vayrac
☎ 05 65 37 38 39

Open daily exc. Mon. Apr.-Oct. By appt. Located in an old hunting lodge, this is a farm-inn that manufactures small amounts of top-quality, **pure-nut oil**. During the winter months and every Saturday in summer, the Castagné family demonstrates the fine art, with a commentary. The nuts that they harvest are crushed and the hydraulic press produces a beautiful, delicately perfumed, pale-coloured oil.

Haut Quercy by train
Depart from Martel station
☎ 05 65 37 35 81

Spotcheck
D2-3

Lot

Things to do
Visit an oil mill
Visit the Cavagnac artists

With children
Discover the world of reptiles
Get lost at Labyrinthus
Haut Quercy by train

Within easy reach
Souillac (9.5 miles/15 km SW), p. 180
Rocamadour and the Merveilles trail (15.5 miles/25 km S), pp. 170 and 174

Tourist office
Martel:
☎ 05 65 37 43 44

See the Dordogne from an unusual angle. This old railway line, running from Bordeaux to Aurillac, traverses the cliff face overlooking the valley at 260 ft (80 m). At the end of the 19thC., it carried as much as the barges. This 4.5-mile (7-km) stretch takes you from Martel to Saint-Denis and back, with a choice of steam or diesel engine.

Cavagnac
6 miles (10 km)
N of Martel
Art galore
Hameau Pélissié
Open Apr.-Sept.

Five very different art forms are on show at Puy Troubadour – **sculptures** by Lucien Ghomri (☎ 05 65 32 02 10), **glass windows** by Marc Baujard (☎ 05 65 32 02 37), **glass-blowing** by Steven Jackson, **ornamental knives** by Patrick Hupp (☎ 05 65 32 00 35), and **paintings and frescoes** by Henry Bonnet-Madin (☎ 05 65 32 00 69).

REPTILES AT REST
Reptiland
N140 (about 0.5 mile/800 m from Figeac)
☎ 05 65 37 41 00
Open 10am-6pm, July-Aug., 10am-noon and 2-6pm, other months. Closed 5-31 Jan. and Mon. (exc. July-Aug.).
Admission charge.

Did you know that the iguana has three eyes, loves oranges and bananas, and was around long before prehistoric man appeared? And did you know that the Massasauga dwarf rattlesnake has an extraordinary venom that helps blood to clot and is often used in dentist's surgeries, in tiny amounts, to stop bleeding? These are just two of the remarkable discoveries that await you at Reptiland, an educational park that is home to almost 200 animals – lizards, snakes, tortoises, crocodiles, scorpions and snakes – can be seen here in peaceful surroundings. The track game is a must too.

Green Iguana

Rocamadour
the miracle city

The history of the city of Rocamadour, which sits in the wildest of the Lot valley's causses, is written in its stone buildings, its cliffs and its holy letters. The second most important listed site in France after Mont-Saint-Michel, its delightful medieval houses, the dizzying panoramic views and the natural atmosphere of its animal parks are a jewel of civilisation amid the wild emptiness of the surrounding country.

Château de Rocamadour

Shrines

The town is named after the little-known Saint Amadour, who built a primitive shrine, dedicated to the Virgin Mary, in the cliff; originally destroyed in a rock fall, the shrine has been rebuilt several times. The discovery of the Saint's body, perfectly preserved, under the threshold of the cathedral in 1166, made

Rocamadour famous throughout Europe and turned it into a place of pilgrimage. From the top, admire the view from the château before going half-way back down to visit the city, with its seven churches and chapels huddled together on the cliff face. From the top, a lift goes down to the medieval city; it's free if you buy a Pass'Découverte

from the tourist office (adults 74F, children 48F), which offers reduced admission charges for most attractions in Rocamadour and L'Hospitalet.

Eagles' rock

220 yards (200 m) from Château de Rocamadour car park
☎ **05 65 33 65 45**
Open daily 10am-6pm, July-Aug.; 10am-noon and 2-6pm, Apr.-Nov. Closed 11 Nov. and Dec.-Mar.

Admission charge.
On the high plateau stretching behind the Château, take time to visit the aviaries at the Rocher des Aigles (Eagles' Rock). This place is home to about 100 birds of prey, and the flight of the great vultures, which soar to over 3,000 ft (1,000 m) before flying down again to rejoin their handlers, can be admired from nearby.

Museum of old toys

Place Ventadour
☎ 05 65 33 60 75
Open daily 10am-noon and 2-6pm, 15 Mar.-15 Nov. Closed 16 Nov.-14 Mar.
Admission charge.
Both adults and children will be fascinated by the Musée du Jouet Ancien, located at the entrance to the medieval city.

About 100 pedal cars, tricycles, scooters, boats and other means of 'transport', dating from the early 20thC. to the 1960s, fill the four exhibition halls. This private collection has been amassed by Christian Delpech, who will enthusiastically welcome you to his museum.

The medieval city

Halfway up the rock is the old city of Rocamadour, protected by its fortified gates.

Spotcheck
D3

Lot

Things to do

Gourmet stop at the distillery
Dinner at Beau Site
Festivals and concerts
Canyon walks
Barouche rides

With children

Eagles' rock
Museum of old toys
Amazing automata
Monkey forest
House of bees

Within easy reach

Cramat (6 miles/10 km SE), p. 178
Martel (12.5 miles/20 km N), p. 168
Saint-Céré (17 miles/ 27 km NE), p. 174

Tourist office

Rocamadour:
☎ 05 65 33 22 00

'BEAU SITE' TERRACES

Restaurant Beau Site
Rue Roland-le Preux
☎ 05 65 33 63 08
Open daily exc. mid-Nov. to end Jan.
The terraces of this restaurant, in the very heart of the medieval city, offer not only stunning views over the surrounding valley but delicious dishes of the distinctive local cuisine (conserve of duck foie gras cooked in cloth in Monbazillac wine or loin of Quercy farm lamb in tomato juice with seasonal vegetables, basil and garlic). These remarkable dishes are created by the chef, Laurent Carlier (Set menus 110 and 195F). A bar section offers a faster service, with prices ranging from 60 to 89F.

Leave your car at the entrance, as the city is pedestrianised, and enjoy walking past the splendid houses with their brown roof tiles and the trade buildings along the main street, Rue Roland-le-Preux. At the end of this street is the beginning of the Grand Escalier, the huge staircase which leads to the shrines.

A paradise of fruit and liqueurs

Distillerie du Périgord
Rue Roland-le-Preux
☎ 05 65 33 65 44
Open daily 9.30am-7pm. This smart, top-of-the-range shop offers an irresistible selection of fruit treasures. Its shelves display hundreds of bowls with fruit in alcohol – the Morello cherries are

probably the best – and elegant bottles containing pastis, chestnut liqueur and nut wine. All these delights have been manufactured since 1860 by the parent distillery in Sarlat, and regularly receive awards for their superior quality.

Shows all year round

The town is home to many different shows, possibly the best of which are the classical concerts and variety shows held on Wednesday evenings in July and August in the basilica or the valley, and usually free. Rocamadour also celebrates its famous miniature goat during the cheese festival (Fête des Fromages) on Whit Sunday. Finally, on the last Sunday in September the sky is filled with a display of brilliantly coloured hot-air balloons.

L'Hospitalet
N of Rocamadour
Panoramic lookout

Linked to the medieval holy city by the Voie Sainte, a long, winding path, the ancient village of L'Hospitalet offers a magnificent view of nearby Rocamadour from its belvedere – more than just a viewpoint.

The cave of miracles

☎ 05 65 33 67 92
Open Apr.-Nov., 10am-noon and 2-6pm (9am-7pm, July-Aug).
Admission charge.
The prehistoric Grotte des Merveilles, situated next to the tourist office, will whisk you into a magic world of crystalline rock formations that reflect the underground waterways, and ancient cave-paintings 20,000 years old with clearly recognisable deer and horses as well as human handprints.

Amazing automata

La Féerie du Rail

☎ 05 65 33 71 06
Open daily, with 5-8 shows daily in summer. Closed Nov.-Mar.
Admission charge.
From the outside, you wouldn't believe that this modest building is home to a most remarkable miniature world. The 45-minute tour will show you miniature working models of trains, towns, landscapes, circuses, châteaux, factories and people – all on a fascinating small scale and accompanied by the background noise of daily life.

The house of bees

La Maison des Abeilles

☎ 05 65 33 66 98
Open daily 11am-7pm, July-Aug.; 11am-5pm, out of season, Wed., Sun., public and school holidays.
Admission charge with 1-hour guided tour.
Opposite the Forêt des Singes, 500,000 bees live in a series of hives opened to the public by the bee-keeping association. During the guided tour of the Maison des Abeilles you will see a video explaining the bee's life cycle and assist in a bee-handling demonstration. Afterwards, enjoy a tasting session and visit the shop, where honey, wax, royal jelly, mead and pollen are all available.

A ramble along the canyon

Balades Nature

Information from tourist office
☎ 05 65 33 74 13

Rocamadour and the surrounding area is cut across by several paths, alternating between wild, high country and the depths of the Alzou canyon. There are four interesting trails, of varying distance, open to everybody

House of bees

and known as 'Balades Nature'. Each one is more impressive than the next they will lead you to sources of rivers, waterfalls, long, low walls, an old water-mill and a dolmen. The walks also offer a unique opportunity

to learn about, and of course, appreciate the flora of the protected area of the Causses within its own environment.

Alzou canyon

FORÊT DES SINGES (MONKEY FOREST)
☎ 05 65 33 62 72 or 05 65 38 79 45
Open daily Apr.-Oct.; 10am-7pm, July-Aug., closed noon-1pm, other months.
Admission charge.
In this huge 25-acre (10-ha) park, both children and parents can try to spot a macaque leaping from branch to branch, a female monkey carrying a baby or a whole family of monkeys delousing each other. About 100 monkeys live here in total freedom, and will frequently come to ask the visitors sweetly for some popcorn. This is a remarkable place that should not be missed, all the more so because it is actively involved in helping to preserve the endangered Barbary Apes of North Africa and return them to their habitat.

Barbary Apes grooming one another

Lafage
1 mile (2 km) N of L'Hospitale
Don't spare the horses!
La Grelotière
☎ 05 65 33 67 16
Open all year.
Take the weight off your feet and enjoy a leisurely ride in a barouche carriage. This is probably the best way to discover Rocamadour from the cliff road, which runs through the surrounding countryside right up to Eagles' rock.

Circuit des Merveilles
and Saint-Céré country

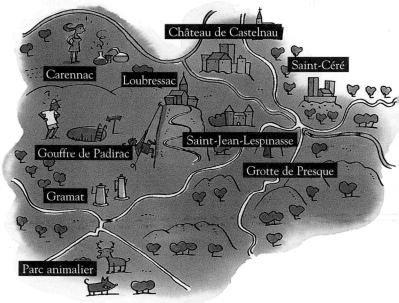

Château de Castelnau

Saint-Céré

Carennac

Loubressac

Gouffre de Padirac

Saint-Jean-Lespinasse

Grotte de Presque

Gramat

Parc animalier

N ot for nothing is this area known as the 'Circuit des Merveilles' ('miracle trail') – it is a miracle of creation and an ideal retreat from the crowds. Come here to see a magical world, with rushing streams and pale, opalescent greenery, the fairy-tale villages of Loubressac and Autoire, and the great pothole at Padirac, the crowning glory of the area.

Saint-Céré

15.5 miles (25 km) NE of Rocamadour

Riverside houses

Sitting between the two branches of the River Bave, Saint-Céré offers the visitor two remarkable locations: the Place du Mercadial (the market square) with venerable timbered houses and the Quai des Récollets, where the mature gardens of the houses run down to the lazy river. The little stone bridges and the chapel bell tower of the Chapelle des Récollets combine to make this a really delightful area.

Place du Mercadial

Spotcheck
DE3

Lot

Things to do

Saint-Céré lyric festival, fairs
and markets
Jean Lurçat's tapestries
Maquis arts and crafts
Golf
Climbing
Gramat pewterware

With children

Presque cave
Padirac great hole
Aromatheque
Maison de la Dordogne
Parc Animalier

Within easy reach

*Causse de Martel (15.5
miles/25 km NW), p. 168
Dordogne valley (9.5
miles/15 km N), p. 180
Rocamadour (15.5
miles/25 km W), p. 170
Le Ségala (10 miles/
16 km E), p. 184*

Tourist offices

Carennac:
☎ 05 65 10 97 01
Gramat: ☎ 05 65 38 73 60
Saint-Céré:
☎ 05 65 38 11 85

Tastes and sounds of summer

In summer, the town is suddenly transformed into a hive of activity by its lyric festival (Festival Lyrique, p. 70) and numerous fairs and markets: the fair is on the first and third Wednesday of every month, all-year round; there is a Saturday morning market; craftspeople visit the town in July; a bric-a-brac fair takes

Maison des Consuls

place on the third Sunday in July; and the potters' market is held in mid-August.

Lurçat tapestries
**Atelier-musée
Jean-Lurçat**
☎ 05 65 38 00 02
Open Palm Sunday-
Sunday after Easter
and 14 July-30 Sept.,
9.30am-noon
and 2.30-6.30pm.
Admission charge.

Château de Montal and golf course

The two square towers (12th and 14thC.) of Saint-Laurent stand tall on the hill overlooking Saint-Céré. Bought by Jean Lurçat (1892-1966) in 1945, they were once the workshop in which his huge and ingenious collection of tapestries was made. Everything in this museum, from the walls with their decorated beams through the scribbled sketches to the finished tapestries, is a testimony to his fascinating life and work.

Atelier de Maquis
304, Avenue des Maquis
☎ 05 65 38 04 80
Open Mon.-Fri. 9am-
noon and 2-6pm
This artists' workshop is an ideal place to find a piece of real quality, as it brings together many artists working in a host of different creative media (glass, sculpture, photographs, lithographs, ceramics, paintings, engravings and others). A fascinating combination of aesthetic beauty and originality.

Saint-Jean-Lespinasse
*1 mile (2 km)
W of Saint-Céré*
Reconstructed château
Château de Montal
☎ 05 65 38 13 72
Open daily exc. Sat.

25 Mar.-1 Nov.,
9.30am-noon
and 2.30-6pm. Closed
2 Nov. to mid-Mar.
Admission charge.
The appearance of this Renaissance château and its magnificent sculpted Carennac stone staircase, one of the best in France, is just as interesting as its history. Sold in pieces to museums all over the world, it owes its reconstruction to the tireless efforts of just one owner. Probably its most interesting feature is the 16th- and 17th-C. furniture. Next to the château is a **golf course** (☎ 05 65 10 83 09).

Place des Consuls, Bretenoux

Saint-Médard-de-Presque

3 miles (5 km)
W of Autoire
Presque cave
Grotte de Presque
☎ 05 65 38 31 04
and 05 65 38 07 44
Open daily 15 Feb.-15
Nov., 9am-noon
and 2-6pm (9am-7pm,
July-Aug.). Closed
Dec.-14 Feb.
Admission charge.
Visit lasts 40 minutes.
From tiny columns as thin as
candles to great pillars, this
cave offers a remarkable
variety of formations of all
shapes and colours. Nearby
is the 14th-C. Manoir de
Presque, with its dovecote.

Prudhomat

5 miles (8 km)
NW of Saint-Céré
The red triangle
Château de Castelnau
☎ 05 65 10 98 00
Open 9.30am-6.45pm,
July-Aug., daily 10am-
noon and 2-5.45pm,
rest of the year. Closed
Tues. Oct.-Mar. and 1
Jan., 1 May, 11 Nov.
and 25 Dec.
Near to the fortified bastide
of **Bretenoux** (where the

galleried Place des Consuls
should not be missed) is the
imposing feudal Château de
Castelnau, built of red brick
in a triangular shape and
considered one of France's
finest. It contains a remarkable
collection of furniture and
art from the Middle Ages to
the 18th C.

Carennac

8 miles (13 km)
NW of Saint-Céré
'Something smells good'
**Distillation museum
and 'Aromathèque'**
**At the entrance
to the Parc du Château**
☎ 05 65 10 91 16
Open daily 10am-1pm
and 2-7pm.
Carennac is well worth a visit
– to see its narrow streets and

old, brown-tiled houses, the
art treasures in the old
priory (the cloister and the
chapterhouse tomb) once
directed by Fénelon (1651-
1715) and for the magnificent
view of the Dordogne.
The Musée des Alambics et
Aromathèque will test your
sense of smell and offers a
demonstration of the
distillation of lavender
(4.30pm in high season).

Down the river and back in time
**Maison de la
Dordogne
Quercynoise**
Château de Carennac
☎ 05 65 10 91 56
Open daily 10am-7pm,
July-Sept.; telephone at
other times.
Admission charge.
Everything you always wanted
to know about the River
Dordogne (geology, flora,
fauna, fishing, sailing etc.)
can be found at the Maison
de la Dordogne. This
permanent exhibition, which
covers three floors of the
16th-C. Château de
Carennac, traces the
relationship between man
and the river from prehistory
to the present day. The
sophisticated audio-visual
displays, including 3-D
projection and dioramas, will
help both young and not so
young learn with pleasure.

Château de Castelnau

THE GREAT HOLE

Gouffre de Padirac
9.5 miles (15 km)
W of Saint-Céré
☎ **05 65 33 64 56**
Open daily 1 Apr.-
second Sun. in Oct.
Tour lasts 90 minutes
(timetable available).
For centuries this
remarkable natural
well was a source
of fear for the local
population, who
believed it to be the
dwelling-place of the
devil (p. 75). A boat
ride, 335 ft (103 m)
underground, will take
you along the River
Plane and show you
the mysterious Lac de
la Pluie ('rain lake'), the
yellow and red Grande
Pendeloque ('great
pendant'), the Grands
Gours chamber and
thousands of finely
shaped stalactites and
stalagmites. Near the
cave is the Historial,
with an interesting
reconstruction of the
history of the cave
since the pre-Cambrian
and Tropicorama, an
interesting collection of
cacti, rare plants and
tropical animals.

Autoire
5.5 miles (9 km)
W of Saint-Céré
A spectacular climb

The Lot offers a spectacular
setting for all lovers of
climbing, although some areas
are out of bounds (information
from Cahors climbing
association (☎ 05 65 35 94
06) or Emmanuel Salles
(☎ 05 65 31 38 56). The cliff,
which has a 100-ft (30-m)
waterfall, offers a view of the
gorge and the village of
Autoire, nestling beneath the
slopes, surrounded by
greengage orchards, with the
brown tiles of its roofs
blending in with the ochre
stone of the old houses.
Nearby, in the same style, is
Loubressac, a fortified clifftop
village built like an eagle's
nest, which dominates the
valleys and châteaux of the
region – an impregnable
rampart with an unforgettable
view over Haut Quercy.

Gramat
12.5 miles (20 km)
SW of Saint-Céré
Arsène Maigne pewterware

Les Étains Arsène Maigne
1, Rue Gabaudet
☎ **05 65 38 74 94**
Open daily 9am-noon
and 2-7pm.
Near to the forge, where 77-lb
(35-kg) tin ingots are still
founded and then cast into
iron moulds, this huge shop
displays some 600
reproductions or restorations
of old pewterware. With prices
from 100F to 2,500F, there is
bound to be something to suit
your taste and budget among
the bewildering array of
goblets, plates and dishes.

Floral garden in the animal park

Park of a thousand animals

Parc Animalier
Route du Cajarc (D14)
☎ **05 65 38 81 22**
Open daily Easter-Sept.,
9am-7pm; 2-6pm
Oct.-Easter.
Admission charge.
Almost 1,000 European
animals live in this 100-acre
(40-ha) park, including
wolves, lynx, deer, yak,
jackals, foxes and bison. A
selection of domestic animals
will delight the children and
give them an insight into
traditional farm life. A two-
hour visit also takes in a
floral garden and geological
trail. Don't miss the wolves'
dinner party, at 11.30am
every day in July and August
– a delightful prelude to your
own picnic, which you can
bring along.

Autoire gorge

Labastide-Murat and the Causse de Gramat

Statue of Murat

The Causse de Gramat is undoubtedly the wildest of all the Lot's causses, covered by high moorland and cut across by the canyons of the Alzou and Ouysse. The view from the high plateau extends from the mountains of Auvergne to the Pyrenees. To the southwest, the town of Labastide-Murat is at the junction of the roads that cross the high, bare areas, and despite its sleepy appearance, it is famous for its lively fairs and markets.

Labastide-Murat

*20 miles (32 km)
NE of Cahors*

The Prince's town

Musée Murat
☎ **05 65 21 19 23**
(town hall)
Open daily 10am-noon and 3-6pm, July-Sept. Closed Oct.-June.
Admission charge.

This town is, as its name suggests, a bastide, founded in the 13th C. and named Fortanière or Fortunière. In 1852 Napoleon III allowed the name of the town to be changed to Murat in honour of Joachim Murat (1767-1815), maréchal of the Empire, brother-in-law of Napoleon I and King of Naples. This was a remarkable rise to eminence for this innkeeper's son, whose house has now been transformed into a museum and exhibits furniture, documents and various other objects that belonged to the Prince's family. There is a sharp contract indeed between this modest family house and the château, built in the Empire style by Joachim for his brother André; it's at the entrance to the town, but unfortunately not open to the

Sheep farm on the Causse de Gramat

public. André, unlike Joachim, remained in France, becoming mayor of the town from 1800 to 1815.

Popular fairs

Info. from tourist office
Although many local people have migrated to larger towns, Labastide-Murat is still the agricultural capital of the l southern Causse de Gramat. Its fairs, on the second and fourth Monday of each month in the Place de la Mairie, attract visitors from a wide area. There is a producer's market (marché

Murat's birthplace

LABASTIDE-MURAT AND THE CAUSSE DE GRAMAT • 179

Causse de Gramat between Soulomès and Cagnac

des producteurs) every Sunday in July and August, from 9am to noon, and two bric-a-brac fairs (Foire à la Brocante), in mid-July and mid-August.

Leisure time in Labastide

The popular **footpaths** of the causse take in moorland, sheepfolds, caves and great hollows (information from the tourist office). There is a small **golf course** at **Bourat** (2 miles/3 km south of Labastide-Murat 05 65 21 11 34) and **aeroplane trips** are offered at **Montfaucon flying school** (École de Pilotage de Montfaucon, on the D10, 6 miles/10 km north of Labastide-Murat ☎ 05 65 31 13 50).

Le Bastit
7.5 miles (12 km)
NE of Labastide-Murat
A simply spectacular sinkhole

The action of water on the limestone plateau has, over thousands of years, produced spectacular underground structures. The whole of the plateau is criss-crossed by caves, with grottoes, hollows, wells, chambers and sinkholes. The most remarkable of these is Igue de la Vierge, with a gallery 650 ft (200 m) long and a sinkhole 82 ft (25 m) deep (this is private property).

Séniergues
6 miles (10 km)
N of Labastide-Murat
Ochre and grey

Séniergues is one of the most beautiful villages in the Causse, with its red-grey houses, patterned with ochre, and brown roofs. The 12th-C. church is quite fascinating as it is built in the form of a

View of Séniergues

Greek cross. Nearby is a remnant of the old château, which has been incorporated into a private house.

Carlucet windmill

Spotcheck
D3

Things to do

Fairs and markets
Walking tours
Golf
Aeroplane trips

Within easy reach

*Rocamadour (15.5 miles/25 km N), pp. 170
Circuit des Merveilles (28 miles/45 km NE), p. 174
Gourdon (13.5 miles/ 22 km W), p. 182*

Tourist office

Labastide-Murat:
☎ 05 65 21 11 39

Carlucet
7.5 miles (12 km)
N of Labastide-Murat
Carlucet windmill
Moulin des Anglais
Info. ☎ 05 65 38 72 83
Tours Sun. pm in summer; by appt, rest of the year.
Admission charge.

The existence of this mill was first recorded in a survey in 1168. It's French name means 'the English mill', since its two-stone mechanism is unique in Quercy but found frequently in England, as well as in Aquitaine.

The Dordogne valley in Quercy

focus on beauty

Souillac

Saint-Sozy

Grottes de Lacave

Château de la Treyne

The Dordogne tumbles through this valley with the speed and energy of a mountain river. This section of the valley, although only 37.5 miles (60 km) long, contains a remarkable variety of landscapes and exceptional tourist attractions.

Sainte-Marie abbey church, Souillac

Souillac

22 miles (35 km)
NW of Rocamadour
Three cupolas of Sainte-Marie
Église Sainte-Marie
292, Place Pierre-Betz
Free visits 9am-7pm daily, throughout the year.
Sitting at the confluence of the Dordogne and Borrèze rivers, this town grew up around the remarkable 12th-C. Benedictine Abbatiale Sainte-Marie de Souillac. The abbey church boasts a large nave with three cupolas, an apse and three radiating chapels, and is also well known for its statues, especially those of the prophet Isaiah, Jacob wrestling with the angel and an extraordinary tableau of monsters.

A happy upheaval

In summer, life in Souillac is turned upside down; the medieval city is floodlit, and a train visits the old districts and the nearby banks of the Dordogne (☎ 05 65 32 65 91). In addition, there are a wide variety of special events: a Jazz festival ('Souillac en Jazz') in early July, classical music concerts and the national arts fair (featuring local artists) in July and Aug., and the puppet and mime festival ('Festival du Mime Automate') in August. Pick up a programme from the tourist office.

Lacave

3.5 miles (6 km)
SE of Souillac
Château dining
Château de la Trayne
☎ 05 65 27 60 60
Admisson free. Closed Tues. and Wed. pm (exc. July-Aug.).
Menu prices 220F to 420F.
In the King Louis XIII salon or on the terrace overlooking the Dordogne; you can enjoy the peace and harmony of the

Château de la Treyne

Spotcheck
D3

Lot

Things to do

Souillac fairs and shows
Lacave caves
Dinner at Château de la Treyne
Foie gras production centre

With children

Museum of automation
'Prehistologia' park

Within easy reach

*Rocamadour and Circuit des Merveilles (12.5 miles/20 km SE), pp. 170 and 174
Gourdon (18.5 miles/30 km SW), p. 182
Causse de Martel (9.5 miles/15 km NE), p. 168*

Tourist office

Souillac:
☎ 05 65 37 81 56

French-style gardens and the view of the forest stretching away out of sight. Then sample the delights of fresh langoustine (lobster) pâté, the masterpiece of the young chef, Stéphane Andrieux.

Jurassic Park in the Lot valley
Prehistologia
☎ 05 65 32 28 28
Open 10am-6pm, July-Aug. Telephone out of season.
Admission charge.
The life-size dinosaur models in this prehistory park are enough to make you shiver. A woodland path almost 1 mile (1.5 km) long takes you past a 21st-C. light-and-surround-sound display, and offers you a chance to greet a brachiosaurus or a pteranodon, with its 26-foot (8-m) wingspan, and visit a Neolithic village.

Cave mirages
Lacave caves
2.5 miles (4 km) S of Château de la Trayne
Open daily 9.30am-6pm, July-25 Aug. Telephone out of season.
Admission charge.
At the Grottes de Lacave, thousands of years of calcite deposits have produced spectacular shapes, including those of huge animals, in the 12 chambers 460 ft (140 m) underground. Not only that, but there is a cave with an underground lake, in which

thousands of stalactites are reflected eerily and produce extraordinary underground mirages. A lift and electric train will transport you effortlessly around this remarkable cavern.

Saint-Sozy
9.5 miles (15 km) SE of Souillac
An original taste
Quercy Périgord Fermier
☎ 05 65 32 22 88
Open July-Aug., Tues. and Wed. am, 10am-12.30pm. Gates open 10am Fri.
Free visit to conserve house and tasting sessions.
Traditional skills, culinary secrets and modern production techniques are the

keys to the success of this foie gras and duck fillet centre, which has won several medals at the Paris agricultural show. The foie gras is best eaten semi-cooked, as it keeps all its flavour if simply pasteurised.

PERPETUAL MOTION
Museum of automation
Place de l'Abbaye
☎ 05 65 37 07 07
Open daily 10am-7pm, July-Aug.; 10am-noon and 3-6pm, June and Sept.; 10am-noon and 3-6pm exc. Mon. Apr., May and Oct; 2-5pm exc. Mon. and Tues. other times.
Admission charge.
From the first mechanical toys, such as the 'girl with the bird' of 1890, to 21st-C. androids, the Musée des Automates houses a collection that is unique in Europe: 3,000 toys and robots all programmed to act and interact in a fantastic display of light and sound. The museum is also home to the national automaton and robot centre and a restoration workshop. The shop sells musical boxes and modern miniature automata.

Gourdon and La Bouriane
rich colours and tastes

In sharp contrast to the dryness of the Causses, La Bouriane has several waterways. They wind through valleys dominated by 'pechs' – limestone outcrops to which a few feudal ruins still cling. The pale brown soil is ideal for nuts and cep mushrooms, which are sold on many stalls in the attractive market places.

Medieval street, Gourdon

Gourdon

18.5 miles (30 km)
SW of Rocamadour
Gourmet Gourdon
Farm-produce market,
Place Saint-Pierre, Tues.
and Sat. am out of
season, Thurs. am in
summer, 8.30am-1pm.

Perched on a limestone butte, the white-stone town of Gourdon can be seen from 12 miles (20 km) away. The medieval streets are a delight, and the farmers market (marché fermier) is a must, giving a fascinating insight into the rural life of the area.

'Écoute s'il pleut' water park
Plan d'eau aménagé
Route de Sarlat
This water park, on a 100-acre (40-ha) site, has two lakes offering pedalos, sail boats, supervised swimming beaches, health sessions and a covered bowling lawn. La Bouriane has 10 similar sites, listed in the map 'Plans d'Eau en Bouriane' (available at the tourist office).

Cougnac

1 mile (2 km)
N of Gourdon
Cro-Magnon cave paintings
Cougnac caves
On the D704 towards Sarlat
☎ 05 65 41 47 54

Spotcheck
D3

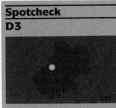

Open daily Palm Sunday-1 July, 9.30-11am and 2-5pm; 2 July-31 Aug. 9.30am-6pm; 9.30-11am and 2-5pm, 1 Sept.-1 Nov. Other times by appt only.

Admission charge.

Seeing Palaeolithic art is always a moving experience, and the Grottes de Cougnac have classic paintings depicting ibexes, mammoths and giant stags. Not only that, but superb stalactites and stalagmites combine with great domes to form a huge chamber of almost uncanny regularity, cut across by an underground river.

Milhac

6 miles (10 km)
N of Gourdon
Going climbing

Milhac is the site of a rock face known as 'Pied Noir' ('black foot'), with 80-ft (25-m) climbing routes. For experienced climbers, a guide to good climbs in the Lot region is available from tourist offices and libraries, describing the département's 10 locations. For novices, the best introduction is to be guided by an experienced professional, such as Emmanuel Salles (☎ 05 65 31 38 56).

Les Arques

18.5 miles (30 km)
SW of Gourdon
Zadkine museum
Musée Zadkine
☎ 05 65 22 83 37/84 81
Open daily 10am-1pm and 2-7pm, June-Sept.

and school and public holidays; 2-5pm, Oct.-May. Closed 25 Dec., 1 Jan., 1 May and 1 Nov.

Admission charge.

Born in Russia in 1890, Ossip Zadkine, who died in 1967, moved into a house at Les Arques in the 1930s. This sculptor's works, influenced by the period in which he lived, combine classicism, cubism and baroque and lyrical styles. Engravings, photographs and documents trace the life of the sculptor, and some of his works are on show in the village and in the church.

Lavercantière

12.5 miles (20 km)
SW of Gourdon
The key to the forest

Things to do

Gourdon farm-produce market
Summer music festival
Cougnac caves
Climbing
Forest walks
Musée Zadkine

With children

Medieval festival
'Écoute s'il pleut' water park

Within easy reach

Dordogne valley (18.5 miles/30 km NE), p. 180
Rocamadour and Cirucit des Merveilles (18.5 miles/30 km NE), pp. 170 and 174
Labastide-Murat (15.5 miles/25 km SE), p. 178

Tourist office

Gourdon: ☎ 05 65 27 52 50
Salviac: ☎ 05 65 41 57 27

Frau guided walk
Information from Salviac tourist office
In the heart of La Bouriane, discover the hidden treasures of the forest, including the legends of the Frau Giant and the Toun, the 'dragonfly ball', the plants with watery feet and many others. Visits may be unguided (pick up a map from the tourist office) or guided.

SUMMER MUSIC FESTIVAL
Info. from Gourdon tourist office
Launched with the aim of promoting music in rural areas, Gourdon's summer music events, which include free concerts in churches and public places, now attract people from far beyond the locality. Choose between classical music, Jazz, chants, dance, theatre, medieval festival (first weekend in August) and a major festival of sacred music – the selection and quality is remarkable.

Quercy's Ségala region
lessons in nature

The far northwest of the Lot region includes the foothills of the Massif Central and the highest point in Quercy, 2,572 ft (784 m) above sea level. Cut across by gorges, upland paths and fast-flowing rivers full of fish, this wild area, on the edge of the Cantal, is also known as La Châtaigneraie (or 'the chestnut grove'). It is ecologically rich, with a wide variety of flora and fauna.

GR 652

Laroquebrou

Lamativie

Sousceyrac

Labastide-du-Haut-Mont

Le lac du Tolerme

Sénaillac-Latronquière

Lacapelle-Marival

also see a squirrel or roe deer spring away into the undergrowth.

Sousceyrac

10 miles (16 km) SE of Saint-Céré

A botanical trail

Sentier Botanique de la Fôret de Luzette

Info. from the tourist office, Place de l'Église

In the heart of the great Sousceyrac forest, 'La Luzette' is a 4.5-mile (7-km) trail for walkers, horse riders and cyclists, marked with signs showing the area's botanical riches. With the help of the tourist office's guidebook, you will discover more than 80 species of trees, shrubs and ferns on this two-and-a-half-hour walk. In the forest, plaques explain the main properties of the leaf or bark to enable you to distinguish the various species. During this educational walk you may

Garden in the gorges

Information from the tourist office

At the confluence of the Cantal, Corrèzes and Lot rivers, the GR652 trail begins an 18.5-mile (30-km) journey along the gorges of the Cère, between Laroquebrou and

Eagle owl

Laval-de-Cère, passing through Lamativie. The flora is remarkable, with snowdrops, narcissi, spring scillas, hart's-tongue, wild garlic, phalanger lily and the rather exotic insect-eating sundew. The fauna is well worth seeing, too. In fact, the area is simply teeming with all sorts of wild life, including short-toed eagles, peregrine falcons, hen harriers, genettes, stone martens and otters. You will find that it is much easier to walk the path in one direction and return on the train. Take some time to visit the tourist office, which has information on many other walks in the region, especially the Vieyres trail (Circuit de Vieyres) with its famous waterfall.

Labastide-du-Haut-Mont

5.5 miles (9 km)
SE of Sousceyrac
This is the highest point in the Lot region, 2,572 ft (784 m) above sea level. The Auvergne mountains, Rodez cathedral and even the Pyrenees are visible from here.

Panoramic map, Labastide-du-Haut-Mont

Lacapelle-Marival

20 miles (32 km)
SW of Sousceyrac
Covered market place
Information from the tourist office
This town developed around its magnificent 13th- to 14th-C. **château** and impressive keep. The distinctive features of this area are the delightful farms with 'bolets', terraces

accessible by an outside staircase with a trellis or wisteria, and, in the town, the covered market, with its 15th-C. stone pillars covered in round tiles. This is the location for a farm-produce market (marché producteur), every Tuesday 5-7pm, with such delights as *pescajounes* (buckwheat pancakes), delicious conserves and cep mushrooms.

A LAKESIDE PARK FOR YOUR PLEASURE
Lac du Tolerme
Sénaillac-Latronquière
5 miles (8 km)
S of Sousceyrac
☎ 05 65 40 31 26
Car-park charge in summer.

Opened in 1990, the Plan d'Eau du Tolerme is an attractive, shady 94-acre (38-ha) lakeside park, with play, picnic and barbecue areas, a West Indian restaurant, botanical trail and health centre. For lovers of water sports, supervised swimming, windsurfing, kayaks and other boats are all available. On top of that, the local sailing and rowing schools offer a wide range of activities as well.

Lacapelle-Marival covered market

Conques and the Vallon de Marcillac

valley treasures

This area has a 'most' of everything. The most beautiful – a golden statue decorated with jewels by pilgrims. The most exciting – the village of Conques with its narrow streets and old lauze-covered houses. The most successful – Sainte-Foy abbey church, one of the most attractive of all medieval buildings. And the most natural – the ruby red Marcillac wine.

Chevet, Sainte-Foy abbey church

Soulages stained-glass windows

Like the stone from Rouergue, his home region, Pierre Soulages, an abstract painter born in 1919, is a powerful presence – built like a rugby player and always dressed in black. Among his major works are the fascinating stained-glass windows at the Abbatiale Sainte-Foy, made of special 'devitrified' glass designed to diffuse light and blend perfectly with the austere atmosphere and symbolism of the church itself. This self-taught artist's work reflects his desire to do away with the superfluous and rebel against all established forms of art and glass-painting. Soulages, who discovered painting at the age of 19 after falling under the spell of works by Picasso and Cézanne, is now one of France's most popular and well-known painters.

Sainte-Foy abbey church

Place de l'Église
Information from tourist office
Open daily 9am-noon and 2-6pm
(7pm in July-Aug.).
Admission free 9.30pm
The Abbatiale Sainte-Foy and its cloister contain some of the most beautiful examples of medieval sculpture, especially the tympanum, with its convincing depiction of the Last Judgement. The

Detail from the tympanum, Sainte-Foy abbey church

cloister contains some of Europe's richest treasures.

Santiago pilgrims

Home to the relics of the young martyr Sainte-Foy, brought here from Agen, Conques has become a major stopping-point on the pilgrims' route to Santiago de Compostela in Spain. Even today, many walkers still follow this historic pilgrims' way, stopping off in the village to be welcomed by the monks. The pilgrims' association, 'Sur les Pas de Saint-Jacques', issues a map showing the route from Le Puy-en-Velay to Conques (☎ 05 65 75 55 75).

Conques music and cinema festivals

Centre d'Art et de Civilisation Médiévale
☎ 05 65 71 24 00
Music mid-July to end Aug.; cinema in Apr.
Every summer, Conques organises a great festival with a medieval theme. Many baroque and classical music concerts are staged in the abbey church, which is blessed with excellent acoustics, and in Apr. each year a week of events linking cinema and the Middle Ages ('Cinéma et Moyen Âge') includes a selection of 20 films, which are usually world masterpieces.

Valady
15.5 miles (25 km) S of Conques
'Rougier' valley wine storehouse
Cave des Vignerons du Vallon
☎ 05 65 72 70 21
Open every working day.
The vineyards of the steep slopes of the Marcillac valley, with their clay and sandstone soil known as 'rougier', produce AOC red or rosé wine with a rich raspberry or blackcurrant flavour. A discovery trail featuring some of the smaller producers is detailed in a guide published by the Marcillac vine-growers' association (Syndicat des Viticulteurs de Marcillac, further information from the tourist office); the trail includes several visits to storehouses as well as free tasting sessions.

Spotcheck
EF3

Aveyron

Things to do

Visit to Sainte-Foy abbey church
Conques cinema and music festival
Marcillac wine storehouse visits and tasting sessions

Within easy reach

Truyère gorges (18.5 miles/30 km NE), p. 194

Tourist offices

Conques:
☎ 05 65 72 85 00

TREASURE OF TREASURES
Sainte-Foy abbey church
Open daily 9am-noon and 2-6pm. Closed 25 Dec. and 1 Jan.
Admission charge.
For 12 centuries, Conques has guarded the treasure of Sainte-Foy, which includes a large and priceless collection of major medieval artefacts. The most remarkable of the relics encased in gold or silver is the statue of Sainte-Foy, a gold masterpiece, encrusted with precious stones, that depicts the saint on her throne. The Abbatiale Sainte-Foy was constructed around these relics, like a magnificent jewel box.

Olt country
where the Lot becomes
a torrent

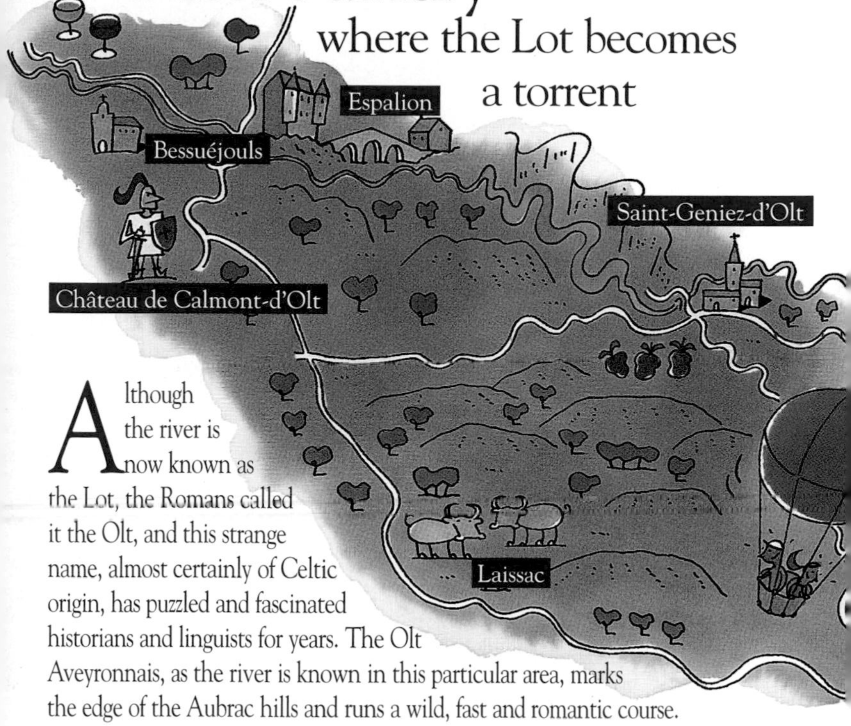

Espalion

Bessuéjouls

Saint-Geniez-d'Olt

Château de Calmont-d'Olt

Laissac

Although the river is now known as the Lot, the Romans called it the Olt, and this strange name, almost certainly of Celtic origin, has puzzled and fascinated historians and linguists for years. The Olt Aveyronnais, as the river is known in this particular area, marks the edge of the Aubrac hills and runs a wild, fast and romantic course.

Old tanneries by the Lot, Espalion

Espalion
**20 miles (32 km)
NE of Rodez**
Pink stone jewels
The pink sandstone buildings of this village include old tanneries with covered galleries and washing slabs, stark old Protestant houses

and magnificent Renaissance palaces. After a stop on the Pont Vieux ('old bridge'), with its three red arches straddling the Lot, visit the two nearby churches, the **Église de Perse** and the charming **Église Saint-Pierre** at Bessuéjouls (2.5 miles/4 km west of Espalion) and its 11th-C. Romanesque chapel, with remarkable interlacing decorations.

An unusual suit
Musée Joseph-Vaylet
☎ 05 65 44 09 18
05 65 44 09 18
Open daily 10am-noon and 2-7pm, July-Aug.; 2-6pm exc. Tues. out of season. *Admission charge.* The inventors of the first-ever diving suit came from Rouergue, and this unusual museum traces the history of their invention as well as displaying Rouergue earthenware and copper items.

Château d'Estaing

Travel back in time

Château de Calmont-d'Olt

Route de Rodez 2 miles (3 km) W of Espalion
☎ 05 65 44 15 89
Open daily 9am-7pm, July-Aug.; daily exc. Thurs. and Fri. 10am-noon and 2-6pm, May, June and Sept.
Admission charge.
Perched on a basalt outcrop, this medieval fortress reconstructs the siege of a château fort and demonstrates the firing of ancient war tools. A knight will welcome children and explain to them how the bow and crossbow were used and how a coat of chain mail was made. For their efforts, they will be awarded a Certificate of Knighthood.

Estaing

7 miles (10 km) NW of Espalion
Estaing wine

Les Vignerons d'Olt co-operative cellar
Zone Artisanale de la Fage
☎ 05 65 44 04 42
Visits by appt only.
This singularly pretty medieval village, dominated by its château, first planted vines in the 10th C. The most common types of white Estaing wine, which is dry and fruity, are Chenin and Mauzac; the rosé and red wines, meanwhile, combine Gamay, Mansoi and Cabernet. These delicate and drinkable wines should accompany all dishes of distinction. You can

discover their delights with a free tasting session at the cellar of the Vignerons d'Olt co-operative.

Saint-Geniez-d'Olt

17 miles (28 km) SE of Espalion
Strawberries

Tanneries, nail factories and sheet-makers all contributed in the past to make Saint-Geniez one of the most prosperous villages in the area. It has preserved its rich architectural heritage, most notably its cloister and chapel, the Cloître des Augustins and the Chapelle des Pénitents, with its painted ceilings, as well as a number of distinctive townhouses. Its speciality is

Spotcheck
F3-4

Aveyron

Things to do

Estaing wine-tasting session
Visit the diving-suit museum

With children

Become a medieval knight

Within easy reach

Rodez (20 miles/32 km SW), p. 196
Laguiole and Aubrac (15 miles/24 km NE), p. 190
Entraygues (17 miles/27 km NW), p. 194

Tourist offices

Espalion:
☎ 05 65 44 10 63
Estaing:
☎ 05 65 44 03 22
Saint-Geniez-d'Olt:
☎ 05 65 70 43 42

strawberries, which replaced grapes after a devastating attack of phylloxera in 1860.

LAISSAC FAIR

12.5 miles (20 km) SW of Saint-Geniez-d'Olt
To watch a local dealer selling a cow is a real spectacle. The Foire de Laissac is one of the largest agricultural fairs in France and one of the most typically French — every Tuesday, hundreds of cattle and sheep are bought and sold by breeders from all over the region. Butchers come here to find the renowned Olt-country Easter bulls. Shortly before the Easter festival, the beasts are groomed and decorated with ribbons, and presented to the butchers to be sold for the festival. This ritual used to mark the end of Lent and the 40 days of fasting.

Aubrac region
highland nature

This unspoilt landscape has a stark beauty reminiscent of the Scottish highlands, particularly in winter. Laguiole, the little capital of this mountainous area, has given its name to a famous pocketknife and a no less renowned cheese made with whole milk straight from the cow.

The restaurant owned by Michel Bras, one of the best in France, serves dishes for everyone.

Wild Pansy

Remarkable flora and fauna

Saint-Chély-d'Aubrac tourist centre
15.5 miles (25 km) S of Laguiole
☎ **05 65 44 21 15**

Guided tours by arrangement.
More than 1,300 different species of flower thrive on the plateau in the high season, and the fauna is almost as varied, with foxes, roe deer, wild boar and stags, whose deep bellow or 'bell' evokes

the atmosphere of the autumn mating season. The ONF, the French forestry commission, offers guided visits showing the ecosystem of the forest and the habitat of the deer.

North of the South

Aubrac Aveyronnais ski-station association
☎ 05 65 51 51 69

When the snow falls, enjoy downhill skiing, snowshoe walking or even

ordinary walking (provided you wrap up warm). The **highland walking trail** (GR 'Tour des Monts d'Aubrac'), which is 93 miles (150 km) in length, can be covered on skis in midwinter. **Laguiole** ski station has 12 chairlifts and **Brameloup** station (18.5 miles/30 km south of Laguiole) has 9 ski tows and a dog-sled track. The Espace Aubrac complex has 125 miles (200 km) of piste in all.

Cabrette, hurdy-gurdy and accordion
Information from Laguiole tourist office

For two days in every year (the third Friday and Saturday in August), Laguiole and the neighbouring villages come alive to the sound of **folk music**, with accordions, cabrettes (traditional goatskin instruments inflated like bagpipes) and hurdy-gurdies. The cabrette is also much in evidence at the **summer-pastures festival** (Fête de la Transhumance), on 25 May (Saint Urbain's day), at the **'Trace du Fromage'**, on the first weekend in Mar., and at the **cross-country skiing race**, where the objective is not so much to win as to down slices of cheese and mulled wine.

A 'buronnier' welcome

Laguiole cheese has been made for centuries in 'mazucs' or 'burons', cheese houses with dwellings attached, in which the shepherds lived during the summer pasture period. During this time, from 25 May to 13 October, three of these burons are open to visitors.

Buron de Canuc
On the D15, 9.5 miles (15 km) from Laguiole and 2.5 miles (4 km) from Aubrac.
Although it is no longer used, the interior of this buron remains intact and offers the chance to taste the famous aligot (adults 50F, children 30F). Be warned, however, this is not a restaurant, so bring your own plates, cutlery and tablecloth (reservations ☎ 05 65 42 29 02).

Spotcheck
F3

Aveyron

Things to do

Downhill and cross-country skiing
Visit the knife factories
Visit an aligot factory
Learn to play ninepins
Michel Bras master chef

With children

Discover the flora and fauna; hear the stag bellow
Folk music festival

Within easy reach

Olt country (18.5 miles/30 km S), pp. 188
Truyère gorges (18.5 miles/30 km NW), p. 194

Tourist office

Laguiole: ☎ 05 65 44 35 94

Buron de Caméjan
Between Aubrac and Nasbinals: take the D219 towards Saint-Geniez-d'Olt, turn right after 1 mile (2 km).
This buron still produces cheese and tomme, and also offers similar aligot-tasting sessions to the Buron de Canuc (reservations ☎ 05 65 44 25 05).

Buron de Théron
Between Aubrac and Nasbinals: take the D219 towards Saint-Geniez-d'Olt, turn left after 2.5 miles (4 km), then right.
This buron is definitely the most authentic of the three. There is no aligot-tasting here, but you can buy cheese made on the premises. It's best to visit between the milking times (that is, between 10am and 6pm).

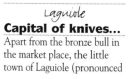

MICHEL BRAS, CHEF AND ARTIST

Ginette and Michel Bras
Le Puech du Suquet
Route de l'Aubrac, 3.5 miles (6 km) from Laguiole
☎ 05 65 51 18 20
Open daily exc. Mon., Tues. pm and Wed. pm.
Closed Mon. pm, July-Aug. Closed Nov.-early Apr.
Set menus 250F (during week) to 700F.
Michel Bras raises Aubrac cuisine to new heights,
turning simple local products into culinary works
of art: gargouillou of new vegetables, roast pigeon
with bitter coffee, crispy bacon with salmon and
pickled onions... The best-known chef in France,
Michel Bras now has a new restaurant, built on
Puech du Suquet, complete with a heliport to
welcome gourmets from all over Europe.

'Layole') is best known for the production of top-quality safety knives. Home to several knife factories, the most remarkable has an enormous blade, designed by Philippe Starck, sticking out of its roof (*see* p. 80).

... and tomme cheese

Laguiole cheese is made from whole fresh milk. Known as 'tomme', with its distinctive brown crust, it forms part of the famous aligot dish. Dating back to the 12thC., it was awarded an AOC in 1961 (*see* p. 39).

Laguiole
Capital of knives...

Apart from the bronze bull in the market place, the little town of Laguiole (pronounced

Laguiole cheese and aligot

Co-operative
'Jeune Montagne'
Route de Saint-Flour
☎ 05 65 44 35 54
Over 30 years ago, a group of young farmers founded a co-operative to relaunch Laguiole cheese. Today, despite producing huge amounts of fresh tomme cheese and aligot per year, they still open their doors to visitors. Tomme and even aligot is sold deep-frozen, having been made in the traditional way according to a recipe by the great Michel Bras (*see above*).

Knife factories

Calmels
3, Allée de l'Amicale
☎ 05 65 44 30 03
The family of Pierre-Jean Calmels, the creator of the famous Laguiole knives, are now running a workshop again (not open to the public); their work received the main prize for regional crafts in 1981.

Le Couteau de Laguiole
Workshop: Place du Nouveau Foirail
☎ 05 65 48 45 47
Shop: 23, Allée de l'Amicale
☎ 05 65 44 39 49

Bronze bull, Place du Foirail, Laguiole

Founded in 1985, this company was the first to relaunch the small-scale manufacture of Laguiole knives, maintaining quality and guarding against inferior imitations.

Le Coutelier de Laguiole
Workshop: Route de Rodez
☎ 05 65 44 34 55
Shop: 8, Place de la Patte d'Oie
☎ 05 65 48 42 29
This workshop sells standard models, knives ornamented with guilloche or those made to unique specifications. The forge hosts demonstrations.

Forge de Laguiole
Route de l'Aubrac
Shop: 8, Allée de l'Amicale
☎ 05 65 48 43 34
The remarkable Laguiole knives designed by Philippe Starck are made entirely by this company, from the forging of the blade to the final polishing. The mounting room and the forge are both open to visitors, and the knives are displayed in the exhibition hall and the shop.

Cassuéjouls
6 miles (10 km)
NW of Laguiole
Ninepins

Forge in Laguiole

This game is played only in northern Rouergue, yet has well over 3,000 licensed teachers. Cassuéjouls ninepins club meets regularly and organises introductory evenings, open to everybody, in the summer. Laguiole club meets at the same time.

Truyère gorges
wild lakes and deep valleys

Thérondels

Mur-de-Barrez

Sainte-Geneviève-sur-Argence

Saint-Gervais

Barrage de Couesque

Le Fel

Saint-Amans-des-Cots

Entraygues-sur-Truyère

Lying between two lava plateaux formed by the ancient Cantal volcanoes, the River Truyère threads a course through a series of deep, narrow, winding gorges, whose beauty is undiminished despite the recent building of several major dams. This wild country forms a perfect backdrop for water sports.

Wonderful walks
Detailed guide to local walks available from Mur-de-Barrez tourist office.
The Truyère gorges are ideal for walkers, with 25 trails of 3.5-12 miles (6-19 km), signposted by the ONF and

View of Saint-Hippolyte, Truyère gorges

listed in a guidebook. Probably the best walk is the trail starting from Sainte-Geneviève-sur-Argence and leading to the 'Bout du Monde' ('world's end') viewpoint; take the D900 to Mels and follow the yellow signs. Almost as good is the trail leading to the Laussac peninsula, where you can freshen up with a swim before taking the return path; south of Thérondels, follow the yellow signposts. A more demanding route takes you to the 'Dent de Chien' ('dog's tooth'); before Saint-Gervais, follow the blue and white arrows towards Monnès.

Entraygues-sur-Truyère
18.5 miles (30 km)
NE of Conques
River Truyère bridge
Before setting out for the gorges, take time to visit this village, remarkable for its splendid 13th-C. Gothic bridge and old quarter. Rue Basse, Rue Droite and Rue du Chemin-de-Ronde are linked by a number of narrow passages.

Place Castanie

Château de Vallon ruins

Le Fel

6 miles (10 km) W of
Entraygues-sur-Truyère

**L'Auberge
du Fel**

☎ 05 65 44 52 30
Open daily Apr.-Nov.
Set menus from 70F.
The tiny village of Le Fel is an
ideal starting point for scenic
walks. Two **walking trails**, one
lasting 1 hour 45 minutes,
signposted in blue, and the
other lasting 2.5 hours,
signposted in yellow, start
from the beautiful church, the
Église de Roussy. After your
walk, enjoy a gourmet stop at
the Auberge du Fel, in the
centre of the village. Take the
opportunity to try the
delicious 'farçou' (a pie unique
to the Cantal region), 'pounty'
(cabbage stuffed with prunes
and tomatoes), duck with
turnips or kid with sorrel.

Barrage de Couesque

4.5 miles (7 km) N of
Entraygues-sur-Truyère

**Visit a power
station**

Espace Truyère

☎ 05 65 44 56 10
Open daily 3-7pm, July-
Aug.; for groups by appt.,
rest of the year.
*Admission free. Visit
alternates with the
Barrage de Sarrans.*
Located inside the Barrage de
Couesque (Couesque dam)
power station, the Espace

Truyère exhibition area
explains the history and
operation of hydroelectric
power in the Truyère valley
with models, films and displays.

Mur-de-Barrez

15 miles (24 km) N of
the Barrage de Couesque

**Frons astronomical
observatory**

**Observatoire
de Frons**

☎ 05 65 66 17 83
Open all year by appt.
Admission charge.
The dark nights of Carladez
are even more interesting
than the days. With no street
lights, the clear sky above this
remote plateau is ideal for
astronomical observations.

Saint-Amans-des-Cots

10 miles (16 km) NE of
Entraygues-sur-Truyère

**Plateau
de la Viadène**

Sandwiched between the
Aubrac mountains and the
Truyère gorges, the Viadène is
a roughly triangular plateau,
not often included in tourist
trails. However, its delightful
waterfalls, vast horizons and
wide-open waters will delight
anglers and lovers of water
sport. Saint-Amans-des-Cots

is a good starting point for
excursions (information
from the tourist office) and
the village of **Vallon** offers
a panoramic view of the
Truyère gorges.

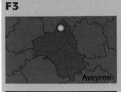

Spotcheck
F3

Aveyron

Things to do

Gorgeous walks
Inside a hydroelectric power
station
Entraygues wine-tasting
Local-cuisine dinner

With children

Astronomy evenings

Within easy reach

Aubrac (18.5 miles/30 km
SE), p. 190
Conques (18.5 miles/
30 km SW), p. 186
Olt country (31 miles/
50 km S), p. 188

Tourist offices

Entraygues-sur-Truyère:
☎ 05 65 44 56 10
Mur-de-Barrez:
☎ 05 65 66 10 16
Saint-Amans-des-Cots:
☎ 05 65 44 81 61

AN EARTHLY WINE WITH
A HEAVENLY TASTE

Méjanassère estate
*D42, Route de Laguiole, 3 miles
(5 km) from Entraygues-sur-Truyère*
☎ 05 65 44 54 76
Open weekends and public holidays
Apr.-June and Sept.-Dec.; open daily
July-Aug.; closed Jan.-Mar.
**The Entraygues-sur-Truyère and Le Fel
area has produced a very drinkable
local VDQS (*vin de qualité supérieure*)
wine since 1965. Its 50 acres (20 ha)
of vines produce smooth red and rosé wines,
while the dry and highly perfumed white wines go
superbly with goats' cheese. At the Domaine de
Méjanassère, Frédérique and Véronique Forveille
will take pleasure in introducing you to these wines.**

Rodez and the Causse Comtal
the land of the Counts of Rouergue

Place du Bourg, Rodez

Since 1960, Rodez has grown and grown. From the promontory on which the old city was built, a sea of modern houses and buildings tumbles down all the way to Aveyron. The old city, still watched over by its impressive cathedral, is full of new, vibrant life. At the gates to the capital of Rouergue, the Causse Comtal, where the Counts of Rodez left a rich heritage, offers wide-open spaces for rest and relaxation within a short distance of the city.

Cathédrale Notre-Dame
Place d'Armes
Reservations for visits to the bell-tower at the tourist office (Place Foch).
This cathedral, built between the 13th and 16thC., is a Gothic masterpiece that dominates the entire city,

a northern intrusion into a southern domain. In summer, you can climb right to the top of the octagonal bell-tower, 285 ft (87 m) high; take time to admire the view of the old city with its ancient houses and gardens.

Venerable old houses
Most of the architectural riches are found in the old city, especially the 15th- and 16th-C. houses such as Maison de l'Annonication on Place du Bourg, which was both a market place and a burial ground until the 14thC.; its bas reliefs have been well restored. Nearby is Maison d'Armagnac on Place de

l'Olmet, with its bizarre combination of Gothic and Renaissance building styles.

Local poetry
Occitan festival and poetry days
Info. from Rodez town hall ☎ 05 65 77 88 49
For four days in mid-July a group of artists, comedians and singers bring the traditional Occitan culture back to life, with events in a variety of halls around Rodez and free shows in the streets. On a different note, May is the time for the poetry days (Journées à la Poesie), during which three prizes of international repute are awarded. One is the coveted Antoine Artaud prize,

named in honour of the 'cursed poet', publisher of *Lettres de Rodez* in 1946, who was a patient in the city's psychiatric hospital.

Salles-la-Source

7.5 miles (12 km)
NW of Rodez
Climb to the source

Salles-la-Source, built on limestone cliffs carved into amazing shapes, has buildings on three separate levels, all centred on a waterfall over 65 ft (20 m) high. The village is also home to an **arts and**

Salles-la-Source waterfall

craft museum (musée des arts et métiers), which retraces the history of the local vineyards (open daily except Saturday morning, 10am-12.30pm and 2-7pm, July-Aug.; 2-6pm, May, June and Sept.; by appointment out of season ☎ 05 65 67 28 96). There are also opportunities to go climbing on the cliffs.

Belcastel

12.5 miles (20 km)
W of Rodez
Beautiful Belcastel

Château open daily mid-June to mid-Sept., week-ends and public holidays Apr.-15 June and 15 Sept.-1 Oct., 11am-12.30pm and 2.30-7pm.

Vieux Pont, Belcastel

Admission charge.

On the banks of the Aveyron, at the foot of the old feudal château, Belcastel is best known for its 500-year-old sandstone and mica stone bridge, the Vieux Pont. The houses, with their floral decorations, galleries and ancient bread ovens look out over the narrow streets or 'calades', which run up to the château. Belcastel has been named a 'Beau Village de France' and certainly justifies the status.

Bozouls

14 miles (22 km)
NE of Rodez
Fly a microlite
Club d' ULM
☎ **05 65 48 86 52**

Imagine yourself flying over an old town built on both sides of

Spotcheck
F4

Things to do

Occitan festival
Poetry days
Bozouls canyon flight
Climbing

Within easy reach

Marcillac-Vallon (12.5 miles/20 km NW), p. 186
Sauveterre-de-Rouergue (18.5 miles/30 km NW), p. 212
Espalion (18.5 miles/30 km NE), p. 188

Tourist offices

Belcastel: ☎ **05 65 64 46 11**
Rodez: ☎ **05 65 68 02 27**

a deep, horseshoe-shaped canyon, a river rushing between reddish-coloured cliffs and a cave reckoned to be bottomless. The cave is known as the Gourp d'Enfer and the ULM club at Bozouls has introductory flights over this amazing place for 150F.

THE FLAVOURS OF THE VIEUX PONT

Restaurant du Vieux Pont
☎ **05 65 64 52 29**

Closed Sun. pm, Mon. and Tues. lunchtime (Mon. lunchtime only July-Aug.). Closed Jan. to mid-Mar.
Set menus 140-350F, children 80F.

This restaurant is situated right opposite the old bridge at Belcastel. Nicole and Michèle, the owners, grew up here and have now turned the house into one of the region's best restaurants, with a subtle mixture of old traditional tastes brought back to life by their seemingly boundless culi-  **nary skills. The menu includes such dishes as cep mushrooms in cream of garlic, grilled duck liver on stewed rhubarb, and fried sea bream.**

Lac de Pareloup

Lévezou region
the great lakes

L ying between mountains and plateaux, the area to the southeast of Rodez is like the Auvergne, with huge expanses of smooth water, produced by the hydroelectric complex at Le Pouget. From north to south, five separate dams have created a total of nearly 4,500 acres (1,800 ha) of lakes.

Lac de Pareloup

23 miles (37 km)
SE of Rodez
The inland sea
Vernhes water-sports centre
☎ 05 65 46 33 33
or 05 65 75 55 40
(out of season)

The Pareloup basin, the fifth-largest lake in France, has an amazing 75 miles (120 km) of tree-lined shores. The view is particularly impressive from the dam, situated on the west side between Le Fraisse and Aures, which can be crossed by car or on foot. For swimming and water sports, the best location is the Base Nautique de Vernhes, on the east side, a water-sports centre with a small beach (beware: no lifeguards) and pedalos, windsurfers, optimist boats and catamarans for hire.

Dine on the water
Emmanuel-III boat-restaurant
Les Vernhes
☎ 05 65 46 31 04
or 05 65 44 32 80
Departures daily May-15 Oct. at noon, return at 3pm, or at 7pm, return by night.
Evening meals available mid-June to mid-Sept. (with reservation).
Admission charge (about 180 F including menu and walk).
Enjoy your lunch or evening meal on board this attractive little pleasure boat as it sails away from the beach at Les Vernhes and glides peacefully across the lake.

Vézins-de-Lévézou

16 miles (26 km)
SE of Vibal
Château de Vézins
☎ 05 65 61 87 02
Open daily exc. Wed., 15 June-15 Sept., 10am-noon and 2-7pm.
Admission charge.
This vast château, with high, semi-circular walls, belongs to the Count of Lévézou de Vézins, who will show you round himself. Combining the medieval style of the 12th-C. fortress with Renaissance and neo-Gothic additions, it tells the story of 800 years of architectural development.

Saint-Léons

7 miles (11 km)
SE of Vézins
Insect city
Musée Jean-Henri-Fabre
☎ 05 65 58 80 54
Open daily 2.30-6.30pm, mid-June to mid-Sept.; Sun. 3-6pm only, Easter-1 Nov.

Statue of the entomologist Jean-Henri Fabre

Admission charge.
Saint-Léons, the birthplace of the eminent entomologist Jean-Henri Fabre (1823-1915), is dedicated to the study of insects. Visit the scientist's birthplace, with its little museum, and follow the nearby botanical trail. Also nearby is the recently opened 'Micropolis' complex, with an area of 26,000 sq ft (2,400 sq m) devoted

entirely to the world of insects in all their fascinating forms.

Castelnau-Pégayrols
22 miles (35 km) SW of Saint-Léons
A real gem
This steeply sloping village is home to no less than five significant historical monuments, including the château and two Romanesque churches. The narrow streets, lined with beautiful old

Castelnau-Pégayrols Romanesque church

sandstone or timbered houses, lend the village, which is not often visited by tourists, a distinct atmosphere and charm.

Spotcheck
F4

Aveyron

Things to do

Vernhes water-sports
Dine on the water
Watch craftsmen at work
Château de Vézins

With children

Discover the world of insects
Tea on the farm

Within easy reach

Millau (18.5 miles/30 km SE of Vézins), p. 200

Tourist offices

Pareloup-Lévezou:
☎ 05 65 46 89 90

Time for tea
Le Sahut farm
(*Just before Castelnou*)
☎ 05 65 62 02 26
Open Thurs. at 4pm, 6 May-30 Oct., by appt.
To taste a real traditional local tea, visit Geneviève Soulié's farm, which offers one of the area's most highly rated 'fourses', with Roquefort cheese, apple paste, caramel tart, ewe's milk and fruit juice. Perfect to round off a visit to the farm and its herd of ewes.

EARTH, IRON AND WOOD
12.5 miles (20 km) N of Vernhes
Maison Créative du Vibal
☎ 05 65 46 81 08/86 55
Open all year by appt.
Admission charge.
See three craftsmen at work in their studios. Blacksmith Claude Villefranque beats red-hot iron into unusual figurines; François Boutonnet demonstrates the turning and firing of earthenware and ceramics; and wood-turner Jean-Louis Courtial is one of the few remaining makers of Aveyron ninepins. The decorative and practical creations of these three masters are original and full of character.

Making a set of Aveyron ninepins

Millau
fits like a glove

18th-C. washhouse, L'Ayrolle

Millau, on the edge of the Causse Noir and crossed by the River Tarn, is the capital of southern Rouergue and a lively business centre. Once the ceramics capital of the Roman Empire, the town is now best known for the fine art of glove-making.

Old mill on the River Tarn

Old Millau

At the entrance to the town, stop to look at the remarkable 15th-C. mill, which is perched on the 12th-C. bridge that spans the Tarn. Then visit the 18th-C. lavoir (washhouse) on Boulevard de l'Ayrolle, which is almost hidden behind a magnificent portico. From Place du Mandarous, the heart of Millau, stroll along the old narrow streets, including the old commercial centre, Rue Droite, with its 157-ft (48-m) bell-tower, a former prison.

A lively evening market

Every Monday evening in July and August, from 7pm to 11pm, the town centre hosts a great evening market (marché nocturne), selling wonderful local produce. The commercial and cultural spectacle draws everyone into the streets, including children, for whom there are special attractions.

The belfry

Glove workshop
21, Rue Droite
☎ 05 65 60 81 50

Open Mon.-Sat.,
10am-noon and 2-7pm.
Millau glove-maker Christian
Canillac will welcome you
to his workshop, where he
demonstrates the craft of
making a glove from the
cutting stage right through
to the sewing. Watch this
master turn a piece of hide
into a piece of art using heavy
scissors, picking knives and
an iron mould of a hand.

Gloves and pots...
Musée de Millau
Hôtel de Pégayrols,
Place Foch
☎ 05 65 59 01 08
Open daily Apr.-Sept.
exc. 1 May, 9am-noon

and 1.30-6pm; daily
10am-6pm, July-Aug.;
daily exc. Sundays and
public holidays 10am-
noon and 2-6pm,
Oct.-Mar.
Admission charge.
Find out all about hides and
gloves at this museum, which
has more than 100 models
and an active glove-makers'
workshop during the summer.
Next door, there is an
archaeological exhibition
of Gallo-Roman pots found
on the nearby site at La
Graufesenque; first-class
reproductions of these pots
are on sale. A twin ticket
(35F) gives you access to
the museum as well as the
archaeological site.

Roman capital of ceramics
La Graufesenque
Archeological site
1 mile (2 km) E of Millau
☎ 05 65 59 01 08
Open daily 9am-noon
and 2-6.30pm, exc. 1
Jan., 1 May, 1 and 11
Nov. and 25 Dec.
Admission charge.
Visit the ruins of the ancient
Gallo-Roman settlement
of Condatomagus, at the
confluence of the Tarn and
Dourbie rivers, where
excavations have revealed the
largest collection of ancient

Spotcheck
G4

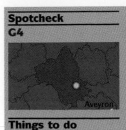
Aveyron

Things to do
Visit a glove-maker's
workshop
Glove museum and
archaeological exhibition
Walking at Chaos de
Montpellier-le-Vieux
Roman archaeological site
Adventures at Roc et Canyon
Ride on camel-back
Larzac Ecomuseum
Discover a honey factory

With children
Causses Botanical Gardens
Monday markets

Within easy reach
*Roquefort-sur-Soulzon (13
miles/21 km SE), p. 206
Causse de Larzac (25
miles/40 km SE), p. 204
Le Levézou (17.5 miles/
28 km NW), p. 198*

Tourist office
Millau: ☎ 05 65 60 02 42

pots in the world. Here, in
the 1stC. BC, over 600 pottery
workshops created high-
quality vessels of red clay that
were exported all over the
Roman Empire. The
archaeological site also has

A PETRIFIED CITY

Chaos de Montpellier-le-Vieux
10 miles (16 km) NE of Millau
☎ 05 65 60 66 30
Open daily Easter-1 Nov., 9am-6.30pm.
Admission charge.
The Sphinx, the Bear, the Harlequin, the Mycaenean Gate and the Arc de Triomphe are all names given to the extraordinary limestone rock formations, carved out by wind and rain in the Causse Noir, at Chaos de Montpellier-le-Vieux. You can visit this 'petrified city' by mini-rail or on foot, with several trails between 30 minutes and 2 hours, or take a round-trip by driving down to the Gorges de la Dourbie along the delightful C4 (not suitable for caravans or camper-vans), coming out at Roque-Sainte-Marguerite.

the remains of ovens, drying houses as well as dwelling houses and a 45-minute tour with a ministry of culture guide is available.

Canyon sports centre
Base Sportive Roc et Canyon
Out of season:
55, Avenue Jean-Jaurès, Millau.
In season: Route de Nant, E of Millau, between the Tarn and Dourbie rivers.
☎ 05 65 61 17 77
Open all year.
This sports centre takes full advantage of its thrilling setting. If it's water adventure you're after, try canyoning or white-water rafting, canoeing or speedboats. The more daring can try climbing, hang-gliding, paragliding or caving, while the more down-to-earth are welcome to go horse-riding, walking or mountain biking.

Scented gardens
Jardin des Causses
Parc de la Victoire, Avenue Charles-de-Gaulle
☎ 05 65 59 50 68
Open daily 7am-10.30pm.
Admission free (dogs not allowed).
Set in a shady park, this delightful botanical garden includes a display of typical Causse landscapes reproduced in miniature. Some 120 separate species of plants, including several rare ones, decorate this peaceful and informative walk.

A gourmet institution
La Vieille Fontaine
1, Place de la Tine
☎ 05 65 59 29 00
Closed Sun.
out of season.
Set menus ranging between 140-340F.
This restaurant, located right in the centre of the town, has become something of an institution, serving such gourmet treats as haunch of game and crusted spaghetti with morels. The main meals are certainly worth the trip,

Botanical garden, Millau

Veyreau
12.5 miles (20 km)
NE of Chaos de
Montpellier-le-Vieux
Honey farm
Le Mas Nau:
Jo Blanchecotte
and Joël Blanc
☎ 05 65 61 12 02
(by appt)
Take the country roads – the diversion is worth it and try some of the region's best honey at the Le Mas Nau farm. Not only is the honey organic, it has won several gold medals, and the shop also sells mead, honey vinegar, spiced bread, almond paste and lots of other sugary surprises.

but unfortunately, the quality of the desserts do not quite match the superb standard of the first courses.

House of rural history and culture
Maison du Larzac,
Écomusée de la Jasse
☎ 05 65 60 43 58
or 05 65 60 87 67
(out of season)
Open 10am-7pm,
mid-June to mid-Sept.
Admission free.
At this sheepfold, situated at the gateway to the Grands Causses, there is a panoply of Larzac life for the tourist to discover. One exhibition relates the struggle of the people of the Causse de Larzac to preserve their wild country through a mixture of co-operation, perseverance and passion for their region. The stone arches of the sheepfold house an a remarkable exhibition concerning the rural way of life in the Causses and its pastoral traditions. You can even buy some interesting local foods to eat on site with a picnic, or some farm products, traditional crafts and books.

CAMEL RIDES!
Méharées des Grands Causses
La Blaquière, Verrières
☎ 05 65 47 69 66
Open all year (booking essential).
No, you're not dreaming – there is a camel train passing slowly through the Aveyron countryside. In fact, the dry landscape suits them. Riding a camel can be a little bumpy (and it's a long way to the ground) but whatever your age, don't be afraid to take one of these extraordinary humped creatures for a walk out of the ordinary. They are, believe it or not, delightful animals. One word of advice: best to book in a group.

Causse du Larzac
cradle of the Templar cities

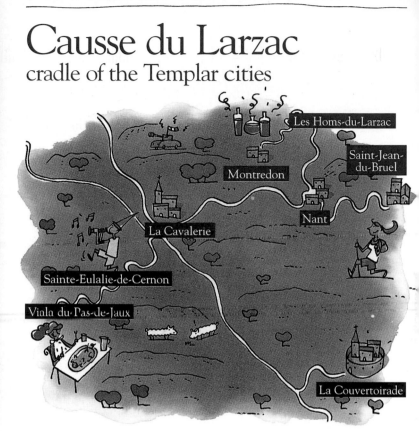

The largest of the Grands Causses limestone plateaux, measuring around 400 sq miles (over 1,000 sq km), is also the best known in France, thanks to the local people's 10-year battle against Paris bureaucrats who wanted to make it the site of a military camp. Since their victory in 1981, its image as a remote, deserted plateau, windswept and cold, has changed little. However, in fact, the landscapes of this causse are dotted with oak, beech, box tree, juniper and stipe woodland and it is also home to the former cities of the Knights Templar.

La Couvertoirade Templar castle

La Couvertoirade
25 miles (40 km) SE of Millau
A medieval city in miniature
Maison de la Serpione welcome centre
☎ **05 65 62 78 73**
Open daily 10am-7pm, July-Aug.
Guided tours. Telephone out of season.

Sheltering within the ramparts of La Couvertoirade are the architectural treasures of the Knights Templar and Knights Hospitaller. This tiny medieval city is best seen on foot, walking the maze of narrow streets, covered passages and picturesque open squares. Along the way you will see splendid 15th-C. houses with outside staircases, 17thC. townhouses and a great many craft shops.

The shepherd's bag
La Couvertoirade
Info. ☎ 05 65 99 36 60
Open daily 10.30am-1pm
and 2-6.30pm, Easter-
All Saints' Day (1 Nov.).
The only essential equipment
of the Causse shepherd was his
bag – solid but supple, with
brass buckles, in which he
would protect his clothes.
For over 20 years now, in his
shop Le Sac du Berger ('the
shepherd's bag'), Jean-Pierre
Romiguier has been carrying
on this time-honoured
tradition. The current design
dates back to the 17thC.

Animal power
Musée de la
traction animale
☎ 05 65 62 26 85
Open Apr.-Nov., 10.30am-
1pm and 2.30-6pm.
Admission charge.
Located at the entrance to the
town, this museum houses a

memorable collection of 60
carts and carriages for both
country and town, as well as
harnesses for horses, oxen,
dogs and goats. In the entrance
hall there are a number of
stalls run by Aveyron jam-
makers and local farmers.
Outside you'll find a series
of remarkable polystyrene con-
structions depicting famous
churches, cathedrals and
châteaux, including St Peter's
Basilica in Rome and, of
course, La Couvertoirade itself.

Sainte-Eulalie-de-Cernon

Living
Templar cities
Larzac summer festival ('Les
Estivales de Larzac') brings
the tiny cities of the Causse to
life, with medieval fairs and
historical firework shows at **La
Cavalerie** (☎ 05 65 62 78 73),
night shows and tours at **La
Couvertoirade** (☎ 05 65 62
11 62), story-telling evenings
and medieval banquets at

Viala-du-Pas-de-Jaux (☎ 05
65 59 95 35), and concerts and
stories at **Sainte-Eulalie-de-
Cernon** (☎ 05 65 62 79 98)
and **Saint-Jean-d'Alcas**
(☎ 05 65 49 26 02).

The hidden Larzac
ONF Millau
☎ 05 65 60 16 40
or Saint-Jean-du-Bruel
☎ 05 65 62 28 77
There is a range of **country
trails**, lasting from just a few
hours to a week or more. In
July and August the ONF
(National Forestry
Commission) also offers guided
tours of Causse de Larzac and
Causse Noir lasting half a day.

A rock resembling ruins, Larzac

Spotcheck
G5

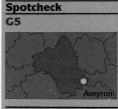

Aveyron

Things to do
**Discover La Couvertoirade
Causse walking trails
Aromatic-plant cultivation**

With children
**Museum of animal power
Templar city festivals
Architectural model
exhibition**

Within easy reach
*Millau (25 miles/40 km
NW), p. 200
Roquefort-sur-Soulzon
(25 miles/40 km W),
p. 206*

Tourist offices
**La Couvertoirade
town hall:**
☎ 05 65 58 55 55

HOMS PASTIS

Les Homs-du-Larzac
*Between Nant and La Cavalerie
on the D999. At Liquisses Basses,
follow the Route de Montredon.*
☎ 05 65 22 56
Open daily exc. Wed., July-Aug.,
2-7pm. By appt out of season.
In this remote location at the heart
of the Causse du Larzac, Maria
and Pierre-Yves cultivate aromatic
and medicinal plants, dry them with
the greatest of care and then turn
them into drink infusions or use them
to flavour other products. Their star
product is Pastis des Homs, an aperitif delicately
flavoured with anise, liquorice and a variety of other
plants. You can also taste Causse eglantine, a 16°
proof rosehip-flavoured aperitif, sloe gin and mint-
flavoured vinegar.

Roquefort country
home to a famous cheese

Although most French people will be familiar with Roquefort cheese, a little introduction may be needed for us. Roquefort is a blue cheese that has been made for centuries by natives of the village of Roquefort-sur-Soulzon and is now known over almost the whole world. All around the village, the reddish soil of the 'rougier de Camarès' colours the Grands Causses regional nature park.

Viala-du-Tarn

Roquefort-sur-Soulzon

Le château de Montaigut

Saint-Jean-d'Alcas

Saint-Sernin-sur-Rance

Saint-Félix-de-Sorgues

Sylvanès

Roquefort-sur-Soulzon
13 miles (21 km)
SW of Millau
Roquefort cellars association
Société des Caves de Roquefort
☎ 05 65 59 93 30 or
05 65 58 58 58
Open daily 9.30am-6.30pm, July-Aug.;
9.30-11.30am and 1.30-5pm, out of season.

Closed 25 Dec. and 1 Jan.
Admission charge.
Visit the underground cellars in which the famous veined cheese is matured (p. 38). In the cellars, the thousand-year history of the master cheese-makers is told with animated models, a sound and light show and a video. Visitors follow the production of the cheese step by step, rounding off with a tasting session.

Shepherds' paths
Rising high above Roquefort-sur-Soulzon, the **Plateau de Combalou** (2,595 feet/791 m above sea level) has two memorable walking trails with

magnificent views, old shepherds' huts and needle rocks. Choose from the Sentier de Trompette or, for the more determined, the Sentier des Echelles, a tough 3.5-mile (6-km) trek lasting 2.5 hours. Ask for details at the tourist office.

Viala-du-Tarn
15 miles (24 km) NW of Roquefort-sur-Soulzon
The 'raspes' of the River Tarn
Mas de la Nauc
☎ 05 65 62 59 12
Open Easter to mid-Oct.
Leaves daily at 10.30am, 2pm, 4pm and 5.30pm.
The 'raspes' are great slabs of black schist rock, covered with broom, which hem in the green waters of the River Tarn. To discover this wild

landscape, inaccessible on foot, board the 'Héron des Raspes', moored at Viala-du-Tarn; the 1.5-hour journey takes you to the Barrage de Pinet (Pinet dam) and back, via the pretty little village of Saint-Rome-du-Tarn.

Saint-Jean-d'Alcas

5 miles (8 km) S of Roquefort-sur-Soulzon
In the footsteps of the Templars
This ancient Templar city is quite delightful – a village of greystone buildings in the shelter of a magnificent

SYLVANÈS,
TEMPLE OF MUSIC
Abbaye de Sylvanès
18.5 miles (30 km) SW of Roquefort-sur-Soulzon
☎ 05 65 98 20 20
Open daily 9.30am-noon and 2-6pm. Closed Sat. and Sun. am Nov.-Mar. *Admission charge.* This magnificent Cistercian abbey, founded by a converted 12th-C. brigand, is a centre for musical and cultural gatherings, as its acoustics are second to none. In the summer, Sylvanès stages an international festival of sacred music, called 'Chants et Liturgies de la Mer' ('sea songs and liturgies'). The abbey is also a teaching, research and training centre and hosts conventions of religious chants and music.

enclosed fortress, which has been perfectly restored.

Saint-Sernin-sur-Rance

20 miles (32 km) SW of Roquefort-sur-Soulzon
Aveyron cuisine
Carayon
☎ 05 65 98 19 19
Open daily for lunch and dinner. Closed Sun. eves and Mon. out of season. Connoisseurs of good cooking come from afar to sample one of the seven set menus offered at this restaurant, located in a pretty little village over-looking the Rance river. There is a range of Rouergue specialities (82-300F), with the goose and mutton dishes highly recommended. The best place to eat is on the panoramic terrace overlooking the swimming pool.

Saint-Félix-de-Sorgues

15.5 miles (25 km) S of Roquefort-sur-Soulzon
Bambi country
Ferme de Drulhe
☎ 05 65 49 03 88
Admission free.

Druhle farm, perched on a rocky outcrop overlooking a vast tract of wild country, has a 375-acre (150-ha) animal park where, in addition to the traditional farm animals, stags, hinds, fallow deer and mouflons roam freely among the rocks. There is also a lake, home to a variety of ducks and geese.

Spotcheck
FG5

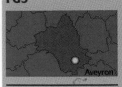

Aveyron

Things to do

Visit the Roquefort cellars
Combalou shepherds' paths
Concerts at Sylvanès abbey
Château de Montaigut

With children

Ferme de Druhle animal park
Tarn river ride

Within easy reach

Causse du Larzac (to the E), p. 204
Millau (12.5 miles/20 km NE of Roquefort), p. 200

Tourist offices

Camarès:
☎ 05 65 49 53 76
Roquefort:
☎ 05 65 58 56 00

Gissac

12.5 miles (20 km) SW of Roquefort-sur-Soulzon
Château de Montaigut
☎ 05 65 99 81 50
Open daily Easter-1 Nov., 10am-noon and 2.30-6.30pm (10am-6.30pm, July-Aug.); open to groups by appt, rest of the year. *Admission charge.* Built in the 10thC., this clifftop feudal château offers a splendid view across the 'rougier', the red-soil countryside of the region. Inside, you can walk through arched halls and visit the guardroom, the kitchens, the medieval chambers and a museum and country house.

Château de Montaigut and the 'rougier'

Villefranche-de-Rouergue
in the land of the bastides

In the west of Aveyron, between the Lot valley, the Causses and the Aveyron gorges, stand the three royal bastides of Villefranche, Villeneuve and Najac. It's a pleasure to stroll round these places, where people take the time to live well and eat well.

Villefranche, historical capital of Rouergue

Take time to appreciate the layout of this huge 13th-C. bastide, which has a number of architectural jewels, notably the Chapelle des Pénitents Noirs, a small, round chapel, topped with two pinnacles. Inside, take a look at the painted wooden arch and the richly ornamented gold-leafed reredos. Villefranche, once the capital of Quercy and Rouergue, is still a lively centre for the agricultural trade, and its Thursday-morning market in Place Notre-Dame is well known for its traditional atmosphere and delicious local produce.

Cloister, Saint-Sauveur charterhouse

Saint-Sauveur charterhouse

0.5 mile (1 km) S of Villefranche-de-Rouergue
Open daily 10am-noon and 2-6pm.
Admission charge.
It is well worth a detour to see the magnificent Chartreuse Saint-Sauveur, a pearl of Gothic architecture built by a rich 15th-C. merchant. Constructed in just eight years, it required no fewer than 5,000 stonemasons to complete it. The little cloister, built in a flamboyant style, is particularly memorable.

Graves

1 mile (2 km) NW of Villefranche-de-Rouergue
Château de Graves
☎ 05 65 45 13 18

A penitent

Open Mon.-Fri. July-Aug., 10am-noon and 2-6pm.
Admission charge.
The pale stone walls of this small 16th-C. Renaissance château are particularly impressive seen from the summit of the nearby hill. The château has an attractive square courtyard and a terrace overlooking the gardens.

Villeneuve

7 miles (11 km) N of Villefranche-de-Rouergue
Villeneuve tinware
Étains du Rouergue
☎ 05 65 81 64 03
Open daily exc. Sun.
This bastide boasts a beautiful galleried central square and

Les Pénitents Noirs chapel

the Église du Saint-Sépulcre, with its 13th-C. frescoes, sacred treasures and rotunda. Don't miss the Étains de Rouergue shop, which has over 450 different high-quality items made of tin, including decorative art and tableware.

Najac

11 miles (18 km) SW of Villefranche-de-Rouergue

River leisure centre
Base de Loisirs

1 mile (2 km) from Najac (follow signs for Camping de Najac)
☎ **05 65 29 73 94/ 72 05**
Open daily 9am-noon and 1.30-6pm, July-Aug.; by reservation out of season.

Pike

The Aveyron river hurtles past at the foot of this charming medieval village with its 13th-C. **royal fortress**. In the wild waters, full of trout and pike, you can fish, canoe or go white-water rafting (not in summer), or even try your hand at river boarding, a

Place du Faubourg, Najac

strange sport which involves trying to stay upright on a pair of floats.

Foissac

13 miles (21 km) N of Villefranche-de-Rouergue

Walking through prehistory
Préhisto-site
☎ **05 65 64 88 99**
Open daily 10am-6pm, July-Aug.; 10am-noon

and 2-6pm, June and Sept.; 2-6pm, Apr., May and Oct. Closed Sat.
In the caves and parks of Foissac you can discover various prehistoric remains as well as the 'Préhisto-site' centre, where the dwellings, lives of our most distant ancestors are reconstructed. In summer, you can even sit down to a prehistoric meal, with lamb and pork grilled in a pebble ditch, mushrooms and peas, followed by a wheat and honey dessert washed down with mead. Afterwards, walk off your meal along the 3-mile (5-km) Circuit des Dolmens (dolmen trail, starting opposite the town hall ☎ 05 65 64 61 16).

Spotcheck
E4

Aveyron

Things to do

Wild-water activities
Rouergue tin products
Visit a Renaissance château

With children

Foissac prehistoric park

Within easy reach

Sauveterre-de-Rouergue (25 miles/40 km SE), p. 212
Decazeville (25 miles/ 40 km NE), p. 210

Tourist offices

Najac: ☎ **05 65 29 72 05**
Villefranche-de-Rouergue:
☎ **05 65 45 13 18**
Villeneuve:
☎ **05 65 81 79 61**

PAUSE IN PARADISE

Hôtel-restaurant Longcol
La Fouillade
12 miles (19 km) S of Villefranche-de-Rouergue
☎ **05 65 29 63 36**
Open daily. Closed mid-Nov. to mid-Feb.
Everything about Longcol is remarkable. The stunning location, with its swimming pool overlooking the valley. The blue-roofed building complex housing the hotel and the restaurant, with its elegant decor, adorned with oriental antiques. The impeccable manners of the staff and, last but certainly not least, the fresh, imaginative and refined cuisine, giving locally produced ingredients an other-worldly taste. The chef, Francis Cardillac, produces his masterpieces with dedication and discretion. Undoubtedly, one of the best restaurants in the region and at an affordable price (Set menus 145F (lunch, except Sunday), or 195-245F).

Decazeville basin

the 'burning mountain'

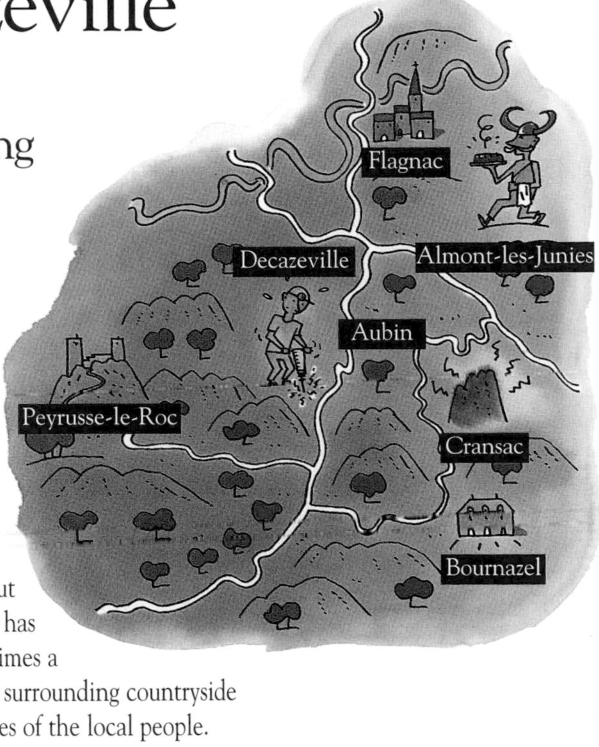

Decazeville was built in the 19th C. to mine a vast deposit of coal found in the area. Although the mine, once one of the biggest in France, has all but stopped working, it has left its mark, sometimes a painful one, on the surrounding countryside and on the memories of the local people.

Flagnac

Decazeville

Almont-les-Junies

Aubin

Peyrusse-le-Roc

Cransac

Bournazel

Decazeville

22 miles (35 km) NE of Rodez
Mine of discovery
Mine de la Découverte
At the southern exit of Decazeville
☎ 05 65 43 18 36
Booking essential (15 days in advance).
Admission charge.
It was in the vast sloping Bassin de Decazeville that the first opencast mine in France opened in 1932. The nearby town, a former mining capital, owes its creation by the Duke Decazes to the nearby 280-million-year-old coal deposit. In the past, the town witnessed some bitter strikes and dreadful explosions and, more recently, has survived a difficult transformation as the mine has all but ceased operations. The mine is best seen from the viewpoint, or you can ask for information about visits at the tourist office.

Aubin

2.5 miles (4 km) S of Decazeville
In the footsteps of the miners
Musée de la mine
☎ 05 65 63 19 16 or 05 65 63 14 11
Open daily 10am-noon and 3-6pm, June-end Sept.; weekends and public holidays 3-6pm, rest of the year.
Admission free.

Statue of miner, Aubin

You enter this museum via a gallery constructed by former miners to discover an amazing underground world, with models, tools, films, displays and reconstructions, including a firedamp explosion.

Cransac

4.5 miles (7 km)
SE of Decazeville
A natural health spa
☎ 05 65 63 09 83
Open daily 7am-noon,
5 Apr.-23 Oct.
The nearby coal deposit has a very strange effect – an underground fire producing super-heated vapour, rich in sulphur, at 280°C (536°F). Hence the expression, 'la montagne qui brûle' ('the burning mountain'). At this health spa, these vapours

are cooled, channelled and used to treat rheumatism, stress, injuries, and to help heal damaged skin. The 'Therm'Découverte' ticket (200F) gives a choice of two treatments (preliminary medical examination compulsory).

Bournazel

11 miles (18 km)
S of Decazeville
Florentine château
Château de Bournazel
☎ 05 65 80 26 04
Open daily 3-7pm,
July-Aug. Public holidays and Easter out of season.
Admission free.

Sculpted friezes, château de Bournazel

The Renaissance Court of Honour, with its ingenious stonework, will leave you spellbound. This is a Florentine jewel in the middle of Rouergue, with intricate antique columns, friezes, medallions and garlands.

Peyrusse-le-Roc

12.5 miles (20 km)
SW of Decazeville
Proud ruins
Open daily July-Aug., with torch parades once a week. Open Sun., public holidays and Easter out of season.
Admission charge.
This former medieval stronghold once guarded the silver mines and its many ruins are still identifiable as a huge **fortress**. There are three walking tours.

Almont-les-Junies

7.5 miles (12 km)
NE of Decazeville
Viking grub
Restaurant Ferrières
☎ 05 65 64 04 65
The Viking recipe of 'stockfish' (dried fish) was adopted by the Rouergue region in the 18thC. and has now developed into the modern 'estofinado'. This is a traditional Decazeville basin dish, similar to the French dish 'brandade', made with dried or fresh cod, potatoes, eggs, garlic and nut oil. Almont-les-Junies, home of the Restaurant Ferrières, offers this delight as a special dish from October to May, together with stuffed chicken and 'Aveyron fouace'.

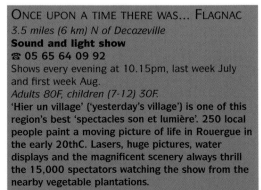

Aveyron fouace

E3-4

Things to do

Discover the coal mine and the miners' lives
Visit a Renaissance château
Cransac thermal health centre
Visit a medieval fortress

With children

Flagnac sound and light show

Within easy reach

Conques (13 miles/21 km NE), p. 186
Figeac (15.5 miles/25 km NW), p. 164

Tourist office

Decazeville:
☎ 05 65 43 18 36

ONCE UPON A TIME THERE WAS... FLAGNAC
3.5 miles (6 km) N of Decazeville
Sound and light show
☎ 05 65 64 09 92
Shows every evening at 10.15pm, last week July and first week Aug.
Adults 80F, children (7-12) 30F.
'Hier un village' ('yesterday's village') is one of this region's best 'spectacles son et lumière'. 250 local people paint a moving picture of life in Rouergue in the early 20thC. Lasers, huge pictures, water displays and the magnificent scenery always thrill the 15,000 spectators watching the show from the nearby vegetable plantations.

Sauveterre-de-Rouergue and the Viaur valley
jewels of the Ségala

Place Centrale and galleries, Sauveterre-de-Rouergue

Until 100 years ago, the Ségala was still cut off from the world, growing nothing but rye, its inhabitants content to eat brown bread and chestnuts. This isolation ended in 1902, when the railway arrived via the Viaur viaduct, bringing fertiliser and machinery. Today, the Ségala is considered one of Rouergue's finest areas. The best place from which to explore it is Sauveterre-de-Rouergue, one of the southwest's prettiest bastides.

Ségala country, near Saint-Martial

Sauveterre-de-Rouergue
A gem of a bastide

Sauveterre derives its name from the French 'sauveté', meaning 'restricted city' (*see* p. 56), and is one of the best preserved and restored fortified towns in southwest France. At Pentecost (Whitsunday), the town organises craft and book fairs, and on All Saints' Day (1 November), they hold a chestnut and cider festival.

Unicorn

La Licorne
Place aux Arcades
☎ 05 65 72 02 48
Open 10-12.30pm and 3-7pm.
This little shop, located under the arches, is widely known for its copies of medieval tapestries (prices 300-10,000F). The gentle colours and noble materials combine to make excellent tapestries, bedspreads and cushions.

Beautiful food
Le Sénéchal
☎ 05 65 71 29 00
Closed Mon., Tues. and Thurs. lunchtime (Mon. only July-Aug.). Closed Jan. to mid-Mar.
Set menus 140-480F (Aveyron produce tasting sessions).
Behind the Place aux Arcades, take time to visit Michel Truchon's restaurant, Le Sénéchal. Enjoy the fillet

TRIPOU TRADITION

Maison Charles Savy, La Naucelloise
Naucelle
☎ 05 65 69 20 20
Open 9am-noon and 2-6pm Mon.-Fri., 9am-noon Sat. Open all day Sat. 14 July-Aug.sam. toute la journée.
The traditional Rouergue dish 'tripou', developed in the 19thC. by farmers' wives, almost died out in recent years but has now been brought back to prominence by Charles Savy, who won the national prize for the best tripou in 1966. Containing calf's caul, haunches and leg, simmered gently in a white-wine sauce, with carrots, tomato purée, celery, spices and flavourings.

of duck breast, with its caramelised, lightly cracking skin contrasting exquisitely with the soft, tender meat. Round off with iced nougat with liquorice and apricot sauce. Great to look at and great to taste.

Naucelle

9.5 miles (15 km) SE of Sauveterre-de-Rouergue
On holiday with Toulouse-Lautrec
Château de Bosc
☎ 05 65 69 20 83
Open daily 9am-7pm. Visits by appt out of season.
Admission charge.

The Château de Bosc is an ochre-stone manor house with lauze roofs, local-stone walls, red shutters and a distinctive rustic charm, surrounded by floral gardens. As a child, Toulouse-Lautrec spent several holidays at the house, which belonged to family friends. Although the museum does not contain any of the painter's major works, it shows lesser-known drawings by his father and uncles, as well as several of the artist's sketches and mementoes from his life.

Pradinas

6 miles (10 km) NW of Sauveterre-de-Rouergue
Pradinas animal park
Parc Animalier de Pradinas
☎ 05 65 69 96 41
Open 2-6pm Sun. and school holidays, 14 Nov.-15 Mar.; 11am-7pm weekends and public holidays, Apr.-June; 10am-8pm, July-Aug.; 2-7pm, Sept. to mid-Nov.
Admission charge.
More than 250 cattle and deer live in this 50-acre (20-ha) wooded, valley park, which can be visited either on foot or by mini-rail. See the exhibition of antlers from animals world-wide, which includes a series of antlers from the same stag, 'lost' once a year for 18 years. Also in Pradinas, the **museum of rural traditions** (Musée des

Aveyron

Things to do

Craft and book days
La Licorne tapestries
Toulouse-Lautrec château

With children

Pradinas animal park

Within easy reach

Rodez (18.5 miles/30 km NE), p. 196
Villefranche-de-Rouergue (28 miles/45 km W), p. 208

Tourist office

Sauveterre-de-Rouergue:
☎ 05 65 72 02 52

Traditions Agricoles) shows the harshness of life in the Ségala years ago (☎ 05 65 59 94 52; open 2-6pm, July to mid-Sept.).

Viaduc du Viaur

11 miles (18 km) S of Sauveterre-de-Rouergue
The iron arch
Opened in 1902 after seven years of construction work, the 1,500-ft (460-m) Viaur viaduct, arching 380 ft (116 m) over the wild gorge below, finally ended the isolation of the Ségala region. The arch, with its 720-ft (220-m) span, was the work of Bodin, a pupil of Eiffel.

D